PRAISE FOR

From the Farm to Arlington

"*From the Farm to Arlington* is a wonderful journey and an endearing story, not just of a man and a patriot, but the loving family and life lessons he left behind. This book is a relatable adventure for any person who loves their country and values their family."

—**Andrew Och**, Author of *Unusual for Their Time: On the Road with America's First Ladies Vol. 1&2*

"*From the Farm to Arlington* is our country's story. Clay Custead weaves his father's remarkable journey with clarity, strength and an abiding respect for the commitment and courage of a generation that fought the wars, made the peace, and defined our national identity. Custead's work shows us that a single individual can trace his finger along the contours of our times, and, in the process, give us lessons worth embracing."

—**Greg Fields**, Author of *Arc of the Comet*, 2018 Kindle Book of the Year in Literary Fiction Nominee

From the Farm to Arlington:
Memoirs of an American Patriot

by Clayton Bard Custead

© Copyright 2019 Clayton Bard Custead

ISBN 978-1-64663-019-6

All rights reserved. No part of this publication may be reproduced, stored in a retrieval system, or transmitted in any form or by any means—electronic, mechanical, photocopy, recording, or any other—except for brief quotations in printed reviews, without the prior written permission of the author.

Published by

210 60th Street
Virginia Beach, VA 23451
800–435–4811
www.koehlerbooks.com

From the Farm to Arlington

MEMOIRS OF AN AMERICAN PATRIOT

CLAYTON BARD CUSTEAD

VIRGINIA BEACH
CAPE CHARLES

To our mother, who raised us all to be good people

And to the United States Marine's FOX Company, whose grave sacrifices saved our father's life.

CLAYTON CUSTEAD

Table of Contents

Introduction 1

Chapter 1—My Story 10

Chapter 2—Family Roots 13

Chapter 3—A Southern Farm 23

Chapter 4—Childhood on the Farm 32

Chapter 5—Bonnie 45

Chapter 6—Racism 50

Chapter 7—The Great Depression 56

Chapter 8—Enlistment 60

Chapter 9—World War II 71

Chapter 10—Camp Pendleton 79

Chapter 11—Korea: The Inchon Landing 82

Chapter 12—Korea: The Frozen Chosin 89

Chapter 13—Korea: Griffin Goes Insane 114

Chapter 14—Marriage 119

Chapter 15—The USS Banner 125

Chapter 16—National Naval Medical Center 135

Chapter 17—Noyes Drive 144

Chapter 18—Fort Belvoir 154

Chapter 19—Antarctica 161

Chapter 20—Return to National Naval Medical Center 183

Chapter 21—The Vietnam War 195

Chapter 22—Letters to Home 215

Chapter 23—Retirement 227

Chapter 24—Three Wars Later 231

Chapter 25—My Legacy 237

Epilogue 243

Appendix A—Service Record 246

Appendix B—Performance Reports 249

References 252

It Is the Soldier

It is the Soldier, not the minister
Who has given us freedom of religion.

It is the Soldier, not the reporter
Who has given us freedom of the press.

It is the Soldier, not the poet
Who has given us freedom of speech.

It is the Soldier, not the campus organizer
Who has given us freedom to protest.

It is the Soldier, not the lawyer
Who has given us the right to a fair trial.

It is the Soldier, not the politician
Who has given us the right to vote.

It is the Soldier who salutes the flag,
Who serves beneath the flag,
And whose coffin is draped by the flag,
Who allows the protester to burn the flag.

CHARLES MICHAEL PROVINCE, U.S. ARMY

Introduction

THE GENESIS OF THIS BOOK was our father's stroke. All our lives, he regaled us seven children with tales from his childhood spent on a farm in the Deep South and his twenty-eight-year career serving in the United States Navy. At times, his stories seemed almost too fantastic to be true. The repetitiveness of every single detail of these stories over many years, however, gave weight to their veracity. We often encouraged him to write down these tales, usually after hearing either the same anecdote again or a new one for the first time. We knew his stories were unique and should be captured in writing, if for no other reason than to preserve an important part of our family history. He told us often how he desired to record his memoirs, but he never seemed to know how to get started. Sitting next to his bed in the emergency room the night of his stroke, I realized we had finally run out of time. I knew his speech and writing ability were now permanently impaired and decided that night to help him record his life's stories.

As a man, my father can best be summarized as a martinet—a rigid, military disciplinarian who demands complete obedience. I was in the seventh grade at Kensington Junior High School in Maryland when I first came across this strange, French-sounding word on a spelling quiz. This word, *martinet,* struck me from the first time I encountered it and it has stayed with me through my entire life as it allowed me, for the first time, to understand my father. It was the very essence, the very embodiment of my father, a man who saw life's choices only in terms of right or wrong. The world to him was either black or white; there existed no grey area. He was a man who imparted upon his five sons and two daughters the now seemingly outdated concepts of chivalry and honor. To my father, there was nothing more contemptible than a man who did not dutifully devote 100 percent of his attention and love to his wife, children, and country.

Growing up, I was terrified of my father, and at times, I mistakenly thought I hated him, especially as I became a young man and naturally started to yearn for independence. His unyielding discipline never ceased, nor did my absolute fear of him. When he addressed me, I concentrated my attention on the tips of my toes. Doing so allowed me to maintain a neutral expression and avoid eye contact. My father viewed direct eye contact by one of his children as a sign of disrespect indicating a need for immediate correction. A neutral expression was a guard against him detecting any attitude, which would prompt him to ask, "Do you want me to wipe that smirk off your face?" The most nerve-wracking moments occurred when my father commanded me to look him in the eyes despite the unstated but understood rules against this behavior. He only did this while saying something like "Do you understand? Look at me and tell me you understand." I dared not follow his commands while every fiber of my being told me that to look him directly in the eyes might shorten my life span.

At slightly over six feet, two inches tall, my father had remarkably long, ape-like arms. I remember that none of us were ever out of his reach. At the dinner table, if any of us said something my father disapproved of or otherwise misbehaved, he would reach out with a humiliating flick of his finger aimed at the side of our heads. The offense may have been something as innocuous as asking Mom to bring the salt shaker in from the kitchen (we learned early that our parents did not wait on us, but that it was our duty to wait on them) or complaining about the food being served. A flick might also punish poor manners, such as taking the last of some food without first inquiring if anyone else would like it. That flick carried a big punch, not due to the physical pain, but because of the accompanying humiliation. It was always followed by a few moments of everyone looking down at their dinner plates in silence until normalcy would naturally return.

I often overheard my father brag to other parents that only a few of his children had ever dared have a temper tantrum, and if it did happen, it had only happened once. He responded to the resultant puzzled looks by explaining. If any of his children had a tantrum, no matter where, even in the checkout line at the grocery store, his response was so swift, violent, and out of proportion that not only the child but his sibling witnesses never considered echoing the offense. My father seldom raised his voice or ever repeated himself. On the few occasions he did, you knew all hell was about to break loose. During the rare times our family went out to dinner, strangers would often go out of their way to stop by our table to complement our parents on what incredibly well-behaved children they had. I am not saying we were perfect, but you might have mistaken us for *The Sound of Music*'s Von Trapp family, only without the lederhosen.

Growing up, I showed signs I was a little out of the ordinary because of the way I was raised, even for the 1960s. For my father, growing up on a farm meant he could work beyond an average man's point of collapse. He possessed an incredible work ethic, born of a mental toughness, which allowed him to ignore pain, hunger, and fatigue until the job was done. He passed this indefatigable work ethic down to his seven children. Seeing his children idle or at play seemed to irritate him to no end. My childhood recollections include washing woodwork or windows every weekend. Each day after school and each evening after dinner, we all had chores such as vacuuming, washing the dishes, or cleaning the kitchen floor. People who came by our house could not believe how clean it always was, especially for having nine people living in it. There was never even a pair of shoes by the back door.

Being raised on a farm means learning to be self-sufficient. My father certainly was, and this was another wonderful trait he handed down to his children, especially his boys. There were only two things my father paid a professional to do: mount and balance tires and align the steering. This was only because he did not own the expensive equipment. Everything else, he did himself with his boys' assistance, including rewiring the house, rerouting gas lines, fixing the plumbing, repairing our slate roof, carpentry, constructing brick patios, pouring concrete walkways, gardening (of course!), flooring, felling 150-foot oaks, fixing anything with a motor or an engine, and on and on. He even, at times, hand-built sofas and chairs, sewing the upholstery himself.

It was Dad's ability to do anything around the house that enabled a Navy master chief with seven children to live in a beautiful neighborhood with doctors and lawyers. Dad's meager income otherwise should have precluded us from settling there. When our family of eight (the ninth member, Becky, was born soon after) first moved to Parkwood Drive in Bethesda, Maryland, we were met with contempt and derision from most of the neighbors. Our house, which we initially rented, was the scourge of an otherwise idyllic upper-middle-class neighborhood. The neighborhood was a stone's throw from downtown Washington, D.C. and ran along scenic Rock Creek Park. The house had been a rental for some twenty years, mostly to military families, and was an embarrassment to the neighborhood. Once the neighbors realized Dad was a master of every trade and a man of undeniably high IQ, they often stopped by to ask him how to do something around their house or asked him to look at a car not starting. If a car needed it, my father could get it started without fail. Besides being a master electrician, plumber, carpenter, and gardener, the man was also a master mechanic. I watched him make a head gasket out of a Wheaties cereal box. I saw him pull a starter motor from one of our cars in the dead of winter and rebuild it on the kitchen table by fashioning a bushing out of a washer using a file and a pair of pliers. In both instances, the repairs did not cost a cent.

Dad trained each of his boys not only to work with their hands but to take great pride in doing so. He was fond of saying that anyone with a high school diploma was capable of performing any of the trades, be it electrical, plumbing, carpentry, or auto repair. I am sure my four brothers would agree that though we are all white-collar professionals, we derive great pleasure from working with our hands, creating something we can admire. There is tremendous satisfaction gained from knowing that you finished a basement, remodeled a bathroom, shingled your roof, or built a deck better than any contractor would have. Of course, saving thousands of dollars because you know how to work with your hands is a definite plus.

Over the years, as my father changed the house from an embarrassment to one we could all be proud of, our neighbors grew to like and respect the Custead family. The neighbors also admired the way my parents raised us to be extremely polite and respectful of elders or anyone in authority. Growing up, I often overheard other parents say things such as, "Why can't you be more like the Custead kids? They are so polite, respectful, and courteous." The character traits my father (and mother) was unyielding about and most adamantly enforced were manners, courtesy, consideration, and respect for others. Education was, of course, of paramount importance to him as well.

One vivid memory having to do with my father happened when I was fourteen and the Vietnam War had just ended. It was at a point in my life when I was resenting my father's strict discipline. I was with my girlfriend Sally at the Walter Reed Army Convalescent Center, Forest Glen Annex in Silver Spring, Maryland. Sally was a good-looking blonde with a long, full mane and a very mature figure; she looked great in jeans. I was a six-foot, 175-pound athletic young man. We both appeared much older than we were, especially in the dark of the night. We had just come out of the base movie theater on a moonless night when two military police officers, patrolling the base on a golf cart, decided to have some fun by roughing me up a bit in front of Sally. They approached us aggressively, separating me from Sally, and gave me a hard time, asking me what I was doing on base. They said that I had to leave or that I would be locked up but that Sally could get a ride home with them. Being very young and raised to be downright frightened of authority, I felt threatened and scared. They demanded I produce identification. It was then that I pulled out my military ID card, issued to all military dependents. The card listed my father as Hospital Corpsman Master Chief (HCMC) Elmer Custead, U.S. Navy. After reading this with the aid of their flashlight, the situation changed drastically and immediately. They asked where my father was stationed. I told them that he had just returned from Vietnam and was a Master Chief at Bethesda National Naval Medical Hospital. I remember how strange it was that their behavior changed so abruptly. They went from yelling at me nose to nose, to gently touching me on the shoulder and speaking in a friendly tone. They did not apologize directly but did so with their newfound sincere kindness. That night, for the first time in my life, I got an inkling that there was something special about being the son of my dad, a man I thought I hated.

Much to my surprise and amazement, my father apologized later in life for being such a "hard ass." My mother and father were at my house for dinner, and the three of us were sitting out back on the patio. I was in my early thirties at the time with two young sons. I admit, the reason he was there wasn't because I enjoyed his company, but simply out of a sense of obligation to include him in my children's lives. Our relationship at the time was cold and distant. He correctly detected a chip on my shoulder when I informed him, "I am not going to raise my boys to fear me." In truth, I was making excuses for one of them being disobedient and misbehaving. He looked at me with an expression I had never before seen. His facial expression and tone indicated he desperately wanted me to understand and approve of how he raised us — something I had never experienced in our rather distant relationship. Pleading for me to understand, my father said, "I am sorry you feel I was hard on you. Either seven children were going to run the home, or I was. It was the only way to maintain order. It would have been chaos otherwise."

The change in my relationship with Dad was a journey that began in earnest after a series of three significant events. The first was becoming a father myself. It was after the birth of my first son I remember telling my father I loved him for the first time. I could tell the words made him a bit uncomfortable as he responded in kind, but I was glad to say it nonetheless. He just wasn't a very affectionate man. In truth, I don't remember him telling me as a young boy that he loved me either. The closest he came would be to say, "Son, I am very proud of you." We still were not close, but telling him I loved him was a first step in realizing being a good father was not always easy and did not come with an instruction manual. That moment on my patio when he opened his heart to me marked the second turning point in our relationship. My father revealed to me for the first time a sensitive, caring side; telling me what I thought of him mattered deeply. The third and most impactful was the occasion of his stroke. It was only then, knowing he could have died, that I realized what a great man my father was and how lucky I was to have been raised by him.

This brings me back to the night of his stroke in September of 2007. Sometime during the night at the hospital, I told Mom and my sister Becky to go home and get some sleep. I knew Mom had been stretched thin dealing with my father's failing health for some time and I wanted to give her a night's rest. I lied and told them I was going to be leaving soon. Instinctively I understood that I could not leave the side of this man. Little did I know how things were going to change in the distant and cold relationship I had with my father. He was the most feared and respected disciplinarian I had known, the ultimate martinet. Now, after his stroke, his disoriented and bewildered state confused and frightened me. I found my eyes moist with love, worry, and concern. He did not know who he was or where he was. He kept trying to focus on everyone's faces, not recognizing anyone around him. He looked at me and called me Homer, the name of his long-deceased brother. I realized that this man, who had always been truly fearless, was now visibly scared. He had been in charge all his adult life, and now he was perplexed and frightened. I knew I had to stay by his side and be there for him. I could not allow him to wake up feeling abandoned, scared, and alone. I fell asleep sometime after they had sedated my father, on a hard, plastic chair with my head against the wall.

That night, my father's long-lived dream of one day recording his life story ended abruptly. He had run out of tomorrows. His speech was damaged and would only be repaired with hard work and the aid of a speech therapist. Until this time, I may have seen my parents once or twice a year, despite living only twenty minutes away; I was no better keeping in touch by phone. I felt I was a horrible son, and I knew in the deepest recesses of my mind that one day I was going to regret not spending more time with them. I seemed to think, as my father did with his book, that there would always be another tomorrow.

It was in October of 2010, shortly after my father had convalesced from his stroke, that I decided to help him write his life story. I started having breakfast with my mom and dad every Saturday morning and came to enjoy their company. I brought a tape recorder to each of these visits, and together, we went through boxes and boxes of memories my father had kept over the years. He ultimately recovered well from the stroke. He remembered with amazing clarity details from 40, 50, or 60 years ago, but often struggled to remember what he had just talked about or he would have a hard time finding the right word. My Saturday morning breakfast meetings were nearly uninterrupted for close to two years until my father passed away. I continue this tradition with my mother to this day. During this time, my mom and dad morphed from mere blood relatives who I rarely saw or spoke with to great friends whose company I truly enjoyed. I now feel blessed that I was given this opportunity to get to know and love them.

What follows is a labor of love to make my father's dream a reality for his family and for anyone else who may enjoy the tales of a farm boy raised in the segregated South during the Depression, who grew to be an honored veteran of three wars, and a beloved father. In truth, I am not a professional author but a financial executive in the private sector. Mine is a job that requires far more than forty hours a week, one that does not afford me the experience or time to perform in-depth research to corroborate my father's tales. I thought of subtitling my father's book, "A Farm Boy's Tales," for two reasons. First, because my father always humbly referred to himself as a simple farm boy, and second and more importantly, the use of the word "tales" connotes an un-researched, unproven story. I did make frequent use of the Internet to bring historical perspective to the reader and to check the accuracy of key facts. In the end, I know my father would be happy and proud to have his life's experiences recorded for his family.

As I said, I can't remember telling my father that I loved him until my first child, Joseph Bard, was born. It was only after I became a father myself that I came to understand what a special man my father was. Even then, the realization did not happen overnight. That gradual process started that moonless night at Walter Reed and culminated decades later with the writing of this book. Looking back, I now realize that, while I feared and respected my father, he had never struck me out of anger or punished me when I did not deserve it. The hate I thought I felt for him as a young man was resentment; resentment toward him for forcing me to be a responsible, courteous, and respectful young man, traits that have served me well in my life and career. Upon Dad's passing, I knew in my heart that he had always treated me fairly and that he had sacrificed and dedicated his whole life to his family. I am a better man for having been raised by him and for having learned from him the outdated concepts of duty to family and chivalry.

CHAPTER 1

My Story

NO ONE WANTS TO HEAR an old man start a story by saying that kids these days don't know what hardship is, but in many ways, that is one of the driving forces behind me wanting to share my life. My seven children and their children have never known war, hardship, starvation, and even death on a scale known by my generation. Their millennial children, my grandchildren, cannot comprehend that in the not-too-distant past, men, women, and children starved to death in this great country of ours. Sadly, they cannot begin to understand the magnitude of suffering caused by both the Great Depression and World War II. While they learn their grandfathers fought and died in distant lands, they have little understanding of the abstract concepts of freedom, liberty, and the inalienable rights for which their grandparents fought and died.

As an eighty-two-year-old man, I am of course suffering from poor health. I was born on December 13, 1928, one year before the stock market crash of 1929 and the start of the Great Depression. My eighty-two years have been hard yet richly rewarding. While I have recently suffered a stroke, which has impaired my ability to collect the right words, my mind is still sharp. My legs have long been weak due to nerve damage brought on by exposure to Agent Orange during the

Vietnam War. While I can get around decently, I must always have ahold of a cane because my legs can buckle unexpectedly. The rest of my ailments have been with me since long before the stroke. I think my body's decline started earlier than most due to the tremendous physical toll demanded of it over a lifetime of back-breaking work on the farm and in battle.

While my life shares many characteristics with those of my generation, it is much different in many respects. Raised a simple and humble farm boy in the Deep South during the Great Depression, I journeyed on an unplanned trip around the globe, a trip that included three wars, sea duty in the South Pacific, and a tour in Antarctica. A movie of my life would have to incorporate a bit of *To Kill a Mockingbird, The Grapes of Wrath, Saving Private Ryan, McHale's Navy, Ice Station Zebra,* and perhaps a little of *Cheaper by the Dozen.*

I was raised on a prosperous farm in central Florida. My family were Yankees from Pennsylvania via Santa Barbara, California; as such, we were always considered outsiders despite my father being a church and community leader. My father, a remarkable, righteous man in his own right, would today be termed "enlightened," as he fought against the injustice of racism and assisted the poor with his own time and money. Our family was, for the most part, self-sufficient during the Depression, and our farm was a relatively safe island in a sea of poverty, death, racism, and hardship.

Like most young men of my generation, I left high school and the farm eager to fight in World War II. At the time, I was experiencing nightmares that the war would come to an end before I could get in on the fight. As an eighteen-and-a half-year-old eleventh grader, and with my parents' permission, I joined the Navy during the tail end of World War II on July 1, 1947. This date may sound as if it was after the war had ended, but many different dates measure the end of the war. Harry Truman did not officially declare it over until 1951. At the time of my enlistment, there was still fighting going on all over the globe, especially in China, where I served. Little did I suspect when

I enlisted as a high school dropout that, years later, I would leave the Navy highly educated in the newly formed field of nuclear medicine. I retired a highly-decorated Hospital Corpsman Master Chief, a rank achieved by less than one percent of enlisted men. A corpsman is the Navy's equivalent to an army medic. During my twenty-eight-year career, I served in combat in World War II, Korea, and Vietnam. I was awarded medals, ribbons, and commendations for a distinguished career that included five years as a Navy corpsman serving with the United States Marine Corps and for seven years of sea duty. The number of veterans who have served in all three of these wars, especially in a combat role or in a war zone as I did, is astronomically small. According to the website VA.gov, in 2000, there were 171,000 out of 9.2 million living veterans that served in all three of these wars, less than 2% of the total. The Navy was an adventure that took me all over the planet, including the South Pole, and truly lived up to its slogan "Join the Navy and see the world."

CHAPTER 2

Family Roots

MY MOTHER, MARY, WAS FROM Erie, Pennsylvania, and my dad, Homer, was from Meadville, Pennsylvania. Dad's lineage was mostly English with some German stock, while Mom's side of the family had immigrated from Germany. The oldest known ancestor on her side is John Joseph Bard, who was born in Germany in 1700 and immigrated to the United States in 1720. My middle name, Bard, has been handed down from father to son for eight generations. It is the name I gave to my middle son, Clayton Bard, who has now passed it on to his firstborn, Joseph Bard.

My parents met when Dad traveled to Erie to find work, shortly after the turn of the century. They married and moved to Oswego, New York, on January 1, 1908, where Clara was born, the first of their nine children. Their next move took them 3,000 miles to San Francisco, California, looking for work. At the time, San Francisco was a boom town. Dad performed day labor in citrus groves until he saved enough money to move on to Santa Barbara; there, he worked as a tenant farmer on the Richter family's land before he purchased his first orchard farm growing citrus, olives, pecans, and fruit. My father was a natural-born leader, active in the farming community of Santa Barbara. It was without any effective local government at the time and was, in many ways, still the Wild West. My two oldest brothers, Oliver and Homer, were born in Santa Barbara in 1910 and 1912, respectively. By all accounts, my mother hated it there. Before she could let the children out to play, she had to scout the area with a shotgun to kill rattlesnakes. They were so numerous that in just the two years they lived there, Mom killed 30 rattlesnakes. That shotgun is still in the family, hanging on my son Clay's den wall.

Mom was so unhappy and so afraid for the children's lives that one day upon my dad's arrival at the house for lunch, she had their buckboard (a light four-wheeled carriage) loaded and hitched to the horses. She was adamant about leaving that day with the three children. She could not abide one more day of risking the children's lives with deadly rattlesnakes. My dad was able to talk her from the buckboard with the promise that they would leave the next day. He arranged a power of attorney with a friend to sell the farm, and they headed east for Florida. My father was so respected as a community leader that this gentleman who sold the farm on his behalf refused to take any compensation, saying it was an honor to be asked to assist. The farm was sold within three months, and the entire proceeds were sent to my mother and father who had by then traveled across the country by train to relocate in Florida.

I guess Mom's ultimatum was not completely out of the blue, because I remember stories of Mom having applied for land in Florida under a homesteading program; however, my recollection on this is not very clear. They tried farming a couple of places in Florida before purchasing what was to become the family farm where I was raised. The location they ultimately settled on was in Mannville, located in Putnam County, about eighty miles west of Jacksonville. They eventually chose the forty-acre family homestead because of its high elevation, two gigantic oaks weeping with Spanish moss, and the lake down in back.

Dad started a very successful citrus farm but changed to truck farming when the Depression hit. In the beginning, at the height of the farm's citrus sales, he owned a citrus packing house at a rail siding that allowed him to ship multiple boxcars of citrus north every week.

Like any farm, we had the typical barnyard animals, including horses, mules, cows, pigs, and chickens. Numerous cats and dogs were always present as well. The farm became very prosperous, and even during the Depression, my family was spared the horrible hardships the surrounding community and the rest of the country faced. Homer and Mary's children never went to bed hungry and always had adequate clothes to attend school. My dad was so prosperous that he was often first in the county to purchase the latest products, including a refrigerator and even the first truck in Putnam County with wide, balloon-type tires.

Despite the horrible death rate of children under five in America at the time, all nine of their children survived infancy and prospered through the Protestant work ethic they inherited and by taking full advantage of the opportunities offered by the American capitalist system. Homer and Mary were honest, hardworking, church-going people. The type of dedicated people with strong moral fiber that produced what news anchor Tom Brokaw coined "The Greatest Generation."

My mother was an exceptional woman. She was born in 1890 to a family so poor that her parents gave her away as an indentured servant to another family at age eight so she could obtain clothing and food. She was one of the most remarkable women I have ever known. Perhaps because she was denied it as a child, the education of her children was of paramount importance to her. She was educated in school through perhaps the fourth grade, after which she taught herself. Yet people who read her letters, written in beautiful prose with meticulous handwriting, often remarked that she must have been very well-educated. I always knew her to have a dictionary within easy reach. At home, she held spelling bees and asked her kids questions to encourage a learning environment.

She was also always cooking. My wife, Lois, remarked that when she joined the family, she could not get over how much food Mom prepared at every dinner. A typical one would include two to three salads, pickles, meat, two to three vegetables, pies, and cookies. She cooked on a big iron stove with seven burners that had been wood-fueled in the early years before being converted to gas.

Mom passed away in 1975 at age eighty-five, but not before dementia had started to invade her mind. I am not sure we ever heard a cause of death, but we think that it was heart failure or pneumonia. Dad had passed away five years earlier in April of 1970. He was five years older than Mom, so they both died at the age of eighty-five.

When my mother died, I felt nothing, and it was the same when my father died. Dad died while I was overseas. I wrote Mom that I would not be home because I was closing the U.S. Marine hospital in Da Nang, Vietnam. My mom and dad were so well known in Mannville that I knew everything would be all right. At least that is how I rationalized it.

I have always wondered whether I am human when it comes to certain emotions, or more specifically, a lack thereof. Some have said I have ice water running through my veins. I attribute my inability to feel to the fact that I have seen so much death in my life, at least a thousand times more than the average person. Death is something for which I have unknowingly developed a defense mechanism. My son Clay shocked me when he pointed out that every time the topic of death comes up, I chuckle or even laugh heartily. He said that the moment he realized it, he came to understand how I drew cold stares from those around me for laughing out loud at funerals. At the time, Clay, and many others, I presume, had just thought I was an insensitive lout. No one had ever noticed this quirk in me before Clay did, not even myself. My wife suggests that my brother Earl's early death was the only time a loss had a visible effect on me. Earl was forty-two when he died from complications from a ruptured appendix and was buried at Arlington National Cemetery. Of all my brothers, I was the closest to Earl, as he was just two and a half years older than I was.

The older kids thought my father was a terrible taskmaster. I am sure he had mellowed with age as Dad was always wonderful to me, the second youngest of nine. He assisted me with my projects, both in school and business, including helping me with my herd of cattle. Dad was a product of his time in that he was never an affectionate man; however, in later years, Dad was quite visibly smitten with my baby sister Ruth's child, Mary, because she lived with them in their senior years.

Before becoming a farmer, Dad was by trade a master carpenter. He had a huge wooden chest full of expensive tools that he kept in the barn. I don't know what my father's education level was, but he was knowledgeable and a born community leader. Besides performing investigations for the local court as a coroner, Dad was also a Federal Housing Agency (FHA) building inspector and the head of the local draft board. It turned out the FHA built only one home in Putnam County in thirty years, but my father was the inspector. He was also the treasurer of First United Methodist Church of Interlachen and a self-taught master electrician who helped a great number of neighbors introduce electricity into their homes. In the early days, the only electricity was direct current (DC). It was one wire and one ground in a continuous loop. A solid, continuous electrical current had to be maintained. If one bulb on the circuit went bad, the whole circuit would be bad. Dad was the first in the county to understand the new wiring concept of alternating current (AC). Electricity was amongst the many trades I learned from my father, probably from the time I was eight years old. I am so comfortable around electricity that I rarely turn the circuit breaker off before working on live wiring.

In announcing the fiftieth wedding anniversary of Homer and Mary in 1968, the local newspaper published the following description of their family:

- Clara, registered nurse (college educated, born in Pennsylvania in 1908)
- Oliver, Agriculture in Plant City, Florida (college educated, born in Santa Barbara, California, in 1910)
- Homer, Real estate, Orange Park, Florida (born in Santa Barbara, California, in 1912)
- Mary, employed at the Florida School for the Deaf and Blind in St. Augustine, Florida (born in Mannville, Florida, in 1914)
- Paul, a farmer with his father (born in Mannville, Florida, in 1916)
- George, city bus driver in Los Angeles, California (born in Mannville, Florida, in 1918)
- Earl, Chief Petty Officer in the Navy (born in Mannville, Florida, in 1925)
- Elmer, Chief Petty Officer in the Navy (born in Mannville, Florida, in 1928)
- Ruth, employee at Darden's Restaurant (born in Mannville, Florida, in 1931)
- 25 Grandchildren and 11 great-grandchildren

Our family was large, which was not unusual for the time. Mary had given birth to nine children over twenty-three years, starting at age eighteen in 1908 with Clara, and ending at age forty-one in 1931 with Ruth, the baby of the family.

Clara was the firstborn and the oldest girl. She was a university-educated nurse and midwifed my birth. Her husband, Herbert Wilkening, was in the business of buying run-down tobacco farms, turning them around, and selling them for a profit.

The only family vacation I ever remember was when my parents took us north to Pennsylvania to attend a family reunion when I was about twelve. On the way up, we stopped at my sister Clara's house in Tennessee. It was on this trip that I met Clara for the second time, the first being twelve years earlier on the day of my birth. Some vacation! My brother-in-law had Earl and me working on his tobacco farm from sunup to sundown. It was harder work than being back home on our own farm. After we gladly said our goodbyes, we proceeded north to our family reunion in Pennsylvania. It was at this family reunion that I met my cousin from my father's side, Clark Gable, perhaps one of the biggest celebrities in the country at the time, having already starred in the blockbuster film *Gone with the Wind*. It was here that I first saw snow, which I thought was more impressive than meeting Mr. Gable. Unfortunately, I never met either set of my grandparents. They had all passed before I was born.

Oliver was the second child of the family and one of the most successful financially, eventually becoming the official horticulturist for the state of Florida. Oliver's farm was in Plant City, Florida. He married Ellen Futch, who came from an extremely wealthy, landowning family. I remember going over to the Futches' enormous cattle ranches. My dad used to enjoy taking me on the two- to three-hour drive over narrow paved and dirt roads, just wide enough for one Model A, to sightsee their three beef slaughterhouses, some of the largest in the country.

Homer was the third child and, like Oliver, became wealthy. Mechanically inclined, his story started as a Greyhound Bus master diesel mechanic. During World War II, a very wealthy admiral from the nearby Jacksonville Naval Air Station contacted Homer and gave him two choices. He could either volunteer to be a civilian manager at the air base as a plane engine mechanic or he would have him drafted as a seaman the next day. Naturally, faced with such a choice, Homer chose the civilian manager route and went on to spend twenty years working at the base. His dealings with this admiral did not end here, however.

In 1949, the state of Florida passed a law requiring all free-range cattle to be fenced in. The area was growing, and free-range cattle were becoming a nuisance. Mr. Moats, Homer's father-in-law, needed to find a fenced-in area for thousands of heads of cattle. Mr. Moats and my father each lent Homer $1,000 to help pay for about 3,000 acres along the St. Johns River from the same admiral who had made Homer a civilian manager at the base. He paid about $1.25 per acre; the bank financed the balance of the purchase price.

The admiral thought the land was never going to appreciate or that it might even depreciate due to World War II ending. Just the opposite happened. It shot up in value to the tune of thousands of dollars per acre, making Homer a millionaire. Developing buyer's remorse, the admiral sued Homer to reacquire the land, arguing that the sale was not legal. In the end, Homer prevailed, but only after several years and at great cost.

Mary was the fourth child of the family and, like me, did not finish high school. She married Dalton Sanders, who delivered ice with a horse-drawn wagon. He eventually became a huge chicken farmer, producing tens of thousands of chickens. They never became wealthy, however, because Dalton refused to break the price control laws in place at the time. He would sell chickens to people who would resell them for two to four times what they paid Dalton.

Paul was the fifth of Homer and Mary's children. He took over the family farm, starting with ten acres my dad gave him as I was leaving to join the Navy in an agreement that he would come back and run the farm. By this time, my father was becoming too old to run the farm himself, and with me leaving, he needed help.

Dad deeded Paul another ten acres on March 5, 1955, in consideration for $10, and twelve more acres on December 28, 1967, in consideration for "love and affection." Paul worked the farm alongside Dad for years before taking it completely over when Dad became too old. He built his family home on the first ten acres and was there to take care of Mom and Dad as they aged. Homer purchased what was left of the farm, about eight acres, for around $8,000 in 1967.

My brother George, the sixth child, joined the Army and was a survivor of the D-Day landing in Normandy and the Battle of the Bulge. I only vaguely remember George being at home because he was ten years older than I was. After the war he settled in Los Angeles, California. He married a wonderful woman with a sparkling personality, Lila Mae. Lila Mae was quite a character. She was a celebrity stalker and could talk her way into any high-society party in Hollywood. She snuck me into a couple of those parties. She worked at one of the national jewelry stores, Robinsons, I think, and helped me buy my wife's engagement ring.

Of my eight siblings, I was closest to my older brother Earl, the seventh child, who also served in the Navy. He enlisted and spent four years in the Navy during World War II and was asked to re-enlist during the Korean War because of his specialized training as a boatswain mate. Sadly, he died at the young age of 42 during one of my parents' trips north to visit him at his duty station in Norfolk, Virginia. He was in dire need of medical attention but refused it, saying he would go to the hospital after our parents' visit. He ended up dying from a ruptured appendix.

Ruth, two years and eight months younger than I, was the ninth and last child. She was the baby of the family and treated as such, becoming spoiled rotten in my opinion. She went to the same one-room schoolhouse that I did, and, like me, never finished high school. She could turn on and off her slow Southern drawl at will and was an exceptionally pretty young lady.

Since I was in the final batch of three, I have very little memory of my older brothers and sisters living at home, apart from Paul, thirteen years older than me. He lived at home until his thirties when he got married. As far as I was concerned, my siblings were Paul, my older brother Earl, and my baby sister Ruth. Of those three, Paul was not so much a brother as a tormentor. Every day he stayed at our house was a day too long for me. He seemed to relish picking on me and sometimes he could be just flat-out mean. The oldest three, Clara, Oliver, and Homer, might as well have been distant relatives. George was twelve when I was born, so he was out of the house by the time I was six.

Remarkably, my mother never saw all nine of her children at one time until the tragic death of her ten-year-old grandchild, Ray, the son of Mary and Dalton. He was killed when he accidentally stepped on a downed high-voltage power line. I was about eighteen at the time because I remember that my older brother George had just returned from fighting in Europe and I was preparing to join the Navy. I am sure my mother and father did not find much happiness at having the whole family together for the first time under such terrible circumstances.

CHAPTER 3

A Southern Farm

THE CUSTEAD FARM WAS IN the small town of Mannville in north-central Florida, approximately 45 miles east of St. Augustine, just off State Highway 20. The two nearest towns were Interlachen, about four miles away, and Palatka, which sits on the shores of the St. Johns River in Putnam County, twelve miles distant. When the family moved to Mannville around 1915, Palatka was like many Western frontier towns in the early 1900s in that it became a focal point for land seekers and businessmen expanding into the countryside. Citrus, cattle, lumber, tourism, river cruise boats, and stagecoach tours were major attractions in Putnam County at the time. Palatka hosted five large hotels for tourists in its heyday, one of which was later converted into the county hospital. Interlachen, the nearer of the two towns, was a sleepy, quiet place filled with nice second homes owned mostly by rich Yankee snowbirds seeking a respite from harsh northern winters.

Lawlessness, as in most frontier towns, was also a problem in Putnam County. As I was growing up, I knew well our own Judge Green and Sheriff Revel. I don't recall any outlandish stories about them, but it was common knowledge that the county jail rarely housed a white person. The local jail population was always stocked with enough black men to supply two chain gangs. The county only had two trucks, each with a trailer and four armed guards for moving the chain gangs around town. If they ever found themselves short of free labor, they would simply arrest a few more blacks.

Over the years, my parents added to the family farm until it became maybe twice its original size; with subsequent sales of acreage, at the time of their deaths, it was once again forty acres.

In the early years, we were primarily a citrus farm, but that ended in a bad way when the large citrus corporations collaborated with the U.S. Government to put smaller farms out of business. Dad plowed over our citrus groves after this bleak period in the farm's history and converted the farm to produce. The Custeads became truck farmers, which, by my definition, meant we took our numerous vegetable crops to market via truck. In any given year, we might have had over thirty varieties of produce depending upon the market, including multiple types of the same vegetable, such as three varieties of mustard greens.

Dad sold in markets all over the area, from daily sales to the corner grocery to major shipments to Jacksonville where brokers purchased and shipped his crops to northern markets via rail.

The farm was a purely capitalistic enterprise in the sense that Dad always attempted to take advantage of changing market conditions. If poultry or beef prices were rising, we would invest in that livestock. Hogs were a staple of the farm. They were bred both for personal consumption and for sale, as their meat was cheap and always in demand. A couple of times a year, we butchered a yearling steer, sold the hind quarter to the grocery store, and canned the rest. At butchering time, Dad insisted we boys took our turns with the rifle and the skinning knife to the throat. It was a rite of passage into manhood for a farm boy.

If eggs could bring in revenue, then Dad would build chicken coops and have Mom sell eggs. The farm's resources were always for sale in any shape or form. Dad even sold clay soil off the farm to the state highway administration, which used it for making dirt roads in an otherwise sandy environment.

The farm also had a pecan orchard, which survived throughout the farm's history. The trees were located just to the left of the driveway on about an acre of land. Many years later, my wife Lois and I were driving in Maine while on vacation when we fell in behind a pickup with a camper bearing a Putnam County tax sticker. We followed it for several miles until it pulled into a campsite. Did I know them, or did we have mutual acquaintances? As soon as I established that I was from Mannville, they said they lived four miles to the west. After not being able to come up with any family names we knew in common, the lady turned to her husband and said, "Mannville was where we met the little old Jew lady selling nuts. She argued over price and gave us light nuts" (light nuts have a paper shell—meat with no body and an oily taste). It had to have been my mother they bought the nuts from, as our farm was the only one with pecan trees in Mannville. These pecans this lady spoke of were of such inferior quality that we would not even give them to our neighbors. Typically, they were ground up and fed to the livestock. I was perplexed as to why Mom would have sold them. Of course, this was a time when she was well into her senior years, and dementia could have started to take its toll on her before anyone realized it. We left the couple still complaining about the "cheating Jew woman" selling her low-quality nuts. I did not have the boldness to tell her that she was speaking of my mother. We were pleased under the circumstances to have met them anyway.

The farm had a good size lake behind the house, and there were dozens more in the area, which meant alligators. Although they were rare around the farm, it was still legal to shoot alligators, even for some years after I had joined the Navy. If they wandered onto the farm, they generally ended up on our dinner plates. We shot them for their hides and to protect our chickens and livestock, but a side benefit was eating the delicious tail meat. We also enjoyed eating frog legs and crayfish.

★ ★ ★

My father built the family home one room at a time. It started as a log cabin and, as the years went by, he added four bedrooms. By the time the house was complete, the only evidence of its genesis was the white-painted log walls in the living and dining rooms. Otherwise, from the outside, it looked like any typical wood farmhouse. I spent my childhood sharing a room with my next oldest brother Earl. My younger sister Ruth had her own room, as did my older brother Paul, who was living with us while he was in his thirties. Even though Mom and Dad had nine children, their births were so spread out that four bedrooms were always enough. The home was heated by propane, which we ran only for an hour or so at a time during the cold winter months, just enough to take the chill out of the home and long enough to eat dinner and bathe. Once or twice, we may have run it through a particularly cold night. Of course, there was no air conditioning in the summer. If you did not grow up there, you would find central Florida in the summer unbearably hot and humid. Florida is just the opposite of the North where people basically hibernate during the short cold winter days and become active during the summer. Looking back, I wonder how I slept in that oppressive humidity. Now I am spoiled and acclimated to air conditioning, but back then, I had no problems sleeping in 100-degree heat with 100 percent humidity, as it was all I ever knew.

As usual in a farmhouse, the kitchen was the most important and largest room, the center of all activity. It not only served as my mother's factory for moneymaking endeavors, but it also served as the source of hours upon hours of my mother's efforts at keeping the family well fed. My mother had the largest stove I have ever seen. It was originally a wood-burning, cast iron stove that doubled as the main source of heat for the home. It was later converted to gas when Dad installed a large propane tank beside the house and ran gas lines inside. Its oven was so large that Mom could bake six loaves of bread at a time. As a young man, I was six feet, three inches and had almost zero body fat despite being very well fed. I stuffed my stomach with lettuce, green onions, just off-the-stock corn, peas, beans, strawberries, and the like every day while working in the fields. Often if I had been out there, I wasn't even hungry when called to supper. While much of our diet consisted of farm-raised vegetables, each meal always had a small amount of meat as a side dish, not as the entrée. A typical dinner might include a small portion of protein with three to five different fruits and vegetables, always followed by dessert.

Mondays were set aside each week to bake that week's bread. We also churned butter from the dairy cow's milk. Making butter, like so many kitchen-based activities on a farm, was a factory-like operation. Whether I was six or sixteen, I often helped Mom make both the bread and the butter. I would do the churning and the kneading of the butter to get the water out of it. It had water because Mom would put ice into the churn to compensate for the Florida heat, helping the cream to solidify faster. We would then salt the butter to taste. We always churned extra for Mom to sell.

Mom's kitchen started with an icebox. My brother-in-law Dalton arrived once a week in a mule-driven cart to deliver ice in wet burlap wraps. Ice was a luxury afforded to those that could incur the cost of an icebox. Later, my parents became the first in the county to purchase a Sears refrigerator. I remember my parents giving guests and neighbors who came by to see the refrigerator an ice cube as a treat to suck on. This sounds strange today, but back then, an ice cube was quite a novelty.

★ ★ ★

Over the years, Dad not only acquired additional acreage, but he sold and gave away land. Some of the land he acquired had small cottages. I remember him giving about three acres to Captain Norris, an elderly retired Salvation Army captain, and his wife. Dad not only gave them the land but also built a house for them simply because Captain Norris was an old man in need of assistance. Three days a week, Dad would bring Captain Norris fresh vegetables so the captain could sell them for a couple of dollars. It was Dad's way of giving this elderly couple some money in a manner that would not offend them. It is hard for today's generation to understand, but at one time, receiving a handout from anyone was a source of deep and sorrowful embarrassment.

He also sold timber-rich land that was not good for farming to Mr. Durden, a man my father repeatedly referred to as "an extremely moral man." I am not sure why Dad always said this, but others must have also admired this man, as a local road was later named in his honor. Around this time, an acre was going for $2.25. Mr. Durden was a logger, not a farmer, and since Mr. Durden was in the timber business, he would often clear farmland for my dad, always insisting on paying my father for the value of the timber removed. He had six enormous oxen he used in his timber business. Many times, Dad would call for Mr. Durden's oxen to assist in freeing trucks and farm equipment from deep sand and mud. Overall, it was one of the most mutually beneficial relationships my dad had with his neighbors.

In 1945, a family of city slickers with two teenage sons named the Kayhills moved to Interlachen. I believe the mom had been a schoolteacher, and their dad, I think, was a chemist. The family wanted to organize a Boy Scout troop. They obtained a charter, even though there were only five boys spread across West Putnam County. My dad drew the line, however, at purchasing uniforms, so the Kayhills purchased a Boy Scout cap for me. The newly arrived Kayhills could not comprehend the distances we boys lived apart from one another or the daily chores that were our responsibility.

Nonetheless, we finally agreed upon a date for a Saturday overnight fishing and camping trip. We had a ball catching a lot of good-sized fish, followed by cleaning and cooking them over an open fire. All was well until dusk. We locals had developed an immunity to the mosquito and spider bites, but the poor Kayhills were eaten alive. I still remember how bad off they were, taking two weeks to recover.

After that, we never heard another word from them about a second Boy Scout camping trip.

Around the same time the Kayhills showed up, a mysterious man appeared in the small cottage built on twenty acres behind the farm that Dad had sold decades earlier. The mutual fence crossed over our western boundary. Various owners and tenants had lived in the cottage over the years, but the house had recently been vacant for some time. This mystery man was powerfully built and appeared quite wealthy. He did not drive and, therefore, did not own an automobile. When an agent from Palatka showed him the cottage, he leased it, then rode back to the county seat and purchased furniture, kitchen utensils, and bedding, all for cash. He claimed to be English and had the accent but would not say anything more about himself.

The mystery man received numerous shipments of crates and barrels of laboratory equipment. Years later, while working in the naval labs, I realized he possessed many of the same apparatuses.

In no hurry, he would wait until my parents were going to Palatka and ask to ride along, insisting they accept a dollar. He always maintained the same routine: first going to the Western Union office and then going to the package store to purchase a few cans of tuna. After a few weeks, he quit walking the miles to the Mannville post office and allowed us kids to pick up his mail. He always had a dime or nickel waiting for us. Because we did this chore for him, we learned his real name. He told us that we should never reveal it to any stranger and, if anyone should ever ask, to say that we never heard of him. We had no idea from whom or what he was hiding.

He also paid us kids to catch non-poisonous snakes. We would walk along the lake shore with him and, using our bare hands, grab snakes that had captured his interest. This was long before I had developed my phobia of snakes. He also paid us to go out in the fields or pastures and capture specific insects. They were worth five cents apiece. We were living high on the hog with all the nickels, dimes, and pennies that we earned from him. I hung around his lab and observed what I later realized was histology techniques for embedding tissue of insects with paraffin for sectioning for microscope slides. I learned somewhat about what our mysterious neighbor was doing; he had a market selling microscope slides to universities and the like. He started showing me checks that he received in the mail, and most were for hundreds of dollars. He was making a king's ransom for the time.

One day, I told him about the newspaper headline my dad had shown me about the newly developed atomic bomb dropped on Japan. "Impossible," he said, sending me to fetch the newspaper. He read it and then said, "Tell your dad that I have to get to Palatka ASAP. It is imperative that I catch a northbound train today." He left more suddenly than he had arrived two years earlier.

As if anticipating a hurried departure, the mysterious man had already prepared instructions and a power of attorney, notarized in Palatka by a judge. A letter of explanation stated he was hiding from a wife in Boston who was, by court order, entitled to a percentage of his earnings. He had lived in England for several years before appearing in Mannville. He maintained a checking account at Palatka National Bank. The bank's president, Mr. Bush, was a family friend who attended our church. Mr. Bush had previously taken Dad into his confidences, so Dad was not surprised by the events as they unfolded and oversaw the packing and shipping of his laboratory. The letter of instruction told Dad to accept or dispose of the household contents as he saw fit. After all was settled, Dad was entitled to a fee of $200 from the sale proceeds.

Another neighbor for whom my father always had high regard was Mr. White, a black man who became very prosperous through his admirable work ethic and character. He performed dirty, arduous work no one else wanted to do. The Whites lived on a small half acre in the black section of town, but they had a nice home with indoor plumbing, which drew curious spectators, both black and white. Mr. White gathered Spanish moss, which hung on nearly every tree in the county. He would lay it in huge piles in his yard until it started to rot. Once rotting, he would hang the slimy, decaying moss over wires he had slung back and forth over his small property. After the rotted moss dried, he would cover his mouth and nose with a cloth diaper and beat the dust out of it until there was nothing left hanging but the fiber. He made his living selling this fiber, which was primarily used as stuffing in furniture. Once the war effort got underway, the fiber became much in demand for seat cushions in military vehicles. I can't remember a single white man ever doing this very hard, very time-consuming manual labor. Mr. White eventually became very well off and sent each of his seven children to college and graduate school. His kids became nurses, medical doctors, lawyers, and teachers, a tremendous achievement for a black family during the Depression, especially one from the South.

CHAPTER 4

Childhood on the Farm

GROWING UP ON THE FARM involved hard, back-breaking, and sometimes dangerous work. Waking up before the sun, working sixteen-hour days, and going to bed after sundown was all I ever knew. Discipline and school were also an important part of farm life, but what I remember the most was the fun I had when I wasn't working and the delicious food our farm produced.

Fond memories included times when Mom made a game of canning and jarring a wide variety of foods, including tomatoes, fruits, peas, pecans, beans, snap beans, and corn. Some of these competitions were just between Mom and the kids, and sometimes they turned into social events that included Dad, neighbors, and church members. Often, we peeled and stripped citrus to make marmalade. Strawberry and blackberry preserves and jellies were a regular staple in our home.

One of my favorites was fresh sweet corn. We were careful not to overmature it, and Dad planted it in staggered plantings so that we could enjoy it over an extended period. Mom occasionally boiled some for breakfast and placed a couple of ears in our lunch bag;

we enjoyed it for supper and even as a bedtime snack. Nowadays I often comment to my suburban neighbors that the produce from supermarkets cannot hold a candle to the vine-ripened, farm-fresh vegetables and fruits I grew up eating. Our farm-raised lemons, for instance, were so sweet, we ate them like oranges.

When it came to sweets, my favorite was homemade citrus rind candies. We made them by steeping the rinds in simple syrup (sugar and water) with mint and other condiments. We cut the rinds into narrow strips and, after cooking in the sweet base, stored them for months in sealed jars. We enjoyed these homemade candies year-round. Mom and Dad gave them as gifts to attendees of the church Christmas party and our neighbors and friends. It was a rare day when one of Mom's candied citrus rinds did not end up in our lunch bags. These were the Depression years, but the Custeads always ate well during those years.

Fun did not always revolve around food. Every Saturday, Ruth, Earl, and I would rotate turns going into Palatka with Mom and Dad. This was a tremendous treat because we got to buy candy or see a movie. As Ruth grew into an attractive young lady, my parents took Ruth with them every Saturday so she would not be left unsupervised. I was really hurt because, at the time, I didn't understand my parents' reasoning.

We also found time to be foolish kids. White and blue herons were everywhere in the marshlands and shallow waters. For years, we young boys made a sport of creeping up on them and getting as close as possible before rushing the final yards in an attempt to grab them by their necks. In the rare instances in which we were successful, we kept control of their long necks to keep the birds from gouging our eyes out. What a challenge! Of course, we always let them go free after our conquest.

★ ★ ★

Growing up on the farm also entailed its share of danger, especially for an accident-prone kid like me. When I joined the Navy, Dad joked that he was glad to see me go because my medical bills had cost him a fortune. Fortunately, we had a great small-town doctor by the name of Dr. Thornton who worked at the county hospital in Palatka.

The first time I met this talented doctor, I was about eight years old. I had fallen into a concrete watering trough and broke my right arm in three places. Both forearm bones next to the elbow and the bicep bone were broken, which was the worst possible combination. Setting the arm with the correct alignment is extremely difficult, requiring great skill. The first doctor, Dr. Bell, tried for several hours before suggesting the arm be amputated at the elbow. My dad was not going to have that without a second opinion, so we went to see Dr. Thornton. This turned out to be the best decision my dad ever made as far as I am concerned. Dr. Thornton took several x-rays to get the bones set properly. He set the bones, took an x-ray, set again, took another x-ray, and so forth until he was satisfied he got the bones aligned as best as possible. He put the arm in a downward position in a cast and affixed a small bucket full of cement as a weight to pull on the bones. For months, I had this ridiculous bucket attached to my hand twenty-four hours a day, seven days a week, and had to figure out how to bathe and sleep with this contraption.

Several years later, when I was fifteen or so, I suffered another serious injury requiring the great skill of this country doctor. I had almost chopped my foot off. I was felling small pine trees for corral fence railings one morning before breakfast. I was out by myself with a horse harnessed to a sled, which we used to drag heavy stuff around the farm. My dad had his ax, which he kept razor sharp. It was a standing order never to use that ax. Of course, since it was the sharpest in the barn, I decided I would borrow it. I was using it to chop off branches from trees that I had felled. The blade bounced off a limb and went straight into my bare foot, almost splitting it in half. I was dressed like I was nearly every day on the farm; barefoot, overalls, and no shirt.

I saw blood squirt several feet straight into the air. I hobbled over to the sled and sat down facing backward. Holding my foot together with both blood-soaked hands, I screamed "Giddy up! YAH! YAH!" The damn horse would not break into a gallop despite my constant yelling. Since I was holding my foot together with both hands, I could not use the reins to whip the rump of the horse, who pulled the sled back to the barn at a slow trot. When I was within yelling distance of the house, I started shouting for my father. Dad came running out of the house as any parent would when they sense panic in the voice of one of their children. Dad wrapped the foot tightly to stem the bleeding and took me to Dr. Thornton, who operated on the foot, sewing three tendons back together. Again, his medical skills matched that of any large-city hospital surgeon. Despite an injury that could have crippled me for life, I never had a problem with my foot afterward, even though I spent years at sea and at war on my feet. For that matter, my right arm never gave me any problems either. Years later, while undergoing my physical for my naval recruitment, the doctor looked at an x-ray of my arm and said, "It looks like it was a terrible break, but the bones are perfectly fused and cellular." Dad never did mention me bloodying up his prized ax.

The final remembrance of this talented country doctor involved a trip to his office after I developed a horribly infected foot combined with lockjaw. Back then people typically got lockjaw by incurring a bad infection, usually from stables or rotten teeth. I believe I got the infection when, dressed as usual in overalls and bare feet, I jumped a barbed wire fence and cut my foot. It grew hugely swollen, and I was not able to walk on it. Dr. Thornton lanced it and drained cup after cup of pus. He then irrigated the wound, thoroughly cleaning it. Within a few weeks, the foot was back to normal. The lockjaw cleared up a few days later once the infection was under control.

While my dad always paid with cash, I knew Dr. Thornton's poorer patients often paid with such items as chickens or eggs. Most people in the county could not afford medical care at the time.

★ ★ ★

    My father was a strict disciplinarian. Growing up, I was belted a couple of times, but only one time did I not deserve it. That was on my baby sister Ruth's fourth birthday. That would have made me about five and Earl about eight. Mom, who rarely ever purchased clothing from a store, had purchased a cute little dress for Ruth from a department store catalog. Normally she made all our clothes from bolt cloth. The only items we regularly purchased from the department store catalog were overalls and shoes, which we wore seven days a week, both on the farm and to school. After supper, Mom told Ruth and me to get a bucket of English peas. Mom wanted Ruth to change out of her birthday dress so it would not become soiled. Ruth raised such a stink, crying up a storm, that Mom relented and allowed her to wear the dress to pick the peas. However, Ruth was only to carry the bucket, and I was to do the picking, further ensuring the dress would not become dirty.

    Ruth and I were on our way back to the house with a full bucket of peas. We had been successful in keeping Ruth's birthday dress from getting a single smudge on it. On the farm, we had big irrigation and drainage ditches. We fashioned bridges across these ditches using railroad ties, enabling trucks and tractors to cross them. Unbeknownst to us, brother Earl was hiding under one of the bridges lying in wait for us with a stockpile of mud pies. He ambushed Ruth and me as we crossed. Ruth was bawling hysterically as I pulled her by the hand toward home, both of us covered in mud. Just shy of the house, I looked up to see Dad enraged. He gave me a bad whipping with his belt. Mom ran out to stop Dad because Ruth, seeing how angry Dad was, had run into the house and told Mom that Earl was the culprit. Later, after we were cleaned up, Dad apologized to me. Earl, on the other hand, spent the night in the fields. He did not gather enough courage to come back until 4:00 a.m., when he received the licking of his life!

One time, we had relatives from Erie bring us apples. These were a delicious treat in Florida, as we did not often get the chance to enjoy this northern crop. Typically, the only apples we enjoyed were ones we got in church at Christmas in a bag of treats. One afternoon, we were visited by our impoverished and elderly neighbor, Captain Norris and his wife. We had been eating the apples for days, and there were only a few remaining. My dad wanted to offer this neighbor an apple when he noticed the few remaining apples had disappeared. I had eaten all three without asking, sneakily and selfishly. The next thing I knew, Dad was giving me a licking with his belt right in front of the visiting relatives and Captain and Mrs. Norris. After he finished, he asked me why I had been beaten. After two or three wrong answers, I got more of the same. It took me a while to arrive at the correct answer before Dad was satisfied. The correct answer, of course, was that I was rude and selfish to eat the last of the apples. It was tough having to come up with it, though, under such duress.

Dad only whipped his boys. Of the two of us, Earl was more of a troublemaker. One time he forcibly rolled me in a puddle of horse urine. Though Ruth often deserved a whipping, as she was quite the hothead, she never got the switch. One time when Ruth was probably fifteen and I was sixteen, she got so mad at me that she came after me with a butcher knife. At the time, I was picking up pecans and started running for my life, zigging in and out of the trees trying desperately to lose my pursuer. I can't for the life of me remember what I did to set her off.

★ ★ ★

Chores on the farm started at four or five years of age. There were many things I was tasked to help with as a small child. When our horses were in harness working for several hours, Dad would give me the chore of attaching feed bags to them and supplementing the feed every couple of hours. They enjoyed the feed and worked much better when they could eat while working. This was a job that gave me great pleasure, and being the youngest brother, I had it for many years. Dad also attached a portable radio to the horse collars. They seemed to enjoy the sound of music or the human voices and remained settled, working better. Sometimes, after Earl had used the team, we would remove their harness and take the horses to cool down by swimming with them in the lake. We would mount bareback and ride them into the water, holding onto their manes or the end of their tails and letting them drag us.

As a small boy and on through my teens, I loved feeding and watering the chickens as well as collecting their eggs. At the height of our egg business, we stacked the wire baskets used to hold the eggs outside because there were too many to store inside. To deter predators during the night, we placed cracked corn in metal trays around the eggs. Any step onto these trays would make such a racket as to scare predators such as foxes away. To entice the chickens into the safety of the coop at night, we scattered feed over the concrete floor inside the hen house and then locked the door once they were all inside.

Dad constructed quite an elaborate set of chicken coops complete with heat derived from solar-heated water for the younger birds. Mom oversaw selling eggs and chickens. She used the money to purchase shoes and clothing from the Sears Roebuck catalog. Fryers not sold for fifty cents (sometimes less with haggling) became fried chicken for our table. Old hens that were no longer laying eggs were used for cooking a dish of chicken and rice.

I probably acquired my attentiveness to the barnyard animals from my mother, especially the chickens and ducks. Ducks, when it comes to nesting and egg-laying, are very secretive, and their nests are damn near impossible to find. Sometimes, a hen or two would abandon the henhouses and strike out like a duck to find a secluded spot to lay eggs, but they were never quite as good at hiding their nests as the ducks. One of the things that Mom and I would purposely do when feeding the chickens was to keep an eye on the ducks and hens that would come running for food from their hiding places. This is how we tricked them into revealing their well-hidden nests. Mom would replace the older eggs with fresh eggs so that the hen or duck did not desert it. In the evenings, she would hold the eggs up to candlelight one at a time to determine their freshness. If they were not fresh, she would cook them, mix them with grits, and make feed for the dogs, cats, and hogs. If the ducks continued to lay eggs, we would add their nest sites to our daily egg-collecting rounds. This routine would last probably two to three weeks before snakes and large birds started beating us to the eggs.

Eventually, the chicken business dried up, and Dad removed all but two of the sixty-foot henhouses. We used these remaining two to store and sort tomatoes as they ripened. These tomatoes were sold to the six or seven local family grocery stores in the area. The excess, by the truckload every couple of days, was taken to the large produce market in Jacksonville. By the time I started to attend high school, it had become my responsibility to drive the tomatoes to market in the mornings before school. I would depart for Jacksonville with a full truck at 2 a.m. and then drive the empty truck straight to school. I did this twice a week all through high school. I always felt that the teachers gave me a break in my grading because they respected the fact that I was working so hard for the family farm.

★ ★ ★

Living on a farm meant having to deal with everything nature threw at you. Besides the normal worries about rainfall and crop-eating pests, I remember on two occasions witnessing mosquitoes swarming like honey bees when their queen flies off to seek a new home. The first time I witnessed this, it was shortly before dark. We were still working in the fields when we heard the swarm coming. We could see them soon after we heard them; they appeared as a low, slow-moving grey cloud. Dad, from experience with such phenomena, yelled for us all to run for the house. Once in, we kept the screen doors shut and turned off all the lights. Thankfully, most of the swarm kept moving past our farm.

The second time, it was again dusk, and again, we high-tailed it inside. This swarm was much worse than the first. From inside, we sprayed poison through the screens at them. The entire length of the front of the farmhouse was screened in, and in the morning, dead mosquitoes were an inch thick on the outside of the screen. We scraped them off using a flat grain shovel. All in all, we filled three-bushel baskets with dead mosquitoes.

Another hardship we faced for years was a result of the environmental catastrophe taking place in the Midwest, the Dust Bowl of the 1930s. The dust from the Midwest blew over our farm for weeks at a time for two or three years. It settled on everything inside the house, causing never-ending cleaning, especially on the beds and in the kitchen. Worst, it hurt us financially because the dust settled on the crops, choking them of sunlight. Our salvation depended upon good rainstorms to clean the plants.

★ ★ ★

We never locked our doors in Mannville. The only crime was committed by nomadic gypsies who rolled through town a couple of times a year. They used the same tactic over and over. They drove by the farm, then circled back on foot and stole anything they could get their hands on, including chickens, hams, sweet potatoes, you name it. The dogs on the farm were for hunting and pets, not guard dogs. Ironically, I never really liked to hunt; for some reason, I never enjoyed it as a pastime. It was different with gypsies though. Several times, maybe eight or so, I took my dad's shotgun, loaded it with rock salt, and shot the gypsies we caught red-handed either coming out of our curing house with a ham or the chicken coup with a chicken.

Several times as a young boy, I had loaded a shotgun with rock salt, aimed it at another human, and pulled the trigger. Maybe that was one reason I did not have any compunction about shooting a man once I found myself in combat. I never hesitated in shooting these thieves. Truth be told, I wanted to load buckshot in the gun. Over the years, as I told stories of shooting gypsies to my suburban neighbors while I chuckled at the thought, I often received looks of horrified shock. So I stopped telling these suburbanites this aspect of my life. I came to understand that they could never understand the mindset of a farmer victimized by thieves. From their point of view, I was shooting hungry, desperate people. From my family's point of view, these nomadic thieves could have stopped at our back door and asked for something to eat but chose to steal from us instead. My parents never failed to provide a meal to those polite enough to ask.

★ ★ ★

I had my own rifle as a boy. It was a hand-me-down from one of my older brothers. I guess no one else wanted a single-shot .22. During the season when the berries ripened, I and a gentleman I called Uncle Dave, who was probably 100 years old, sat sentry at each end of the field for days on end to keep the robins from decimating the strawberry crop. As a flock would come down by the thousands, we would fire off shots to scare them away. Then after about twenty minutes, another migrating flock would see the field and try to attack the crop. Foxes also would do a great deal of harm. For fox, though, we laid traps because they were nocturnal.

One morning at about 2 a.m., there was a huge commotion out in the henhouse. My parents went outside to investigate with my mother carrying a shotgun. My dad had originally purchased it for my mom to kill rattlesnakes back in California. My parents started arguing, and my dad attempted to grab the gun from my mother. My mother tried to hold on to it, and in the struggle, it accidentally discharged while they were standing next to the chicken coop. The next morning, they were shocked to find a dead black panther in the coop.

We had another experience with a panther when my brother Earl and I were riding our horses home from a friend's house. Earl had been discharged from the Navy, was married, and lived nearby. He was carrying a .45 pistol in a holster on his hip and had a shotgun strapped to his saddle; I was unarmed. We were walking our horses at a leisurely pace sometime after midnight when the horses became spooked. They started stomping their feet, shimming sideways, and refusing to move forward. We knew that meant a predator of some sort, perhaps a snake, was somewhere in the dark. I happened to look up and found the full moon silhouetting a panther on the branch of a tree hanging over the dirt road. This was the only tree near the road for miles either way. After I pointed out the panther, Earl debated for a moment about whether to dismount and hand me the reins to keep his horse from hightailing it. After a moment of consideration, he thought it best to stay on his horse in case it bolted, as we were still quite a distance from home. Though our horses on the farm were very accustomed to gunshots and tractors backfiring, he wasn't sure if he was taking a chance of getting bucked off by surprising the horse with a gun shooting just above its ears. At any rate, he aimed the .45 and hit that panther with the first shot, dropping it out of the tree onto the dirt road. While I held his horse, he went over, shot it again to make sure it was dead, and then dragged it off into the undergrowth so that the horses would pass. That shot from horseback in the dark of night was an incredible display of marksmanship.

★ ★ ★

I never realized how good my education was until years after I enlisted in the Navy. For the first two and a half years of schooling, I walked the four miles to the elementary school in Interlachen. This ended abruptly when a second grader named Carrie Rash was hit by a car and horribly injured while walking to school. After this incident, they reassigned the kids in our neck of the woods and put us on a bus to a one-room schoolhouse in Hollister. My first teacher in Hollister was Ms. Sykes, who died in childbirth shortly after my arrival. She was replaced with Mrs. Mabel Houston, who became my teacher for the remainder of grade school. I was the only student in my grade all eight years, which meant that I received one-on-one instruction. Mrs. Houston was a good Southern gal with as strict a disciplinarian zero-tolerance policy as I have ever seen. She borrowed books from the libraries of five counties and read to us as many of those books as she could, not only the classics but pop-culture books like Zane Grey. She read, read, and read.

At Hollister School, every child had to have one hour of physical training every day, which was fine, but it made school one hour longer. This extra hour meant we got home an hour later, which in turn, meant us farm kids had to work an hour later into the evening. We had lettuce to cut, beans, strawberries, or turnips to pick and produce to load for the market. We did not leave the fields until the truck was full, no matter what time of night it was. This often meant working by lantern well past nightfall.

Every Friday afternoon, the four of us boys picked up the trash and raked the leaves around the Hollister schoolyard. We also had to rake out and burn the waste in the outhouse. The five girls had to clean the classroom, blackboards, floors, and front twin doors. Every school day, all nine students proudly took turns putting up and taking down the American flag from our huge flagpole.

In high school, I took the same bus as I did for grade school but stayed on it a while longer to get to the only high school in the area in Palatka. Sometimes I would skip my last class to go to the movies on Lemon Street (now St. Johns Avenue). If the film broke too many times, or if the movie was too long, I might miss the school bus home. If that happened, I would hitchhike to my bus stop and then walk the half mile home. As the bus picked up students from several grade schools, I often would beat it home. Most of my rides were generally with people I knew. One driver always insisted on driving me to our front door. For his kindness, I would usually reward him with a few potatoes or turnips or something. This was okay with my parents because it got me home in time to work in the field and get my chores done.

CHAPTER 5

My Best Friend Bonnie

BONNIE WAS A TWO-YEAR-OLD Tennessee Walker that my dad surprised me with on my thirteenth birthday. He brought her back from a trip selling crops up north in Kentucky. She was a beautiful mare with a red coat. She was trained for the Tennessee gait, but I never had her perform it since I did not know how. She was supposed to be a pleasure horse for me, but that term does not exist on a farm. Dad thought she should earn her oats. Dad tried to put her to work plowing a couple of times, but she was never one to be harnessed. Dad was the only one who could control her in a harness and eventually decided she was not worth the trouble, as he had to manage her every minute of every hour in the field. It was more tiring for Dad than it was for Bonnie.

It was up to me to buy my own tack. I traded a very expensive solid brass saxophone for a very, very cheap saddle and bridle. I think the trade was with some cousin of a cousin. She got the better deal, but I did not care. I knew I was never going to be able to play that saxophone.

Bonnie had four other problems in addition to not wanting to plow. First, she was frightened to death of water. Second, she did not like being mounted. I had to climb her in a split second. The minute I place my left foot into the stirrup, she started shying away. The third problem was she had never seen barbed wire before. The bluegrass pastures of Kentucky where she had been raised had only had board fences. Lastly, she did not take lightly to being tied to a hitching post. Bonnie was eventually able to overcome these challenges, but it made for a rough couple of years in the beginning. Dad had to put a twitch on her nose more than a couple of times to sew up gashes from the barbed-wire fencing. Until she became accustomed to this new type of fencing, she kept trying to run right through it.

Even with these problems to overcome, she was a wonderful pleasure horse, and race-horse fast. God, could she go. When she became spooked, I would have to hold on to her mane for dear life until she came to a stop, miles away and after jumping fences and other obstacles. As for her fear of water, we had self-professed professional cowboys from all over the area show up to help. Each one was sure they could train or force her to go into the water. I knew from riding her that if she could smell water, no matter how far away, she would shy away. As these cowboys tried in vain to ride her into the water, she became worse. She started to associate water with punishment. One of the so-called experts did not try anything fancier than hooking up block and tackle to pull her into the water. That attempt ended with her rearing and bucking so violently that she broke loose from her halter and bolted.

When I was sixteen, three years after Dad had given Bonnie to me and she had become my best friend, I was the one who finally solved her fear of water. I knew of a clear-water, spring-fed creek so clean I often drank directly from it. Since there was no decaying debris around it, I knew the scent would be minimal or nonexistent. I took her at full gallop into the stream on a day when there was no wind. It was probably ten yards across and one to two feet deep. Bonnie came cresting over the berm of that stream at full gallop, and before she knew it, she was standing in the middle of it, shaking uncontrollably. I spent perhaps fifteen minutes in the saddle petting and talking to her in a soothing voice. After a while, she stopped shaking and put her nose down in the water, drinking and blowing bubbles. I got off and gently rubbed her nose, continuing to caress and talk to her. Then she started to paw at the water. At this point, I knew I could walk her around in it and did so for about thirty minutes. Bonnie never shied from the water again.

While Bonnie and I had a great deal of fun and adventure together, I also had a couple of close calls with her. Once I had a bad spill while riding her on an all-out dead run, which could not only have severely injured Bonnie but could have killed me as well. The dirt road we lived on was right next to train tracks and a small lake, which was down a four-foot bank. Bonnie, at a dead run, got tangled up in some trash telephone or electrical wire coiled up next to the road. She went down hard in a heap. We tumbled over and over before ending up down the bank in the water. Bonnie was able to climb out of the water, but I was left unconscious. The only reason I did not drown was because of the quick actions of some black gentlemen. They were down the road playing dominoes at the country store. While they were far enough away that we were out of eyesight, they knew instinctively something bad had happened when the sound of a horse's hooves, running at full speed, came to an abrupt stop followed by complete silence. They knew that a horse always transitioned from a dead run to a gallop to a trot. When they did not hear this transition, they knew something was wrong and came running to my assistance and saved my life. I awoke in the Palatka hospital three days later, again under Dr. Thornton's excellent care, having no recollection of how I got there. Luckily, I had bad head trauma and half the skin on my neck scraped off but no broken bones, despite Bonnie rolling over me going down that embankment.

The other close call with Bonnie involved an eight-foot water moccasin, which became the origin of my absolute fear of snakes. After Bonnie was successfully bred at the nearby Rodeheaver Ranch (now the Rodeheaver Boys Ranch), my dad dropped me off with my saddle and bridle to ride Bonnie home. My three- or four-month-old collie mix puppy came along. It was probably a twenty-mile ride over dirt roads. Trotting and walking, it should have taken about four or five hours. The puppy, who was probably thirty pounds at the time, jumped up on my lap when tired and would jump off when she saw something that interested her. This, of course, caused my arms to get scratched up. Sometime around midday, several hours into my ride home, I fell asleep in the saddle with the puppy on my lap.

I was jolted awake when Bonnie bolted to the left in a violent, sideways jerk. I opened my eyes and realized I was five feet in the air in a sitting position and there was no longer a horse under me. I hit the ground damned hard. I found myself lying almost on top of a huge moccasin. Luckily for me, the puppy took several bites from the snake that were intended for me. She immediately engaged the moccasin in a fight, which took the snake's attention away from me in those first few precious seconds as I gathered my senses. Once the surge of adrenaline kicked in, I was able to roll away from danger, even though I'd had the wind knocked out of me and was hurting and dazed. With the adrenaline still coursing through my veins, my heart pounding out of my chest, and my breathing hard, I picked up an old fence post and beat the snake to death. Afterward, I remember laying the snake out, and it stretched across the eight-foot-wide dirt road. I located Bonnie about a hundred yards away eating grass by the side of the road. Luckily, I had been training Bonnie to stay put when the reins were dropped. It looked like my training had paid off, as I was still a couple of hours from home. While I was walking toward Bonnie, the adrenaline was wearing off. I started to check myself to see if I had been bitten. I remember feeling panicked because I had red scratch marks all over my arms. Were they from the collie, or had I been struck?

The next thing I knew, I woke up staring into the sky through the Spanish moss-covered trees. Judging from the angle of the sun,

I had been lying on my back unconscious for several hours. To this day, I don't know what happened to me. I either fainted from fright or simply went into shock.

Luckily, the puppy was still there and seemed no worse for her violent encounter with the moccasin. She had saved my life. I should have been struck during those first few seconds after hitting the ground. I was disoriented, had the hell knocked out of me, and could not catch my breath. If I had been bitten, and if Bonnie had bolted, I probably would have died in those woods. My dad had not gone straight back to the farm, so no one knew I had been out there lying unconscious. Even after I got back on Bonnie, I was still scared to death and shaking. I was not sure why I had passed out and thought it might have been because I had been bitten. I placed the collie over my lap, held on to her tightly, and kicked Bonnie into a gallop. I probably galloped for ten to fifteen minutes before becoming worried that I would kill her because she started to sweat profusely in the Florida heat, her red coat covered in white froth. From that point, I walked and trotted her for the remaining hour until I got home.

I jumped off as soon as I arrived and ran into the kitchen, telling Mom what had happened. Dad still wasn't home, but Mom was frightened by my ordeal and looked me over from head to toe until she was satisfied that I had not been bitten. My collie became terribly sick once we were home and suffered for a few days but eventually recovered.

Bonnie's foal was born about a year later in the stable in the middle of the night, without any human intervention.

This foal turned out to be a beautiful palomino; gold with a snow-white mane and tail. Just before I joined the Navy, my brother Homer took Bonnie and the palomino foal to his ranch. He rode this gorgeous palomino in parades for years with an expensive black leather saddle and bridle covered in silver studs.

CHAPTER 6

Racism

IN THE DEEP SOUTH, THE "cracker" was one step lower than the established Negro, which was the accepted term of the time for African Americans. The term *cracker* has an interesting origin. It comes from the nickname slaves gave to slave foremen who "cracked" the whips. Crackers, as I knew them, were the product of generations of whites who made their living stealing hogs and moonshine from each other, and timber from Yankees. They were often illiterate and married their first or second cousins. Often their paper shacks, located on property they did not own, lacked even an outhouse. They shared them with pigs and fowl and often defecated just outside their front door. Crackers made up the largest portion of our society. "Yankees," like my family, were a tiny fraction of it. One of my brothers married a cracker, but only after her father showed up nearly every day at our farm, with a shotgun over his arm, looking for that "Yankee" who had defiled his daughter.

An eight-mile-wide swamp separates Putman County into west and east sides. Judge Green appointed my dad as coroner for the western side. Every time there was a murder or death in West Putman, Dad would perform an investigation. As a kid, I often tagged along on these investigations, which made me a witness to death and the brutal side of life at an early age.

In many instances, if the sheriff and judge were satisfied, Dad's report comprised the entire record. I witnessed several occasions when my dad's determination was that a death was the result of accidental drowning or a drunken knifing or shooting. Often, the sheriff didn't investigate crimes because the jail was full or he didn't want to feed more prisoners. Sometimes he would say that justice had already been served or that the sheriff's office didn't need to waste their time and money over a feud that appeared to be over. Of course, this being the Deep South, the sheriff and judge did not care about black-on-black crime. The enforcement of the law and justice was reserved for whites only.

My parents did not fit into the politics of the South. The Custeads were very progressive for both the era and the environment in which they lived. I am not saying we were perfect because we all have our prejudices, but we respected and admired many local black families, more so than the crackers who were so prevalent in the area. Looking back, the black kids I considered friends were anything but. What I did not understand as a young boy was that blacks treated me, a white kid, with polite respect out of a need for self-preservation. They were afraid to cross societal boundaries and kept to themselves for both protection and security. To this day, older blacks adhere to this tradition taught to them by their parents. Even now, when I travel back to Putnam County, I am struck by the continued practice of the older blacks eating outside of restaurants in sweltering heat instead of the air-conditioned dining area inside.

My dad was a very principled man who acted upon injustices. He taught me that, in life, doing the right thing usually ended up being the more difficult choice. We were Yankees from Pennsylvania by way of California, not prejudiced crackers. My dad went to Judge Green and demanded to see the county's property tax records after learning that the black children's school was a dilapidated wooden structure with no indoor plumbing, electricity, or even a bus. At that time, if a black child could not walk to school, he or she simply remained illiterate. This, of course, was entirely different from the white schools like the one I attended. The judge told my father not to disturb the balance or stir up needless trouble. My father ended up suing for the records at his own expense. He found that the blacks in the county were paying for the white people's nice schools and school buses, with nothing going to the black schools. Some of the richest whites paid no taxes at all. I think he sued in district court because I remember my dad traveling back and forth to Georgia. He sued a second time to force the county to pay for upgrades to the school and to furnish the first school buses for the black children. You can imagine the uproar this caused in this sleepy Southern town. These actions resulted in my dad receiving death threats. I remember Dad saying that a group of a dozen or so black people stood in the courthouse square and told the sheriff and the judge that should any harm come to Mr. Custead, there would not be a white home left standing in Palatka.

When my folks walked down the street in Palatka, both whites and blacks tipped their hats and said, "Good day, Mr. and Mrs. Custead." The blacks, as mentioned earlier, would always be extremely polite and well-mannered while in the company of any white. Being polite and well-mannered meant not being noticed and not being noticed meant staying out of jail or worse. A seventeen-year-old store clerk could call a grown black man "boy" while the man would respond with a respectful "Yes sah." Accordingly, my parents were not treated any differently than any other white by the blacks. However, when it came to the bigoted crackers and other whites, it was much more complicated. The mores at the time in a small Southern town dictated that everyone, including the sheriff and his deputies, address my parents politely because of their social status, even though they must have despised "those nigger-loving Yankees."

I learned many valuable lessons from my father about the unpleasant effects of racism. His teachings on social justice for the blacks were not theoretical or abstract. I learned from my father, a righteous man, and lived by his moral guidance and example.

We often hired day laborers on our farm at harvest time. Whenever we needed laborers, and because my dad favored black laborers, he would drive the truck over to the black section of town and yell out the window that he needed pickers. They would come running and jump into the bed of the truck. The white men were indignant at being paid the same as black men and said so, but it did not matter to my father. He paid a penny or two for each pint of strawberries or a nickel for a bushel of beans; the color of your skin did not matter. I remember the whites only working long enough to purchase a bag of grits, while the blacks tended to be much harder workers, working as long as there was a crop to be harvested. It was primarily women who picked berries, which required delicate hands, while the men tended to harvest the heavier crops requiring stronger backs. I, of course, was out there right beside these day laborers because Dad paid me the same rate as everyone else.

When I was fifteen or sixteen, my good friend Herman Bauer and I were driving my dad's truck home late one night from Gainesville when we came across a horrific traffic accident shortly after midnight about ten to twelve miles away from our farm. On this clear, moonlit night, we could see bodies everywhere along the highway. There were seventeen dead and dying black people along the side of the road after what appeared to have been a head-on collision. Some were moaning for help while others were already dead. The cars were so demolished you could barely tell what kind of vehicles they had once been. We stopped to help, but there was clearly nothing we could do. I kept going to the local Western Union office to try and alert the authorities. We stayed there waiting for hours for help that never came. The sheriff did absolutely nothing for these people because they were black. I am convinced he would rather have gone fishing. A black man driving our neighbor Mr. Durden's pulp truck came upon the scene while Herman and I were still there. He was going fishing, so it was probably just before daybreak. By this time, the few who were alive when we arrived had died. I can't remember this gentleman's name, but I remember him knowing me, addressing me, a teenager, as "Mr. Custead." He helped us load all seventeen corpses onto his logging truck. Disgusted that no one came to help, I had him follow me into the county seat in Gainesville where I instructed him to park in the middle of the courthouse square. By the time we arrived, dawn was breaking. I then drove the gentleman back to his home before dropping off Herman.

After I arrived home, I immediately started my morning chores without having any sleep. The culture of the farm was that chores came before all else. As soon as I finished, I got ready for church. It was not until we were on our way to church that I told my dad about the prior night. My dad said it sounded impossible and my brother and sister didn't believe it.

We never heard a word about the seventeen deceased people we left on the courthouse square. Both cars were from New York, not local people. The sheriff did not care. There was absolutely nothing in the local papers, no news of the event at all. We never heard what became of the bodies, but we assumed the county buried them in pauper's graves.

By the time I was seventeen, I had seen a great deal of death. I was thirteen when I first witnessed a murder. I was riding Bonnie home after visiting a local restaurant that featured a jukebox, a major source of entertainment in the county. The blacks stood outside to eat, drink beer, and socialize because, of course, they were not allowed to sit inside. The black men were teasing me about drinking a beer when two black brothers, the Hamptons, got into a heated argument. I was so frightened of the brothers' fierce behavior that I determined it best I mount Bonnie and get away. One of the brothers had the same Durden pulp truck that had carried the bodies away from the aforementioned car crash.

The dirt road near the restaurant separated at a forked intersection about a half a mile from the restaurant. I was riding home on one of the dirt roads past the fork when Bonnie became skittish because she smelled fresh blood. Looking across to the other bend of the path, I saw one of the Hampton brothers using the truck to drive back and forth repeatedly. Slamming it into reverse and hitting the gas, then slamming it into first gear and hitting the gas. Over and over this went on, the truck going back and forth, back and forth. I instinctively knew I was witnessing a murder. The next morning was Sunday. I did my morning chores as usual, washed up, and changed my clothes for church. It was at breakfast that I first mentioned to Dad what I witnessed the day before. On the way to church, I showed my dad the site of the incident. At first glance, there appeared to be a large grease stain in the sand road. Beside this spot was a deep lake with dark water. What had been left of the body had probably been thrown into the lake. Dad got out of the car and realized he was finding small body parts. The turtles in the water were feasting on what we assumed was the murdered Hampton brother.

Being the coroner, Dad performed an investigation for the sheriff. Nothing ever came of it. No charges were filed and no arrests made. The sheriff did not want to waste any time, effort, or money investigating a black man killing another black man.

CHAPTER 7

The Great Depression

The Great Depression was the life I was born into, and it persisted for the first thirteen years of my life. I was one of the lucky Americans, having been born on a prosperous, self-sufficient farm. We never went hungry and always had more than enough, so much so that my parents could help others less fortunate. There was serious, widespread suffering all around us; people were starving to death. No one in the state of Florida received state aid because there was none to give. Occasionally, hobos traveling the rails and crackers showed up at our back door begging for something to eat; usually offering to perform chores in exchange. Either my mother would bring them a plate of food or my father would take them out to the fields and give them a couple of potatoes or turnips.

We had trainloads of people not only leaving town but also arriving, chasing rumors of work. We referred to these trains as refugee trains. Even if my dad wanted to do more to help alleviate the suffering, he could not; it was too great and widespread. If he gave everything he had away in one day, there would still be suffering the next. I was with my dad at times when he would drive the truck to the train station where desperate, starving people had gathered awaiting the next train north traveling the country looking for work. He would load it with citrus, which was not selling well at the time, and hand out oranges, lemons, and grapefruit to the hungry migrants. These migrants mostly consisted of fathers or brothers traveling alone. However, it was not unusual to see entire families with small children.

At the onset of the Depression, most Americans lost their life savings when the banking system collapsed, further aggravating the desperate plight of American families. My father saved every spare nickel the farm had earned over the years and had placed his savings on deposit in the local bank. The Custeads were fortunately spared from the banking system collapse because the president of the bank, Mr. Bush, was a close friend of my father and a fellow church member. Mr. Bush showed up at the farm one afternoon and told my father to meet him at the bank at 2:00 the next morning, knowing that the bank was going to collapse the next day upon opening. In the dark of night, Mr. Bush unlocked the bank and allowed my dad to withdraw his life savings of $1,100 from the vault, the equivalent of $15,000 in today's dollars.

Rich Yankees had always used several hotels and dozens of large homes in Palatka for winter getaways, but all that changed when the Depression hit. Our Methodist church membership dwindled from dozens to maybe seven active members. Most of the churches closed because there was no money from the remaining members to support them. Accordingly, the county, like most of Florida at the time, did not have church-sponsored soup lines or kitchens to feed the hungry. Death became accelerated due to hunger and disease, aggravated by malnourishment. If they still had a home, family members would be buried in their own yards, not interned into cemeteries. Life was brutal.

As a child, I helped my dad bury a lot of people who had died from starvation. Most were desperately poor, illiterate crackers and blacks who had been barely staying alive before the Depression. These people often lived in tar shacks in the woods and swamps with no heat or plumbing. After they died, their homes simply decayed and reverted into nature. Some of the homes were burned down with the bodies in them for fear of disease. Sometimes we found migrants dead in the woods where they had simply laid down to die. Buzzards circling high overhead dead bodies were so common that I regularly kept a collapsible hand shovel strapped to my saddle. Luckily, I never came across any dead children. Typically, it was the very old who succumbed to starvation and disease.

★ ★ ★

The Depression marked the beginning of the end for our citrus crops. The farm had been mostly a citrus operation, but during the Depression, the acres of citrus were plowed over, and the farm was converted to growing produce.

The citrus market dried up for two reasons. First, at the time, citrus was considered a luxury, not a staple. If people had a nickel to buy food, they could buy a lot more potatoes or collard greens to feed their families than citrus. The second reason was crony capitalism. The big citrus companies, with the help of the federal government and state legislatures, fueled by campaign contributions, colluded to squeeze out the small, independent farmers to take over the market and drive up prices. Large corporations started buying up family-owned citrus farms at distressed prices during the Depression and monopolized the market.

We had always produced huge grapefruit, sweet oranges, and red blood oranges. At one point, Dad was producing so much citrus he could fill several boxcars every two weeks. The end came when my dad had filled eight boxcars of citrus on a northbound train. Three of those boxcars sat and froze in a train yard in New York because the "citrus mafia," the large corporations, made sure no one purchased dad's shipment. This was the last time he ever shipped citrus north. The greatest injustice was that the federal government fined my dad for the frozen citrus. He fought it in court but eventually lost. Dad paid these heavy fines by borrowing from business associates and friends. He was a beaten man and knew he could not fight such government-sponsored corruption.

★ ★ ★

Most of my older brothers and sisters suffered terribly during the Depression because they had already left the relative safety and security of the farm and were fending for themselves. My brother Oliver, almost twenty years older than me, was perhaps hardest hit.

By the time the Depression hit, he was a young man in his twenties living in Pennsylvania among our relatives who owned some large farms. Unfortunately, the northern farms were seasonal. After the annual apple crop or whatever was harvested, there was no work. Oliver was starving to death, living off scraps of food where he could find it. For weeks, in a race against time, he walked and hitchhiked in a weakened state from Pennsylvania back to the family farm. Had he not made it, he might have become one of those unfortunate migrants we found dead in the woods.

Trading on the Custead name, Oliver was able to find work on the nearby Hollister farm in exchange for room and board. At some point, he was bucked off a mule or horse and broke his leg. Because he was too poor to afford a doctor, he had a fellow farmhand set and splint the leg. Upon recovery, he again found work on the nearby Futches' strawberry farm. It was here that he met his first wife, Ellen Futch. Marrying into this family became Oliver's salvation. The Futches were one of the largest landholders in the state. Disney World acquired its land from this family to build its massive theme park. Oliver, a great businessman, eventually became the largest grower of strawberries in the state.

CHAPTER 8

Enlistment

BY THE TIME I WAS fifteen, it was 1943, and World War II was in full swing. Like every red-blooded American boy, I wanted to enlist and teach those Japs that America was not to be trifled with. I was genuinely afraid the war was going to be over before I had a chance to enlist. The desire was so consuming that my dreams were full of military adventure. Sometimes, I would awaken in the middle of the night in a panic from nightmares that the war had ended before I had gotten my chance to get in on the fight. On July 1, 1947, I was eighteen and a half years old and had just completed the eleventh grade. With my parents' blessing and permission, I joined the Navy, a decision that would forever change my life and open to me a world that, as a small-town farm boy, I had no idea existed. As I left on an adventure to see the world, the only thing that kept me grounded to the farm was the regular letters I received from Mom. My first enlistment was for four years. Little did I know that I would make a twenty-eight-year career of the Navy, re-enlisting four times on July 3, 1951, July 3, 1957, May 19, 1961, and February 18, 1965.

The decision to enlist was not necessarily an easy one for me or my parents. Paul would be the last of their boys left on the farm, as Earl was already serving in the Navy. In the end, they gave me their blessing. I knew Dad was getting too old to farm. Mom was thirty-eight when I was born and was now fifty-seven while Dad was sixty-two. I was comforted that I was not abandoning my mother and father: the plan was for my brother Paul to take over the farm in exchange for Dad deeding him ten acres. Dad worked the farm alongside Paul until he died from what I suspect was an aneurysm at eighty-five.

My family always joked that Dad was glad I was going into the Navy because my numerous trips to the doctor cost him more money than all the rest of his kids combined. College was not an option I ever thought about, even though I had two wealthy uncles who offered to pay my way. Twenty years before, some of my oldest brothers and sisters had gone to college, but that had been before the Depression. At the time, I did not believe I was college material. Not only had I been educated in a one-room schoolhouse, but I was the only one in my grade. It was not until much later in life that I realized what a great education I received, and that I might have made a mistake by not going to college before enlisting. The first evidence of this was how I scored in the ninetieth percentile on all the tests I took in the Navy. I simply had no idea how well-educated I was because I had nothing with which to compare myself. I did not realize then that being the only one in my grade in the one-room Hollister schoolhouse was basically like receiving one-on-one tutoring for all those years. At any rate, the argument was academic because college or no college, I could not wait to enlist and fight.

At the time of my enlistment, I had twenty-some head of cattle. Before I went into the Navy, Dad arranged to sell them to our neighbor, Mr. Durden, for $400. Dad had already gotten rid of his cattle, keeping only dairy cows on the farm. I took this money and went on a trip up north to Erie, Pennsylvania, to visit relatives before reporting to boot camp; I was under the rather bleak assumption that I would never see those relatives again. I stayed in a hotel, paying cash for everything, and spending $10 a day like a playboy. The hotel security pegged me as the country bumpkin I undoubtedly was and stole $160 from my room. I had foolishly left it there when I took a cousin to see Lena Horne. When we got back, the hotel room had been ransacked like something out of the movies. I had only about $100 of the $400 left when I got home.

When I went to the recruiting station, I was six feet and two and a half inches tall, and not quite the minimum 150 pounds. The chief at the recruiting station said, "Let's take a break for lunch. I want you to go out and eat about five pounds of food so that you can pass the minimum weight."

I promptly went out and ate two bunches of bananas—about sixteen total. I had never eaten so much food at one time in my life. When I got back on the scale after the break, I made the weight limit by just one pound. This was highly irregular and against regulations, but I was convinced that the chief liked and wanted me. Most recruits in Putnam County were illiterate rednecks with no manners, but I was very well-educated and had been raised to be respectful of authority.

Boot camp was in San Diego, California, but I never finished it. I did not know what gays were at the time, due to my extremely sheltered life on the farm, but I sure found out in a hurry. For some reason, my boot camp contained a large number of homosexuals. Once the Navy discovered this, they canceled boot camp and dismissed us one by one, putting us through individual investigations, spending weeks interviewing us. They spent day after day talking to me before they realized that this simple, naive farm boy had no idea what a homosexual was and let me continue into the Navy. I was ordered to San Diego to attend school to become a hospital corpsman, the specialty for which I had been recruited. Most of the recruits were told just to go home as they dissolved the class.

Even if boot camp had not been canceled, I have always believed the physical and mental discipline of boot camp would not have been a challenge for me since I came from a farm. I was raised working sixteen hours a day for days on end. Two of the things the Navy found out about me in the couple of weeks we had boot camp was that I was an excellent diver and that I had no fear of heights. A requirement for graduating was jumping into water from the height of an aircraft carrier. I became the recruit who had to demonstrate this skill repeatedly to the point of exhaustion. It was forty feet at the time, the equivalent of jumping from a four-story building, but nowadays it's higher because the ships are bigger. The policy was that you were discharged if you could not perform this task and swim away.

After boot camp, I had a little leave, which I used to visit my parents before starting corpsman training. It was during this trip home that I met my wife, Lois.

In August 1947, still eighteen years old, I found myself on a Greyhound bus traveling across the Southwest, returning to Jacksonville with three other sailors, also fresh out of the same boot camp, two of whom I knew from Putnam County. One of the two was my childhood friend, Herman Bauer, and the other I remember having the surname Heini. The third sailor, whose name I don't recall, was headed to another part of Florida.

At that time, it took almost a week to cross the country on a bus since there weren't any interstates. These bus rides were rough, one step above crossing the country in a Conestoga wagon. You wore the same clothes without showering for a week. You either slept in a terminal or, more often, on the bus. I was traveling with the other three new sailors when we found ourselves at a bus stop in Texas for two hours waiting for a transfer. I was asleep on a bench with my legs straight out in front of me when Lois, carrying several pieces of luggage, tripped over my feet, dropping her bags. Lois was traveling from Denver to MacDill Air Force Base in Tampa to help a cousin who was expecting a baby; she was with her Aunt Mickey, her chaperon. I immediately jumped up to apologize and help her with her bags. As I did so, I noticed the other three sailors also had come to her assistance. I immediately knew why. She was drop-dead gorgeous.

Aunt Mickey was probably in her forties and was quite a character; a born matchmaker. After we all boarded the same bus, we stopped for breakfast in Denton, Texas. It was at this point that

Aunt Mickey schemed to match Lois and me up. She told me that she would get Lois in a booth next to the wall and would then leave, allowing me to have a private breakfast with her.

At first, Lois was very shy, and awkward. She immediately overcame her shyness, though she did not have to because I did all the talking. I did find out a little about her; for example, she was the oldest of seven children while I was the second youngest of nine. In later years, she told people she became comfortable with me very quickly and thought I was a fascinating conversationalist. Neither of us had ever really had a girlfriend or boyfriend up to this point. After breakfast, I sat with Lois on the bus until we reached the Florida Panhandle. Lois was supposed to change buses to head south to Tampa at this point. After exchanging addresses, I told her she had to kiss me goodbye before she could get on the next bus. Lois was at the head of the line to get on the southbound bus with me standing in her way. What she did not know was that my three buddies and I had bet a couple of dollars back in Texas to see who could get a kiss from her.

The bus driver got into the act too. He said, "Ma'am, you would be awful selfish not to give that sailor a kiss goodbye. Who knows, he may go off to war and you may never see him again. Therefore, I won't let you on the bus until you give him a kiss." Lois was embarrassed and blushing terribly but finally relented and I won my three dollars.

I wrote my first letter to Lois a day or so later. This was the beginning of a long letter-writing campaign that lasted almost four years before we got married. I wrote her letters almost daily. I continued to write as I worked in the San Diego hospital. I wrote her when I shipped out to the USS *Repose* off the coast of China. And I wrote through the Korean War. We only actually saw each other in person a total of eight days before we married upon my return from Korea.

After my leave to visit my parents, I left for San Diego Naval Hospital to begin my training as a hospital corpsman. At the time I enlisted, the Navy was desperately short of corpsmen. I was originally scheduled to report to a fourteen-month training program. The program, however, had already started by the time I arrived. Since they did not allow late entrants and were desperately understaffed at the hospital, they decided I would receive on-the-job training.

On October 31, 1947, I reported to the hospital and was placed under the tutelage of the doctors and nurses there. My first evening I was working in the emergency room when we received a patient injured in a motorcycle accident. Motorcycles were all the rage then. Every Marine and sailor had one.

The doctor on duty, Captain Driscoll, said, "Custead, you will watch, listen, and learn as I care for this patient. I need help in this hospital. I will x-ray for broken bones, scrub and clean his wounds, and suture his cuts. The next patient, I want you to perform these duties under my supervision. The third patient, you are to do it yourself and show me your work afterwards. After that, you are on your own as far as these types of injuries are concerned."

The first patient had almost scraped his kneecap off. Dr. Driscoll showed me how to debride the wound (removing dead tissue and cleaning), cutting a big star-like shape around it. Next, he took a heavy suture and forcibly pulled the star-shaped hole closed around the kneecap. Afterward, he said, "Now you know what to do; just do it."

That first night, we had three almost identical motorcycle-related knee injuries. And just as he showed me, I cut a large star-shaped hole in the skin around the knee, debrided it, and then got Captain Driscoll, who sutured up the wound. The next one I sutured up myself and then had Captain Driscoll look it over. From that point on, I was on my own for these types of injuries. We followed the same protocol for each new type of injury. This was all in my first night of duty as a corpsman. I don't think any other corpsman had ever been thrown into the deep end like I was that first night. I had a lot of help from others besides Dr. Driscoll, including another corpsman, named Griffin, with whom I would become close friends. Griffin had several years under his belt, and he mentored and trained me as a new corpsman.

My duty assignment at the hospital had me working pretty much around the clock since we were so short-handed. Since the war was winding down in Europe and much of the South Pacific, the GIs were coming home, causing a tremendous baby boom in the States. I can recall someone saying we were averaging 275 births a day. It was like an assembly line. I delivered thousands with my own hands.

About a year into my corpsman career, my life took a drastic turn. At eighteen, I had been promoted from Seaman to Hospital Corpsman 3rd class when the mayor of San Diego brought his twenty-two-month-old daughter into the emergency room because she had busted her lip in a fall. It was nothing serious; I don't recall there being any cut or bleeding, only redness and swelling. He could have treated her at home with an ice compress.

My typically understaffed fifteen-hour shift was composed of two medical doctors, me, and two other medical corpsmen. One of the doctors was established in his career and enjoyed a good reputation, while the other, a recent medical school graduate, had no experience or reputation and had only been in the Navy for a short time. It was sometime shortly after the start of my 5:00 p.m. to 8:00 a.m. shift when this new doctor, a lieutenant, gave me an order to give the mayor's twenty-two-month old baby 10 ccs of 10% solution of sodium pentothal, a rapid-onset, short-acting barbiturate general anesthetic.

I knew right away that this was enough to kill a grown man. We never gave it to any child under ten years old in any dose. I tried to tell him that the order would kill the toddler. He became irate and started yelling at me, "And what medical school did you go to, Custead?"

I remember writing it down so I could find someone in authority to reinforce his order. I searched high and low trying to get the attention of a doctor, but everyone was busy attending to some emergency. I went back to the idiot doctor and asked him to put the order in writing. Again, he became irate and yelled at me, "Just do it! How dare you question my order? I'll have you court-martialed!"

I tried in vain to get ahold of the hospital's chief nurse. I left a message for her to come and support me. Unfortunately, to my incredible regret, I reluctantly followed orders and gave the little girl an IV with a dose of sodium pentothal that killed her. I did not know it right away; I started the IV and left to attend the next patient. When I got back, the chief nurse finally showed up and informed me that the toddler had died. She implied that I was not at fault and that I was too junior and inexperienced to have known better. She knew that the lieutenant was at fault for issuing the fatal order. Afterward, someone had to tell the mayor that his little girl died from her busted lip.

I continued to work my shift through the night. I was working on a very serious situation early the next morning, one with exposed bones and lots of blood, when the same chief nurse came and said we had to leave right away for the commanding officer's quarters. I protested that I could not leave what I was doing, prompting her to find a nurse to relieve me. I was in the middle of putting on a clean lab coat when the next shift's doctor arrived. This doctor was a commander and was both highly regarded and loved by everyone at the hospital. His wife often came in with food to feed us on our long shifts.

Reading the logs from the prior night, he noted that there had been five deaths and asked about the twenty-two-month old baby on the list. After I explained my desperate attempt to get help in not administering the order, he told me to wait for him to change into his lab coat because he wanted to come with me. He asked if I was aware of the stupidity of the order, and I told him I had spent ten minutes arguing with the idiot doctor and trying to get witnesses. I added that on top of everything else, the child's father was the mayor of San Diego. He said, "My God, now I know why we are going to the commanding officer's office."

The meeting was a calm affair. The commanding officer, an admiral, asked everyone individually what had happened in an orderly manner, gathering all the facts. It is important to note that in a military hospital, the military chain of command is never to be questioned. It is no different than being in battle. One is to follow orders or risk court-martial.

After being dismissed, I went to the galley to get breakfast before heading back to my quarters. I had not even sat down with my tray of food when two Marine sentries arrived and ordered me to follow them. They locked me in the nurses' quarters and posted outside the room. I was to remain in quarters, under armed guard, for the next three weeks. In effect, I was under house arrest and not allowed to leave for any reason.

Nurses came in all the time under the pretense of bringing me a cheeseburger or a Coke so they could hear from me what had happened. The incident was infamous and became all anyone talked about at the hospital. After three weeks of constant interviews and interrogations, I was convinced that I was being court-martialed and was headed to the brig. Then, one day, the sentries suddenly came in and said I was free to go. I was dumbfounded and not sure what to make of it.

I immediately headed for the galley where my confinement had all started. Maybe I could finish the meal I had been denied three weeks earlier. Again, as soon as I sat down with my tray, two junior officers walked up to me. This time, however, they said I could take my time and finish my meal and then they would talk to me. I am not sure I ate much because I immediately lost my appetite. I was sure the commanding officer changed his mind about court-martialing me.

When I finished, they escorted me to the personnel office, where I received new orders. I had two hours to pack my sea bag and leave

San Diego. I had received orders to report to duty on the USS *Repose* stationed off the coast of China. I have always joked that I was the first person ever to be "shanghaied to China." They wanted me as far from the San Diego press as they could get me and as quickly as possible. I never did hear what became of the lieutenant who issued those fatal orders.

Fortunately, they gave me a couple of days of leave before shipping out with the understanding that I had to leave San Diego within hours. I took advantage of it to visit Lois in Denver. It had been about eight months since we'd met on the bus, and it was to be only the second time I had seen her in person. The visit was maybe all of seven hours. This time, I dug deep into my pockets and bought a commercial airline ticket to Denver. It was during this visit that I first met Lois' mom and dad. Lois' mom was Lucille Alice Durant (maiden name: Dalrymple), and her dad was William Harry Durant, but he went by Harry. He was a paymaster in a coal yard and spent most of his life working around coal, the major source of heat for homes at the time. He was the only one in his family who had worked full-time during the Depression. He never made much money but was one of the lucky few who had a job. He was the kind of person who not only took care of his large family, but other relatives in need. At one time, he took in his mother and two minor siblings into his modest home.

I fell in love with her parents. I had never seen such a close, affectionate family. My family was from old English and German stock and just did not interact lovingly like Lois' family. All my relatives lived in Pennsylvania, a thousand miles away. At Lois' house, there was always lots of family.

As I was leaving, Lois kissed me for the second time in the eight months I had known her, this time without being forced. There was no real commitment at this point; we occasionally dated others but nothing serious. Lois was not serious about me at this point, but I got the feeling she really liked me.

After spending time with Lois, I had to make it back to Terminal Island in San Francisco, where I was to board a merchant marine vessel that would take me to the *Repose*. Unfortunately, I was late getting back and missed my boat, forcing me to wait a few days for the next transport.

CHAPTER 9
World War II

Photo No. K-31496 USS Repose (AH-16) on 24 April 1966

THE USS *REPOSE* WAS A new, state-of-the-art hospital ship, capable of treating 1,700 patients. The date was November 6, 1948, and World War II was still officially ongoing in the South Pacific, especially in China where the U.S. was supporting, training, and equipping the Chinese Nationalist Army in a civil war against Mao Tse-tung and his Communist army. Many Chinese towns had a small detachment of American Army advisors. As the tide of this civil war turned in favor of the Communists, the U.S. Marines' mission was to locate the American Army advisors, protect them, and bring them back before the Communists started overrunning their positions. The Navy's objective was to support its Marines. About thirty Americans were killed a day during this evacuation of Army advisors, and the mission of the *Repose* was to patrol the Chinese coast and care for the wounded.

It was during my tour aboard the *Repose* in 1949 that the ship was involved in a historic United Nations armada, assembled to rescue British citizens trapped 100 miles up the Yangtze River. This famous battle came to be known as the Yangtze Incident and became the basis for several movies. What began as an attempt to rescue British citizens turned into an operation to rescue the British Navy.

The Communist Chinese took over the oil refineries, which the British had colonized and operated in Nanking, China (now known as Nanjing) for decades. These oil refineries had been owned by the British for generations and were populated with and run by British citizens and their families. The British, with the assistance of a United Nations task force, assembled a huge armada of thirty large warships. Counting support ships, the armada numbered closer to 100, representing eighteen different nations. However, the armada was primarily a British operation, and the *Repose* was one of the seventy or so supporting vessels. The British took this armada up the Yangtze River as a show of force, to make the Chinese back down from confiscating their economic interests in Shanghai and to support the C-class destroyer HMS *Consort*, which was already in Nanking to protect their embassy. The HMS *Consort* had lost forty-nine sailors after being attacked by the Communists and needed assistance. Included in this armada was the famous British frigate the HMS *Amethyst*, whose exploits during this incident were later the subject of the aforementioned movies.

The Chinese brought a tremendous amount of artillery down to the shoreline. I was not nervous, but I figured a lot of casualties might be in the making. The Chinese made a statement that they were not intimidated as they proceeded to shoot the hell out of the armada. The warships were sitting ducks as they could not lower their guns to the shoreline since they were designed for long-range firing. Luckily, the *Repose* did not take any fire from the Chinese who seemed to honor the existence of a hospital ship. This was the first big battle the UN had ever engaged in, and it was a complete and utter rout. After the Chinese were done shelling the armada, every warship was blown to hell. Everything above their gunnels was completely shot off or laid in a twisted, blackened heap. There were no bridges, superstructures, or even gun turrets left on the British warships. The ships were so badly damaged that you could not identify one ship from another; they were just hulls with engines. After this disastrous battle, the fleet turned and retreated for the Yellow Sea, still under a constant barrage of fire.

There was an unbelievable number of casualties. We started taking them on en route up the river and were still taking them on during the 100-mile retreat to the Yellow Sea. British warships were lined up to offload their wounded to the *Repose.* I was on one of four surgical teams working around the clock. This was the first of three times in my naval career where duty required me to go without sleep for five days and nights. The younger of us could take the physical punishment; however, one captain, a surgeon, probably around fifty or sixty years old, collapsed into a coma at the end of five days. There were normally female nurses onboard the *Repose,* but they were taken off before going into battle leaving us shorthanded. The wounded were not prepared for surgery; they came directly into the surgery unit as they arrived. I was below deck the entire time. My responsibilities included a tremendous amount of debriding and stitching of wounds as well as bone setting and casting of broken bones. In some cases, I did minor surgery while the surgeons took care of the major cases. There was no time for x-rays, just emergency medical care to stabilize patients and save as many lives as possible. One of my patients was the son of a British general. We ended up putting a silver plate in his head. I am pretty sure both father and son were in that battle, and the general himself had also been wounded.

The second of the three times in my career I stayed awake for five days and nights again occurred on the *Repose* after the Yangtze Incident. The *Repose* was called upon to steam full ahead to Okinawa in response to a devastating typhoon, which had struck the island, killing thousands of military personnel and their dependents; thousands more were wounded. The major cause of deaths and casualties was the result of tin shrapnel from Quonset huts being hurled by gale force winds.

I was evacuating the survivors, most of whom were wounded, with an M-Boat, which are kept on the *Repose* for shore excursions. It was probably twenty-five feet long, open, and was skippered by a sailor. The survivors were marshaled to an evacuation site that was sheltered from the high surf, making it unnecessary to go up and down the shoreline in search of them. On each of the hundreds of trips, we took eighteen to twenty survivors, depending upon how many were on stretchers versus how many could sit or stand. While the skipper of the boat was relieved often, I did not get out of that boat for five days and nights. I relentlessly went back and forth evacuating women, children, and military men. I was able to patch up a couple of the wounded while ferrying them, but I did not do much because it was such a short hop back to the *Repose* and the seas were high. I saw some horrible injuries, including amputations. I never became delirious from lack of sleep thanks to the occasional ten or fifteen-minute catnaps I got here and there, and I was given sandwiches throughout this ordeal so that I could keep my energy up. The Army was there evacuating as well. The difference between our effort and the Army's was that, while our boat was manned by only me and a sailor, the typical Army ship-to-shore boat evacuating survivors probably had eight men. The Army does everything this way. The Navy trains its men to do a much broader array of tasks while the Army training is very specific.

We took Navy and Marine personnel and their dependents while the Army took care of their own. The survivors were taken back to either Japan or Hawaii. I can't recall the total number of casualties, but it was in the thousands. The vast majority of the survivors were either stitched up or had broken bones set so the number of casualties was not a major burden to the ship's capability. I was unaware of whether this ever made the news, and I never knew what they did with the vast number of dead, though I assume they were buried on the island. Afterward, the *Repose* went back to duty off the shore of China, and I fell into a long deep sleep until I was finally aroused for duty.

★ ★ ★

In addition to being a hospital ship, the *Repose* served as an intelligence-gathering platform. I became friendly with one gentleman who we took on board wearing the uniform of a petty officer 2nd class. He was full of interesting information and stories. We became friends as we spent our downtime reading Tolstoy's *War and Peace* together. It was the first time I had tried to read this complex novel. Only in hindsight did I realize this sailor displayed unusual intelligence and education when he assisted me with understanding this challenging book. His education was clearly more advanced than the typical petty officer. I don't remember his name, so I will call him Brown.

We were in our base port of Tsingtao in China, and there were probably a half-dozen ships taking on and offloading cargo. The *Repose* had two separate commanding officers, one for the ship itself and one for the hospital. One evening, while in port, Brown came up to me and said, "You might want to see this."

I was shocked to see that he had an attaché handcuffed to his wrist. I followed him to the ship's commanding officer quarters. Once we got there, I was stunned at how he walked in without knocking and with an air of authority he had not previously displayed. I thought we were both going to catch hell from the commander for the way he barged into his stateroom. I meekly stood next to the wall, trying to blend in like a chameleon, hoping he did not think we were together. Brown pulled some documents from the attaché and handed them to the commanding officer. He introduced himself as Commander Brown of the Navy's CID (Criminal Investigation Division).

This, of course, got both my and the ship's commanding officer's attention real fast coming from a man in a petty officer's uniform. The ship's commander said, "What the hell is this all about?"

Brown replied, "Take these codes and send them to Washington. They will confirm I am who I say I am. I am here to take command of this ship and confine you to quarters. You are being charged with theft and misappropriation of Naval assets."

It turned out that the ship's commander was using the ship to steal anything he could get his hands on. Mostly, he was taking building materials off the docks of one port and selling them at another. Six or eight other crewmembers were also indicted and arrested in this scheme. The whole episode did not take long; Washington confirmed Commander Brown's coded orders in short order. I sat and watched this whole drama unfold right in front of me. The ship's commander was eventually transferred to a flagship, where he was court-marshaled.

The Russians were in China supporting their Communist brethren and it was almost a daily occurrence that a Russian officer would defect from China. They would be brought aboard the *Repose* for a preliminary intelligence debriefing before being quickly transferred off the ship. Where they went after their short stay aboard the *Repose*, I could not tell you, but I have to believe the high-value defectors were sent back to the U.S. for further interrogations.

★ ★ ★

Before my tour aboard the *Repose* came to an end, I made a feeble attempt to sightsee in China. I figured I would never again get this chance. While in the port of Tsingtao, I took it upon myself to visit

Peking (now known as Beijing) for a sightseeing tour. I hopped on a military transport in my quest to see historical sites I would never have the opportunity to visit again. I had my heart set on visiting the Forbidden City and Tiananmen Square. However, after hitching an eight-hour ride there, I became too afraid to venture out. Everyone I spoke to said I was nuts to sightsee without an armed company of Marines. I got cold feet and went back to the safety of the *Repose* without having seen a thing.

Another historic event I witnessed while stationed on the hospital ship was the looting of China by Generalissimo Chiang Kai-shek. By this time, Chiang Kai-shek had lost his war with the Communists and was fleeing the country, taking China's gold bullion and priceless artifacts with him with the aid of U.S. warships. I spent days along with hundreds of sailors, unloading hundreds of trucks as they continuously pulled up to the docks. We formed fire brigade lines hundreds of feet long from the vehicles to pallets that were then taken by forklift to the ships to be hoisted by crane. As I remember, there was enough gold and treasure to fill thirty U.S. warships.

Once my tour aboard the *Repose* ended, the homeward transport ship was detoured for a brief stopover at Pearl Harbor. When we arrived, the captain asked for volunteers to attend Ernie Pyle's funeral. No one stepped forward except me and a few others. Ernie Pyle was a legend to me. All the remaining men assumed they would be given shore leave in Honolulu if they did not volunteer for the funeral. As it turned out, they all had to remain on board while those of us who volunteered went ashore to witness the re-interment of one of America's biggest celebrities at the time.

Ernest Taylor Pyle was an American Pulitzer Prize-winning journalist. He was a traveling correspondent for the Scripps Howard newspaper chain from 1935 until his death in combat in 1945. His articles about the out-of-the-way places he visited and the people who lived there were written in a style much like a personal letter to a friend. He enjoyed a following in some 300 newspapers. All of us enlisted men worshiped him as a friend of the foot soldier. He did not write about troop strengths and movements or generals; he wrote about the men holding the guns, fighting the war. He wrote about their families, hometowns, and lives. Everywhere he went, GIs treated him like the celebrity he was. When I was a teenager, I enjoyed reading his articles in the Palatka Daily News or the Jacksonville newspapers.

On April 18, 1945, Pyle died on IeJima (then known as Ie Shima), an island off Okinawa, after being hit by Japanese machine gun fire. He was buried with his helmet on and laid to rest in a long row of soldiers, between an infantry private and a combat engineer. The Navy, Marine Corps, and Army were all represented at the ten-minute service. Pyle was later reburied at the Army cemetery on Okinawa and then moved to his final resting place, nearly four years after his death, the National Memorial Cemetery of the Pacific located in Honolulu, Hawaii. His headstone was placed at the front gate in a place of honor. This latter ceremony was like the burying of a head of state. The highest brass from all services, high government officials, and international dignitaries attended. I was proud to have been there to pay homage to this great war historian.

CHAPTER 10

Proposal

In August of 1949, I found myself back in the San Diego area running ambulance duty at Camp Pendleton. My naval records list me at 148lbs, still two pounds under regulation for my height. I was still quite the beanstalk.

Other than the occasional gruesome highway accident, it was quiet at Camp Pendleton. The biggest excitement was when servicemen would steal a tank and drive it into town to get a drink or a pack of cigarettes. It was quite the spectacle to see civilian police chasing a tank through city streets.

With World War II winding down, there was a huge reorganization of the armed services. They were transitioning from a war footing to peacetime. This included freezing my billet (rank). All promotions became centralized Navy-wide, and every corpsman had to take a Navy-wide examination covering close to twenty different disciplines. After diligently studying as hard as I could, I was able to pass the exam and was promoted to Hospital Corpsman, 2nd Class.

While stationed at Camp Pendleton, I found time to visit Lois in Colorado again. The commercial plane ride was financed by my brother George and his wife Lila Mae, who lived nearby in Los Angeles. I otherwise could not have afforded the trip since I was making maybe $120 per month.

Lois and I started to become very close during this visit. I was able to stay a couple of days this time. Her family invited me to a picnic at Estes Park, Colorado, at an elevation of 7,500 feet. We were playing softball when a funny thing happened. Due to the high altitude; this lowlander from Florida passed out while running full speed around the bases. When I came to, my uniform was torn, dirty, and bloody. Lois said I had not been unconscious very long. I remember waking up and asking if I was out. I assumed the first thing they did was to take advantage of me being unconscious to tag me. I wasn't embarrassed because they all knew I was a lowlander and made it seem like an everyday occurrence. It was just another way Lois' family displayed warmth toward one another and family friends.

A while later, Lois returned the favor and visited me at my brother George's house in Los Angeles. I hitchhiked the four-hour car ride to get there. In those days, if you were wearing a uniform, you had no problems hitchhiking; people fought over who was going to pick you up. The roads were full of sailors, Marines, soldiers, and airmen trying to get home from the war. It was the fastest and cheapest mode of transportation. Three and a half years had passed since I first met Lois on the Greyhound bus and we had now seen each other a total of four times. After being together for a couple of days, we became even closer. I was contemplating retirement because I wanted to be with Lois. However, I got word that even if I retired, I would be called back up for the Korean War.

I took Lois to a dance during this trip and proposed to her, giving her a ring that Lila Mae helped me buy at the Robinson Department Store. I got her employee discount on a $300, 0.55-carat platinum engagement ring. I could afford this expensive ring because I had saved every dollar I earned. I was a very boring sailor; I did not drink, smoke, or gamble like most of my peers. Lois was not surprised at the proposal; we both knew we were heading toward marriage. When I proposed, I knew the Navy had frozen my rank and that I was heading to Korea. My utmost desire was to come home alive. When Lois got home, she told her family she was engaged. Her family was probably not ecstatic that she was marrying a sailor, but Lois told me they had always liked me and were happy for her.

CHAPTER 11

Korea: The Inchon Landing

BY THE TIME I GOT orders for Korea, the North Koreans had overrun all U.S.-held positions in South Korea down to Pusan (now known as Busan) in the southernmost tip of the Korean peninsula. To me, my orders were just another piece of paper. I was not scared or nervous, even though I was not going to be serving on the relative safety of a hospital ship as I had in World War II. Instead, I would be attached to the 1st Marine Division, a ground combat force.

I felt proud to join a Marine fighting force, and I knew the Marines thought highly of corpsmen. There has always been a rivalry between the Navy and Marines, even with the close association of the two services. Many people are not aware that the Marines are a branch of the Navy. It is the Navy's job to get the Marines to the beach and to pick them up. The Marines know their lives depend on their corpsmen and the consensus has always been that we are tough in battle. The Marines always treat their Navy corpsman with very high regard and look after them. I heard stories of Marine privates getting beaten savagely by their sergeants for the crime of disrespecting a Navy corpsman.

Upon my arrival in South Korea, I disembarked at the city of Pusan. The U.S. was assembling its forces here for the main invasion at Inchon (now known as Incheon), about halfway up the east coast of the peninsula. I was only there for a few days before preparations for the September 15, 1950 invasion began.

The Inchon landing site was not so much a beach landing as it was a muddy lakeshore landing. The 1st Marine Division landed on the southern side of Inchon, code-named "Blue Beach." The tide there moved in and out hundreds of yards, requiring perfect timing of the landings. High tides brought in up to thirty-three feet of water. Landing craft required twenty-three feet of depth while LSTs (landing ship, tank), on which I was to arrive, required a draft of twenty-nine feet. Each high tide lasted only four hours, which meant that every minute counted. Once the first wave of boats carrying the grunts hit the beach, it would be a minimum of another four hours before the next tide moved in the next wave of reinforcements. It was because of these tides that McArthur's gamble on this landing site paid off. There was not much resistance because the North Koreans did not heavily fortify the shoreline, thinking the Americans could not launch an effective invasion at this site.

As the first wave of U.S. forces was assaulting the beach, they came under heavy fire from a hilltop cemetery above the landing site. As the first wave of grunts hit the shore, big naval guns provided covering bombardment to soften the North Korean defenses. My LST was with the 73rd Marine combat engineering division. We hit the beach four hours later with the second wave since we were carrying heavy equipment. As we were disembarking in knee-deep water, a sergeant five feet to my side had his head, left shoulder, and left arm blown off by high-caliber machine gun fire.

This was my first taste of battle as a grunt. I did not react at all other than to duck and quicken my pace. I did not hesitate for a moment. I simply looked over and dispassionately thought to myself, "Well, there is nothing I can do for him," and kept running for the top of the beach where a slight hill provided cover. I was lightly loaded with just a carbine, ammo, and my medical bags strung over my shoulders enabling me to cover ground quickly.

The bulk of my equipment and supplies was loaded in the jeep ambulance, which had not yet been offloaded from the LST. Most of the grunts were carrying 80 to 120 pounds of equipment and ammunition. They obviously could not move as fast and were completely out of breath as they reached the top of the beach where we all hunkered down for about an hour. Other than that poor sergeant, I don't remember any casualties in my immediate vicinity. The first wave had been successful in clearing most of the resistance, but it was still a dangerous spot. Our orders were to sit tight at the top of that beach until the Marines flanked the hill with the aid of continuing offshore naval bombardment. Once the Marines took that cemetery, the rest of the invasion fleet disembarked without further incident.

★ ★ ★

During the landing, it quickly became apparent many of the World War II veterans among us were unable to function once the reality of the situation set in. I did not realize it at first until it was brought it to my attention. I would guess that upwards of 2,000 of these veterans were incapable of disembarking the landing crafts. They remained behind, unable to muster the will to disembark. They could be identified by their looks, mannerisms, and behavior, but I can't describe it with any justice. Many had the proverbial "thousand-yard stare." Many years later I read an article about the Normandy invasion explaining how the military brass purposely chose troops with no combat experience for the bulk of the initial assault force. They reasoned that an experienced infantryman was a terrified infantryman. I agreed with the article, as it accurately described what I witnessed in those men.

Every man on board the landing crafts, including me, was scared to death, not knowing what kind of resistance we would meet on the beach. Would we be faced with dug-in defenses? Would the beach be mined? When the landing craft ramp came down, would everyone on board be annihilated? It was this anxiety and fear amongst us, before a single round had been fired, that triggered this condition in these battle-weary veterans. Some of the World War II veterans made it off the landing craft but froze later, incapacitated with fear and dread. They were only capable of willing themselves to move off the landing craft and up the beach before they shut down. Some made it to Seoul, and still others made it hundreds of miles up to the Chosin Reservoir before becoming incapacitated. They were battle-fatigued before they even arrived, but it hit them only after the landing craft doors slammed down into the surf.

Every one of those men was moved out of the battle forces and into naval hospitals stateside including an Air Force base in the Southwestern U.S. that had been re-commissioned to housing and rehabilitating these men. They were of no further use to the Navy or Marines since they were incapable of further fighting. I witnessed hundreds of these cases and was required to certify that the shell-shocked veterans I encountered could not go on. The armed services acted very compassionately toward these men; there were no court-martials nor any disciplinary actions. Cowardice was not even a consideration because these men had previously proven themselves in World War II. The services even came up with new terminology designed to minimize embarrassment to these valiant men, who had bravely served their country during World War II but, when faced with having to repeat their wartime experiences, just psychologically shut down. Terminology such as "shell shock' and "battle fatigue", which carried negative connotations, were replace with terms such as "gross stress reaction", which did not confer any stigma. It was obvious to me and all who witnessed it that it was not cowardice, but truly a cause for compassion. These men had already witnessed firsthand the horrors of war that all veterans know can never be adequately described to those who were not there. It is only the uninitiated who go into war willingly.

★ ★ ★

One of the stupidest things I have ever done in my life was to pick up an unexploded missile I found half-buried on the beach. This was, of course, hours after the hostilities died down. I was curious about it since I had never seen one before. I was very lucky; that moment could have been the end of my story. To this day I shudder every time I think of how incredibly stupid I was.

After playing Russian roulette with the unexploded missile, I joined up with my unit for the twenty or so mile march to our first objective, Seoul. My engineering battalion was well behind the initial fighting forces, which had encountered stiff resistance in house-to-house fighting. Once Seoul was secured by the Americans, the citizens treated the U.S. forces like conquering heroes.

Marines taking Seoul. The advance forces had the city under control by the time my platoon arrived.[1]

Since I was driving a Jeep ambulance and the first wave of Marines had secured the city, I decided to do a little exploring. I had no business being where I was and certainly had no orders to be there, but I did not think it would be a bad idea to go into the city and check it out. On the second day of exploring, I made my way to the Gyeongbokgung Palace, better known as the Imperial Palace, the name given to it by the Japanese during their pre-World War II occupation. Here I joined in on my first firefight which lasted about two hours. The unit I happened upon was fighting a holdout of North Koreans entrenched in the palace gardens, surrounded by high, white walls. Fighting was going on all around me as I joined five Marines lying on their stomachs behind a one or two-foot stone wall. Unable to dislodge the North Koreans, the Marines called for offshore artillery. I have read about it in books and seen it on TV, but there is nothing like personally witnessing the accuracy and devastation of an offshore naval bombardment. The Marines called it in from what I think was the USS *Missouri,* which was probably twenty miles away. I remember hearing a shell coming in from the battleship. Its trajectory came awfully close and almost deafened me. The only reason I did not lose my hearing was that I was below the shockwave. I was on my belly, firing from a distance of 500 or 600 feet. I could feel the earth shake as those shells hit. It felt as if I had been completely bounced off the ground, becoming airborne for a second. The first shell landed a few feet short of the palace grounds, the next landed a few feet too far, and the third demolished the North Koreans in the gardens, ending the firefight. The Navy, to its credit, was trying to avoid hitting the palace. The violent, destructive power and resultant craters created by these sixteen-inch shells were something to behold.

Once inside the palace, I witnessed a Marine steal a rare, centuries-old albino leopard hide. Despite soldiers always looking for souvenirs, a lot of these stolen treasures were confiscated by the U.S. military and returned. The most prized souvenir among the Marines was the Luger semi-automatic pistol, the sidearm carried by the North Koreans. These pistols were the Marines' favorite who eagerly searched for them. For them, finding one on a dead North Korean was like finding gold. These Lugers had a great combination of tremendous power with minimal recoil. One evening, I saw a Marine taking bets on what his Luger could do. He had stacked a bunch of helmets on top of each other and proceeded to shoot holes through their front and back sides. I was never interested in war souvenirs, nor did I have time to collect them.

After Seoul was secured, we were ordered to move over 200 miles north toward the Yalu River by way of a little-known place called the Chosin Reservoir. The overall feeling among the Marines and sailors, thus far, was that we had the North Koreans on the run; it was only going to be a few quick weeks to kick their ass and then get back home in time for Christmas. Little did we know what was in store for us.

CHAPTER 12

Korea: The Chosin Few

"Our hands and feet were frozen numb. The wind-borne cold attacked with terrible fury. We shivered violently."

—Lt. Joseph Owen, 7th Marines[1]

AT THE NATIONAL MUSEUM OF the Marine Corps, four battles are memorialized as the most important in the Marines' storied history. The Battle of the Chosin Reservoir, a definitive battle of the Korean War, is one of those four fabled battles. To be one of the "Chosin Few," also referred to as the "Chosin Frozen" due to the hellish freezing temperatures, as we veterans of that battle are known, is to command respect like no other from fellow Marines. The importance of this historic battle is drilled into every Marine during boot camp.

Eighteen thousand Marines of the 1st Marine Division and a similar number from the Eighth Army found themselves surrounded by 60,000 Chinese, becoming the victims of both horrendous intelligence failures and the arrogance of General Douglas MacArthur. The General believed he could end the war quickly by pressing north to the Yalu River, which separates China and North Korea. All the while, MacArthur was dismissing reports of the Chinese massing on the other side of that river.

For seventeen days and nights, from November 27 through December 13, 1950, the 1st Marine Division, commanded by Major General Oliver P. Smith, fought its way to safety in sub-zero temperatures. Outnumbered three to one, the Marines used superior military discipline and strategy to keep from being annihilated. They inflicted devastating casualties on the enemy, though the losses were staggering on both sides. During the retreat, they marched and fought for their lives for seventeen days over eighty miles. They marched on frostbitten, frozen feet from the reservoir back to the port of Hungnam. After this battle, the U.S. withdrew from North Korea, but the war continued until the armistice was signed on July 27, 1953.

According to Wikipedia, "As for the Chinese strength, it is normally assumed that the Chinese had 120,000 troops for the battle since the 9th Army was composed of 12 divisions with a strength of 10,000+ men per division." But during the battle, the 9th Army employed only eight divisions, while all divisions were at 65 to 70 percent strength at the start. Thus, the actual Chinese strength for the battle was approximately 60,000.

An aerial view of the Chosin Reservoir[3]

Wikipedia describes the site of battle as follows:

Chosin Reservoir is a man-made lake located in the northeast of the Korean peninsula. The name Chosin is the Japanese pronunciation of the Korean name Changjin. The name stuck due to the outdated Japanese maps used by UN forces. The battle's main focus was around the 78-mile (126 km)-long road that connects Hungnam and Chosin Reservoir and served as the only retreat route for the UN forces. Yudami-ni and Sinhung-ni, located at the west and east side of the reservoir respectively, are connected at Hagaru-ri, south of the reservoir. From there, the road passes through Koto-ri and eventually leads south to the port of Hungnam.

The road was created by cutting through the hilly terrain of Korea, with steep climbs and drops. Dominant peaks, such as the Funchilin Pass and the Toktong Pass, overlook the entire length of the road. The road's quality was poor, and in some places, it was reduced to a one-lane gravel trail.[4]

The terrain was very mountainous and reminded me of the Appalachians, except I don't remember any evergreens. Where there was vegetation, it was brown, leafless, deciduous trees and brush. The area looked like a snowy, grey moonscape, sparsely inhabited by impoverished farmers.

Wikipedia describes how the weather contributed to the battle:

The battle was fought over some of the roughest terrain during some of the harshest winter weather conditions of the Korean War. On 14 November 1950, a cold front from Siberia descended over the Chosin Reservoir, and the temperature plunged as low as -35 °F (-37 °C). The cold weather was accompanied by frozen ground, creating considerable danger of frostbite casualties, icy roads, and weapon malfunctions.[5]

The wind chill made the temperature feel much lower, as I remember the wind constantly howling through the mountain passes.

The impenetrable Taebaek Mountains split the U.S. forces, with the 18,000 Marines of the 1st Marine Division, the division I was attached to, on the east side and the Eighth Army on the west. The Eighth Army's discipline broke down during their retreat, with soldiers abandoning their weapons, ammunition, and rations, and running for their lives. As the Chinese chased the Eight Army, the abandoned supplies strengthened them. In contrast, the Marines, employing strict military discipline, fought their way out of the encirclement, often coming to the Eighth Army's aid.

This is my story of fighting for my life with the Marines.

I was attached to the 1st Marine Division (about 18,000 men), 7th Regiment (3,000 to 4,000 men), 73rd Engineering Combat Battalion (300 to 1,300 men), Company A (80 to 240 men). Though I don't know for a fact, I always suspected that my company of 240 men suffered some of the highest casualty rates of the entire war during this battle. I know there were only eighty of us left standing when we reached the evacuation port of Hungnam. My platoon's casualty rate mirrored that of Fox Company, which I will talk about later in my story.

We fought our way northward 200 miles into the Chosin Reservoir from our amphibious landing at Inchon. The reservoir was a short distance from the Yalu River, which separates China from North Korea. For weeks, we had been moving units north, establishing supply depots and airstrips along the way. In hindsight, we realized that the Chinese wanted to draw us in before hitting us with their superior numbers. Waiting patiently until the U.S. forces were within spitting distance of the Chinese border, they attacked with everything they had. Their strategy was not to take the U.S. head-on but to attack the entire seventy-eight-mile evacuation route. They planned to splinter the U.S. forces into small groups, thus enabling their superior numbers to annihilate us. As an engineering battalion, we took on heavy fire going north because we were behind the grunts, but in front of the main force, clearing obstacles. On the retreat, the Chinese did not want our engineers to succeed in repairing roads and bridges, which they were blowing up to trap us in place. My unit's objective was to get the main forces across obstacles and on the move so they could not be easy, stationary targets. Sometimes, we bulldozed a creek just long enough to get the Marines and their equipment across. As we retreated from the reservoir, our three big bulldozers kept running due to the extreme cold despite having their radiators shot up. I remember marching for two or three hours behind one of the big caterpillars, which had its blade in the air for protection. Most of the time, however, I was either driving or riding in a jeep ambulance or some other wheeled or tracked vehicle.

While fighting northward towards the Yalu River, we corpsmen often found time to provide much-needed medical care to civilians we met along the way. We often lacked the materials or time to do this but always tried to help whenever the opportunity appeared. On the way to Chosin, a family brought me a thirteen-year-old girl who had a chunk of flesh missing from her buttocks. She had sat on a frozen stone and frostbite had set in. For about three days, I treated this young lady, going back and forth to their little house to change her dressing and tend to her wound. We communicated using sign language, as neither of us could speak the other's language. Their home was tiny but very comfortable for South Korea, and like all South Korean homes, it did not have indoor plumbing. Her parents, who were school teachers, were so thankful they were beside themselves. As my unit moved on, I left the family with additional medical supplies. One of my regrets is that I did not get their names or a way to contact them so I could follow up regarding the wellbeing of the little girl and to find out what became of her and her family after the war.

★ ★ ★

It was a bright Sunday morning when my unit arrived on the west side of the Chosin Reservoir, a few miles from the Chinese border, in an area called Yudam-ni. Helicopters were only used at that time to transport generals and other officers. After a general arrived via helicopter, the pilot offered to take me, a lieutenant who was our unit's doctor, and an overweight chaplain on a joyride to the top of a ridge to check the lay of the land. We were aware of Chinese troops amassing nearby, but no hostilities had broken out yet. Having never flown in a helicopter, I eagerly took him up on the offer. The chaplain was much older, perhaps fifty or sixty, and very heavy. The pilot ribbed him mercilessly about whether or not we would get off the ground with him on board.

Once we landed on our hilltop vantage point, we could see the Chinese armies across the Yalu River. The lieutenant was standing about thirty feet from me, urinating, when the first phosphorous shell of the battle took his head clean off. This is my earliest recollection of how the battle started. I remember looking over and seeing him standing for a second or two, still urinating and blood gushing straight out of his neck several feet into the air before toppling over.

The subsequent barrage then blew the helicopter to pieces as we hit the deck. The Chinese assumed it contained a general. The hilltop would have been maybe a thirty-second flight away, so we were not too far from our unit. We got back by a combination of crawling and all-out sprinting. The Marines always brag about taking their dead with them; no man left behind. All I could do was grab the lieutenant's bloody dog tags and stuff them into my pocket to take back with me.

The initial bombardments were five-inch phosphorus shells. No one could figure out why the Chinese started with this type of ammunition because these munitions are incendiary as opposed to explosive. Typically, phosphorus munitions are used against towns and cities, not troops. What was strange, but normal for me, was that

I never got rattled, even when the lieutenant had his head shot off. After about ten or fifteen minutes, we got back to our unit, which was already under fire. One of the first things the unit did while the battle was raging was torch the hundreds of mail bags that had just been delivered. It was November 27, and Christmas was about a month away, so the mail and packages were voluminous. The pile of mail must have been ten feet tall. It was standard military policy to burn the mail when under fire; we could not risk any potential intelligence falling into enemy hands.

When the chaplain, the helicopter pilot, and I made it back, there was no order. It was complete chaos, no structure whatsoever. Due to the turmoil, the three of us dispersed. I did not even try to locate my platoon. At the time, if there were any operational radios, I was not aware of them. A few of us corpsmen found each other and banded together.

Waves of Chinese tried to overrun us Marines that Sunday morning; they did not stop for nearly three days straight. They attacked us with the only advantage they had, sheer numbers.

We were changing out white-hot machine gun barrels every twenty minutes or so as they disintegrated from the unrelenting, nonstop firing. I was on my stomach for the first forty-eight hours, firing my carbine constantly with Marines on either side of me. My major concern was ammunition. A minor concern, after many hours, was my bladder. I relieved myself numerous times while firing from the prone position. There was no way in hell I was going to stand up; men were dying all around me.

As far as ammo, I always saw to it that I never had less than two spare thirty-round ammo clips next to me. Every time I would get down to two clips, I would yell for ammo, and someone would start tossing it in my direction. During the entire battle, we never ran out of ammo thanks to constant air drops. I threw away three carbines those first three days as I wore out their barrels firing thousands of rounds nonstop. The Marines of the fabled Fox Company, who were located further south defending the Toktong Pass, reported that the elite Chinese troops they were facing were wearing a tightly-braided leather vest under their quilted coats; reportedly these vests were stopping carbine rounds. They either took headshots or switched to the more powerful M1s. I was not aware of whether we had similar problems. I learned later that we were facing Chinese regulars, while Fox Company was facing elite Chinese units.

We were so well-supplied by airdrops that we never needed to scrounge among the dead Chinese for rations, ammo, or weapons. If anything, we were over-supplied when we started our retreat. After three days of holding off the Chinese attacks, we had to burn and explode a lot of supplies to keep them from falling into enemy hands.

Our dead and wounded during the first forty-eight hours were not even a consideration. Every man who could pull a trigger, wounded or not, was firing; we were fighting for our very survival. I know I killed a significant number of Chinese, but I have no idea how many. The extreme cold ended up being a blessing for the wounded. Many injuries that would have otherwise caused a Marine to bleed to death froze and congealed, thus saving many lives. I also heard many Marines tell stories of escaping death when Chinese attempted to fire at them from point-blank range only to have their low-quality Chinese weapons misfire due to the sub-zero temperatures.

After the first two and a half days of mowing down the onslaught of Chinese with around-the-clock firing, the Marines were able to maneuver into multiple defensive positions, separating ourselves from the enemy and allowing air strikes to be called in. The first two days were full of tremendous killing; we burned up a lot of guns. Before this point, the Chinese were so intermingled with the scattered U.S. forces that air support was not possible without strafing or bombing our own troops.

The Marines had established supply lines and air bases as we moved north, allowing us to receive airdropped ammunition and weapons almost immediately, but some supplies were accidentally dropped to the enemy. Enemy capture of our supplies was unavoidable because we were so mixed with them. It was not like we were all grouped against an opposing force. My 7th regiment, combined with the 5th regiment, totaling 8,000 Marines, was scattered over many square miles. The Chinese were all around, among, beside, behind, and between us.

When the U.S. was finally able to call in air strikes on the third day, the Chinese changed tactics in response and only attacked at night, hiding from our planes during the day. The waves of Chinese attacks started each dusk after eerie bugle calls emanating from somewhere out in the darkness. The sound of the bugles raised the hair on my neck as it meant they were coming. The sounds of the horns were a reminder that I was not going to make it out of that reservoir alive. It was during these bugle calls that my gut tightened and I had thoughts that I was not going to see the sunrise. However, once the battle started each night anew, those thoughts vacated my head and survival took over. I attribute my survival to my gut instinct to stay glued to the earth. I can't tell you how many men died simply by raising their head or standing up.

During these night attacks, I was firing at moving shadows in the darkness or at muzzle flashes. I shot, and a shadow went down; I don't know if it was because I hit him or the soldier ducked. I could not keep my eye on him for even a second to see if he got back up because I was immediately aiming for the next shot. It was the only way to keep our positions from being overtaken; they were always advancing with their never-ending supply of men. We raked machine gun fire as they came at us nonstop. As the front lines of the Chinese assault went down, more were behind them, keeping up the charge. The third and subsequent waves often did not even have weapons; they were ordered to pick up weapons from their dead comrades as they advanced. While we were fighting from mostly stationary positions for the first two days, the Chinese onslaughts were successful in overrunning numerous positions. My unit was fortunate; many Marines had been overwhelmed by the Chinese and found themselves fighting hand-to-hand. In my case, the assaults came within twenty feet of us numerous times, but our position held with each night's assault. Many in my immediate vicinity were not so lucky.

Each night, wave after wave, hundreds, thousands, would assault our perimeter. In the morning, it would have perhaps a five-foot-tall by thirty-foot-wide pile of dead Chinese around it. The dead Chinese were so numerous that the heat from their bodies created an artificial fog in the morning. These "dead" Chinese were still lethal; Marines were often killed by living Chinese lying amongst the dead, awaiting a suicide-ambush. I never saw Marines going through the wounded and shooting them, but it is documented that this happened.

Throughout this bloody three-day battle, I never experienced any emotions that even remotely incapacitated me. No shaking, no fear. Other than during the nightly bugle calls, I simply was never afraid despite acknowledging that making it out alive was a long shot. I think the vast majority of the Marines I fought alongside acted the same way. In circumstances like this, your mind and body know what it must do to survive; we were all in the same dreadful situation. We knew we had to kill or be killed. There was no time to be scared.

It was during this battle, fighting to stay alive at night and exhaustively treating the wounded during the day, that I experienced five days and nights of no sleep for the third time. I did not even have a single catnap. Staying awake for that long was not heroism; I did what I had to do. How could anyone sleep knowing that dozens of Marines depended on you to survive their wounds? If I slept during the day, they would bleed to death. If I slept during the night, we would be overrun by the Chinese. It was a simple equation that required no heroism or bravery.

The history books state that my 7th Regiment was defending itself in place for about three days in Hagaru-ri before receiving orders to fight our way back to the sea. That fighting retreat lasted another fourteen days. Standard procedure would have us Marines digging foxholes each time we stopped to defend a position or hunker down for the night. Foxholes, as basic as they are, allow the best chances of survival in a firefight. I never dug one. Even if I wanted to, I couldn't. The ground was frozen as hard as concrete and rocky as well. It was not until the retreat that we were able to pitch medical tents, which is where I found some sleep, sheltered from the freezing wind. I shared the tent with as many Marines and corpsmen that could fit to maximize body warmth. If we had a few square feet to spare, we would pull in another Marine so that all our legs and arms were overlapping one another. The vast majority of the Marines slept in sleeping bags in the snow on rocky, frozen ground with nighttime temperatures reaching -35 degrees Fahrenheit with no protection from the howling winds and drifting snow.

★ ★ ★

Mao, The Unknown Story by Jung Chang and Jon Halliday reported that the Chinese troops were composed mostly of former Nationalist soldiers who had surrendered en masse following Mao Tse-tung's Communist victory in the civil war. These were the same Nationalist soldiers the U.S. was supporting in World War II.[6] I was stationed off the coast of China in World War II where the very soldiers we were currently mowing down by the thousands were, allegedly, the very ones who previously had been our allies. Mao desired to murder these former Nationalists while using them to exhaust American bullets.

Wikipedia adds the following:

Although the 9th Army was one of China's elite formations composed of veterans and former POWs from the Huaihai Campaign, several deficiencies hampered its ability during the battle. Initially, the 9th Army was intended to be outfitted in Manchuria during November, but Mao suddenly ordered it into Korea before that could happen. As a result, the 9th Army received almost no winter gear for the harsh Korean winter. Similarly, poor logistics forced the 9th Army to abandon heavy artillery while working with little food and ammunition. The food shortage forced the 9th Army to initially station a third of its strength away from the Chosin Reservoir as reserve, and starvation and exposure soon broke out among the Chinese units as foraging was not an option at the sparsely populated reservoir. By the end of the battle, more Chinese troops died from the cold than from combat and air raids.[7]

It was not only superior American firepower that killed the attacking Chinese but the cold and a lack of food. Whole Chinese units froze to death. We found dead Chinese wearing sandals, tennis shoes without socks, or canvas shoes. Since they hid from our bombers and fighters during the day, they could not make fires, which would give away their positions. Night blindness due to malnutrition was a large problem. If they had food, they lived off a single frozen ball of rice, and if not, they ate raw tadpoles or made cold soup from pine needles and water. As bad as we Marines had it, the Chinese had it much worse.

I have always suspected the Chinese provided their soldiers opiates. I cannot otherwise understand how ferociously they fought. They seemed impervious not only to the cold and bullets but to hunger. When the Chinese were successful in overrunning Marine positions, they could not hold them. Instead of defending their new terrain, they started scavenging for food and clothing. Many Marines, myself included, were aghast at seeing a dead Chinese soldier lying in the snow who could not have been more than twelve or thirteen years old.

The murder of the Chinese by their Communist officers was an unbelievable crime against humanity. I am certain the typical Communist soldier had two choices: charge and die or be shot in the back by their own officers. Accordingly, the Chinese would continue an assault even though we were mowing them down by the thousands. One of the contributing factors to our survival was that the Chinese soldier followed a single order given to him at the start of the battle, while Marines could adjust and adapt as circumstances changed.

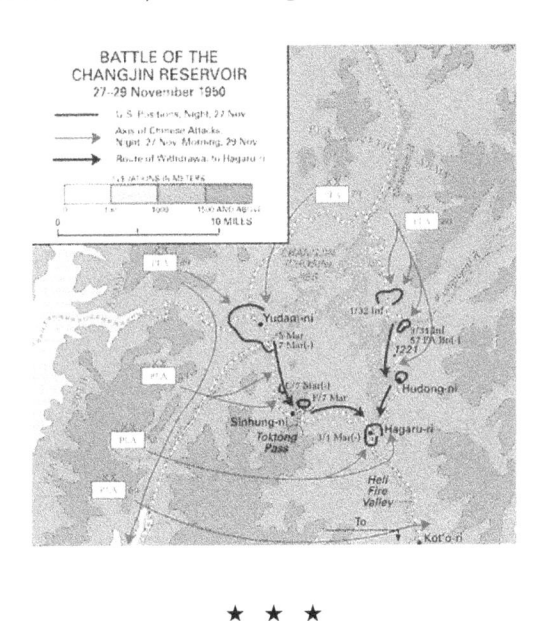

★ ★ ★

After the first three days of holding off the Chinese, we received orders to begin a fighting retreat. Major General Smith famously barked at his leadership back in Washington D.C., "Retreat, hell! We're not retreating; we're just advancing in a different direction." The problem was that the road was mostly a single lane road that went through the narrow Toktong Pass.

A book entitled *The Last Stand of Fox Company,* by Bob Drury and Tom Clavin, describes in riveting detail the 240 Marines of Fox Company's valiant attempts at holding this pass open against overwhelming odds.[9] Over five days, the 240 men of Fox Company were whittled down to eighty effective fighters. Many of these eighty men were fighting to the end despite being grievously wounded or unable to walk due to horribly frostbitten feet. In the end, most of the surviving Fox Company fighters were dragging themselves on their bellies, unable to use their frozen legs. The rest of Fox Company were captured, killed, or too wounded to hold a weapon.

The Chinese threw everything they had at Fox Company. They knew that if they took control of the high ground at this pass, they could slaughter the Marines as they were forced to retreat through this funnel. Unless this pass was held open, the 8,000 Marines up north at Yudam-ni could not escape and would be massacred. The effort to reinforce Fox Company was being made from my position at Yudam-ni in the north and from Hagaru-ri in the South. Only the effort from Yudam-ni was successful. The volunteers from Yudam-ni knew they were volunteering for a suicide mission, and yet they successfully arrived after marching three straight days and nights through enemy territory. They sometimes marched through waist-deep snow, detouring miles around known enemy encampments. The volunteers came just in time as Fox Company could not have survived one more night of Chinese assaults. It is estimated that the 240 Marines of Fox Company killed 3,500 Chinese in defending this critical escape route.

Captain William Barber was awarded the Medal of Honor for his actions as commander of Fox Company. Fox Company held a position known as "Fox Hill" against vastly superior numbers of Chinese infantry, keeping the Toktong Pass open and keeping the 5th Marine Regiment and the 7th Marine Regiment (my regiment) from getting cut off at Yudam-ni. His company's actions to keep the pass open allowed these two regiments to withdraw from Yudam-ni and consolidate with the rest of the 1st Marine Division at Hagaru-ri. The mission from Yudam-ni to relieve Fox Company also led to the awarding of the Medal of Honor to Lt. Col. Raymond Davis, then commanding officer of 1st Battalion, 7th Marines.

This could have been the second time my story ended prematurely. The only reason it did not, along with the stories of 8,000 other Marines, was because of the heroic fighting of the 240 men of Fox Company to whom I unquestionably owe my life. One hundred and sixty of them gave their lives defending those heights above the Toktong Pass. Those eighty who survived were so ravaged by frostbite that most of them had limbs amputated.

While the effort to reinforce Fox Company was successful from the north, allowing the Marines a fighting chance to reach Hagaru-ri, their escape route southward was blocked by the Chinese. Lt. Col. Chesty Puller, commander of the 1st Regiment at Koto-ri, received orders to fight north from Koto-ri to open the road to Hagaru-ri to allow the Marines to escape southward to the sea. His efforts to fight northward were repelled. His men were forced to turn back, leaving the Marines up north on their own to fight every step of the way southward to the sea.

A study I once saw on TV, perhaps on *60 Minutes,* found that in a firefight, only fifteen percent of the men do the actual fighting. The rest are incapacitated with fear, lying in the fetal position and unable to control either their bladders or bowels. During this battle, everyone fought for their lives and the lives of their comrades. However, I did find many Marines in a horrible mental state. Many of the World War II vets who made it off the landing craft at Inchon and to the reservoir shut down once the battle started. We would take them by the hand like small children. Most of these men were identified and weeded out before or during the Inchon beach landing as mentioned earlier. The odd thing was that they did not share any common characteristic other than shutting down. A few were in the fetal position; some were shaking violently, some weakly. Others were catatonic.

The ambulances bore the words *US Marines* and the large International Red Cross insignia on the sides. Up to this point, the world's armies respected the Red Cross insignia worn by medics and corpsman. However, we were instructed to take the Red Cross insignia off our sleeves as soon as we made the Inchon landing. We were warned that the Communist sharpshooters targeted those wearing the Red Cross insignia, in violation of all international norms and laws of warfare. It was in Korea we corpsmen first started wearing the snake insignia, first introduced in 1948, known as the caduceus, on our Marine combat uniform. Corpsmen were a high-value target for the Chinese, as were radio operators and officers.

This came into stark focus at one point during the retreat. I had loaded six wounded Marines into a jeep ambulance that had the International Red Cross symbol on its sides. I banged the back doors to let the driver know that he was good to go. As I turned my attention to other wounded, I heard heavy machine-gun fire in the distance. I looked hundreds of yards down the road to see the aftermath of the ambulance being attacked. I grabbed my carbine and sprinted to the ambulance with others.

As we approached, we slowed and raised our weapons to our shoulders. By this time, the firing had stopped, but we knew we were not going to find any survivors, as the ambulance appeared to have been hit hundreds of times with the rounds going clean through both sides. As the Marines I was with formed a defensive perimeter around the ambulance, I ran up to the driver's door. The driver was mauled beyond recognition by the machine-gun rounds. Next, I ran to the rear double doors and flung them open. Inside I found the bloody remains of what had once been six wounded Marines. The interior of that ambulance was soaked in body parts, bone fragments, brain matter, and nearly eight gallons of blood, which ran out of the back door and onto my knees and down over my boots.

I don't remember what happened to the attackers, but I suspect the Marines tracked them down and killed them. We were appalled that the Communists would violate all norms of war by attacking helpless, wounded Marines in an ambulance. Battle-hardened, I turned and walked back to my patients, as many more needed medical care, leaving the ambulance where it came to rest with the back doors wide open and blood still flowing out over the bumper into the snow.

★ ★ ★

The U.S. forces reluctantly took a lot of Chinese POWs. The Chinese often surrendered just to get something to eat and were a burden to us getting out alive. We would have vastly increased our chances of survival if we had simply killed them. Our national ethos, however, dictated we were obligated to transport, feed, and provide them with medical care, all while desperately fighting their army. My company had about a dozen POWs, all of whom walked up and surrendered to get something to eat and keep from freezing to death. I did not provide any medical care to POWs, but some corpsmen applied a quick tourniquet or speedily sutured a POW's wounds when there was time. I am proud to say I never witnessed U.S. soldiers mistreating POWs.

My memory is foggy about when this happened, but one day during our retreat, a Chinese officer walked into camp and came up to me and two other buddies. Amazingly, I was not even startled as he approached. I guess we were kind of numb to it because we had seen an awful lot of the enemy walking into our camps begging for food. He approached to within five feet and asked for the commanding officer in perfect English. He had his hands up but his elbows by his side. I remember it being chaotic like a subway platform, with people walking in every direction. We talked to him and pointed to a spot about 100 yards away where he could find the colonel. We did not bother to train our weapons on him, tie him up, or even pat him down.

In hindsight, we should have. He was on a suicide mission. He had two grenades under his arms, and as he raised his arms higher, the pins were pulled, blowing himself and the colonel to hell.

★ ★ ★

Poor subsistence farmers sparsely inhabited the region. These farmers had holes in their fields where they stored both animal and human waste that they used for fertilizer. Many Marines had the misfortune of falling into these pits. One big, tough, burly Marine sergeant approached my medical station covered head to toe in this stink. We refused to help him get cleaned up; we wouldn't even allow him in our tent. We instead directed him to a small creek with maybe four to six inches of near-freezing water with ice in it. He stripped naked and rolled around in that stream to clean the human waste and animal manure off. He then came back to our tent completely naked and shivering violently. We gave him new clothes to keep him from freezing to death. No one should ever doubt how tough Marines are.

Most of the corpsmen's provisions were carried by truck or ambulance. We, of course, had a supply of medical provisions in side packs attached to a shoulder harness. In these packs, I kept what we needed and anything useful we could scrape together. Because of the great air support, we were constantly re-supplied; I don't remember running out of any required supplies. We had continual drops of medical supplies, food, and ammunition. At least three times during the retreat, we corpsmen blew up our excess medical provisions to keep them from falling into enemy hands. The most important item we carried was morphine, followed by bandages and large combat pads. I did a lot of suturing before and after, but not during the retreat because there was no time. I kept a lot of morphine in my packs, up to 300 doses of one-gram disposable syrettes. I always kept several morphine syrettes in my mouth so I would have usable morphine that wouldn't freeze.

In the movies, you sometimes see corpsmen purposely delivering a lethal dose of morphine to a Marine who is a goner. This never happened that I am aware of. Never. I would give a lot of morphine to someone to make dying easier for the fellow, but I never intentionally overdosed a Marine. I knew some patients were going to bleed to death and there was nothing I could do about it. They needed surgery, and that was not an option out there. A lot of what we did was psychological. Giving a Marine a dose of morphine often got his anxiety level down and allowed him to get back to fighting.

Another misconception is the idea of triage. In the movies or TV shows like *M*A*S*H,* triage is about taking the worst-wounded first. In reality, triage in the field meant taking the ones who we could turn around and get back to the fighting force first. The origin of this practice was the early Navy, where it was important to get a sailor back to fighting to keep the ship afloat. In our case, getting a Marine back into the fight meant our very survival; if I could get them to pull a trigger again, I was doing my job.

I would guess that eighty percent of the time after a dose of morphine, the Marine stopped worrying about bleeding to death or losing a limb. The morphine syringes were just single dose plastic capsules with a two-inch needle. The most serious injuries were the debrided wounds—open, gaping wounds where the skin had been blown away. These were horrible injuries that caused unbearable pain.

We were lucky napalm and flamethrowers were not used by the Chinese. Burn victims were, for the most part, not a problem as all the battle injuries were either gunshot wounds or frostbite. We were also lucky the Chinese, due to terrain and their speed of attack, did not bring heavy artillery in large numbers. They did not have bulldozers, tanks, and howitzers either, though I did see the Chinese use howitzers further south during the retreat. Big artillery creates such concussive force that often eyeballs are knocked out from their sockets, hanging on the cheek by the optic nerve. Intestines blown out of the abdominal cavity is another common occurrence under heavy artillery fire. Marines had a tremendous casualty rate from frostbite since the temperatures were well below freezing, especially after nightfall. The lucky few who slept did so on rocky, frozen ground in sleeping bags that barely kept them from freezing to death during the night.

Thousands succumbed to frostbite, mostly due to the government-issued boots, which were inappropriate for the weather since they did not breathe. Typically, a Marine's socks would become wet from sweat and then freeze. When the sweat was frozen, the foot would feel dry, tricking the Marine into thinking his feet, though cold, were dry. During the retreat, I changed my socks multiple times a day, but most did not. I kept my extra socks inside my uniform next to my body. They would still be a little damp when I took them out, but they would dry quickly. In the end, I was fortunate to have suffered only a mild case of frostbite. For about four months afterwards, my toes were a little pink and ached, but they eventually healed.

I treated a couple of Marines with gangrene but, for the most part, in the hundreds of cases of frostbite I treated, the toes were blackened and shriveled. I probably cut off 700 boots using eighteen-inch scissors. Often, the fleshy part of the toes stayed in the boot leaving only tendons and dead bone at the end of the foot. Many times, I cut blackened and shriveled toes off at the joints without any sterilization.

Perhaps the strangest and luckiest tale of this battle involved a fellow corpsman who got shot in the mouth while standing next to me. The round was almost spent and only strong enough to knock out one of his front teeth, no other damage. I remember him reaching into his mouth, pulling the tooth out, and holding it up for me to see. He was in just as much disbelief as I was. I later saw his picture in *Time* magazine because he was asked to share his bizarre, lucky story.

As for the dead, we were collecting the frozen bodies and stacking them like cordwood. However, as we became more and more desperate in our retreat, we were forced to leave them behind. At first, we loaded the dead into trucks, taking them with us on our retreat. As we ran out of room on the trucks, we started stacking them in piles with the understanding that the U.S. would come back for them. Toward the end, too weak from starvation and sleep deprivation, we stopped gathering the bodies altogether and left them frozen where they fell. Afterwards, the Graves Registry Service, the unit of the U.S. Army that clears the dead from the battlefield, came in and brought the fallen home.

At one point during the retreat, we received distress calls from an Army field hospital on the other side of the mountain. One of our officers asked for volunteers to cross the ridge to rescue 600 to 700 wounded and medical personnel who the Army had abandoned. On the other side of the ridge, the Eighth Army had completely broken down. There was no order or discipline; they were dropping their weapons and running. I volunteered to climb the pass with about twenty others using fifteen commandeered vehicles. I remember that we were traveling on what barely qualified as a goat trail up inclines so steep we worried about our vehicles rolling over.

We were lucky in two regards. First, the Chinese did not molest us as we were too lightly armed to take on any significant attack, and second, when we got there, we were thankful to find that a lot of the wounded were ambulatory. With only fifteen vehicles, we certainly could not drive them all out of there. We used cargo straps to load as many of the worst cases onto the tops of our vehicles and evacuated these wounded and their medics back the way we came. Those 700 wounded Army soldiers were now in our care as we took them with us on our retreat to the sea.

To this day I can't stand the sight of an Eighth Army insignia, but I respected those Army medics who stayed behind to care for their wounded instead of abandoning them like the rest of their division. If our Marine volunteers had not come to their rescue, those Army medics and their patients would have either been killed or taken prisoner. Those medics were heroes by any definition.

On the seventeenth and final day of this historic battle, I found myself walking with two other Marines about three miles outside of Hungnam, the port city where we were to make our escape to the sea. We were far beyond complete and utter exhaustion, not to mention starved and dehydrated. The only reason we had any will at all to keep walking was knowing that to stop was to die.

An Army military policeman tasked with guarding the perimeter of Hungnam commanded us to stop and give him the password. One of the Marines I was walking with lifted his automatic weapon and, without saying a word, shot him dead. As we walked by the murdered Army MP, the Marine looked back over his shoulder and, while laughing, said, "There is your fucking password!" Amazingly, I did not have any reaction. I just kept walking and was not the least bit disturbed after the hell I had lived through for the last seventeen days. I was sleep-deprived, combat-fatigued, and starving, along with everyone else. Under normal circumstances, anyone should and would have been horrified, but these were not normal circumstances. To be so close to escaping, only to be challenged near the finish line was not going to slow us down one step. Later, as I recollected the incident, I justified to myself that there was nothing I could have done. If I had said or done anything, I am sure I would have been killed by this Marine as well. I never even considered reporting it. My frame of mind at the time did not allow those thoughts to even come to the forefront of my mind. Besides, even if I had, I rationalized, the services protect their reputation and would not allow something like this to become public. Coincidentally, about a month after returning stateside, the Navy distributed a questionnaire trying to determine the extent of combat-related murder among combat veterans. I was not sure if the purpose of the questionnaire was to garner statistics or if it was investigatory in nature. Either way, I lied on the questionnaire, stating that I had never witnessed nor taken part in any such behavior.

★ ★ ★

At the port city of Hungnam, the priority was to set up defensive positions with the second priority being the evacuation of the wounded. While the Chinese had been decimated in their attacks on the 1st Marine Division and were in no condition to attack us at

Hungnam, we did not know that at the time and thus we felt no relief upon reaching it. We all knew we had our backs to the sea and that if the Chinese came after us, we would be trapped.

Wikipedia states:

Some skirmishes broke out between the defending US 7th, 17th and 65th Infantry and the pursuing PVA 27th Corps, but against the strong naval gun fire support provided by US Navy Task Force 90, the badly mauled 9th Army was in no shape to approach the Hungnam perimeter.[12]

Wikipedia goes on to provide a summary of the evacuation from Hungnam:

In what US historians called the "greatest evacuation movement by sea in US military history," a 193-ship armada assembled at the port and evacuated not only the UN troops, but also their heavy equipment and roughly a third of the Korean refugees. One ship, the SS Meredith Victory, evacuated 14,000 refugees. The last UN unit left at 14:36 on 24 December and the port was destroyed to deny its use to the Chinese and North Korean forces. The PVA 27th Corps [Chinese Army] entered Hungnam on the morning of 25 December.

About 105,000 soldiers, 98,000 civilians, 17,500 vehicles, and 350,000 tons of supplies were shipped from Hungnam to Pusan, and they would later rejoin the war effort in Korea.[13]

The wounded were prioritized to get them to Japan for medical care as fast as possible. As a corpsman, I would have been very involved in the process of organizing the wounded and selecting those who needed life-saving surgery to go on the ships first. However, I have no memories from the time the sentry was shot until I awoke aboard an LST, traveling in slow circles at sea. I had been asleep for days. As best as I could put together, I must have collapsed and been carried aboard because I had no recollection of leaving the shore, much less how I came to be in that bunk. The LST was circling because a heavy mine field lay ahead and we had lost the mine sweeper that was supposed to be in front of us.

★ ★ ★

It was only because of the Marines' strict adherence to the military strategy of establishing supply depots and air strips that we made it out alive. Additionally, the Marines leapfrogged from high point to high point to protect the main forces. In the end, the reason 18,000 Marines could fight their way out of being surrounded by 60,000 Chinese was because of U.S. military discipline. The Chinese troops that were not killed by our superior discipline, tactics, and firepower were killed by their own Communist leaders. They were the ones responsible for freezing and starving their own soldiers to death and for commanding them to run directly into our overwhelming firepower.

Wikipedia depicts the impact of this historic battle as follows:

With the entire UN front collapsing, the race to Yalu was ended with the communist forces of China recapturing much of North Korea. The Korean War would drag on for another two and a half years before the armistice was signed on 27 July 1953. Besides the loss of North Korea, the US X Corps and the ROK I Corps later reported a total of 10,495 battle casualties, of which 4,385 were from the US Marines, 3,163 were from the US Army, 2,812 were from South Koreans attached to American formations and 78 were from the British Royal Marines. Outside of the combat losses, the 1st Marine Division also reported 7,338 non-battle casualties due to the cold weather.[15]

Wikipedia offers the following quote from Mae Zedong regarding the aftermath of this battle: "…Casualties had reached a 40,000 high. The Central [Government] expresses its deepest sorrow…"

It continues:

[Major General Oliver P.] Smith was credited for saving the US X Corps from destruction, while the 1st Marine Division, the 41 Royal Marines Commando and the Army's RCT-31 were awarded the Presidential Unit Citation for their tenacity during the battle. Fourteen Marines, two Soldiers and one Navy pilot received the Medal of Honor, and all of the UN troops that served at Chosin were later honored with the nickname "The Chosin Few." On 15 September 2010, the Veterans of the Korean War Chosin Reservoir Battle memorial was unveiled by the United States Marine Corps Commandant General James T. Conway at Camp Pendleton.[16]

CHAPTER 13

Korea: Griffin Goes Insane

I HAD NOW COME FULL CIRCLE. We had been evacuated to the southern port of Pusan, the original launching point for the Inchon invasion. We had to disembark on a large, wide, sandy beach. Trucks, jeeps, and tanks were all getting stuck in the soft sand. A high-ranking officer, I don't remember his name or specific rank, came strutting down the beach, yelling for the whereabouts of "Custead." Told that this officer was seeking me, I quickly found him and asked what I could do for him.

He said, "I was told you are from Florida. I want you to teach these morons how to drive in the sand!"

I then proceeded to hold a class. Using a jeep, I instructed these Brooklyn boys to keep the vehicle in low gear at all times, to avoid using too much gas, and to remain at a slow and steady pace in order to avoid digging the wheels into the sand. I then drove back and forth three times, making packed ruts in the sand for them to use.

It was in Pusan where I had my only opportunity, which would eventually include three wars, to see Bob Hope entertain the troops. I enjoyed his show from a vantage point high up on a pile of tackle in a hanger. He joked he had been waiting three days for the Marines to get there. There were probably thousands outside who wanted to get in. Hope was hostile to the brass and insisted all the officers vacate the best seats in front and let the troops come in. The "boots" loved this!

I saw a second colonel get killed while in Pusan. And again, I had some contributory negligence in his demise. I mentioned earlier in my story that I became close friends with another corpsman 2nd class named Griffin back at San Diego Hospital. While there, he had confided in me that he was an Army deserter, a secret I wish I had not known. Amazingly, he was a captain in the Army before deserting and becoming a Navy corpsman. I guess I should have taken heed of this fact as a sign that maybe he was not entirely a stable person.

In Korea, we ended up attached to the same 1st Marine Division, but in different companies. After we escaped the reservoir and Hungnam, Griffin and I became tentmates. Every night for a week, maybe ten days, I observed Griffin walking the perimeter. He was paranoid that the encampment was about to become overrun by thousands of Chinese amassing somewhere out in the darkness. He would come back each morning and report to the colonel that he caught ten or sixteen or nineteen sentries asleep and demanded that the colonel court-martial them. After doing his perimeter walk one morning, he came back and shot and killed the colonel and the Marine tasked with guarding him.

At first, no one knew what happened. He came back to our tent afterward and proceeded to rant on and on about the lack of security around our encampment. He then left, carrying his carbine with him. I thought he was being unreasonable, definitely a bit agitated, but I did not have any inkling that he had lapsed into a psychotic state, nor did I have any idea what he had just done.

The brass figured out that it was Griffin—my tentmate—who had murdered the colonel, and they came to me looking for answers. I told them, in a state of shock, that I did not see Griffin the night before as he was out on his nightly tour of the parameter and I saw him only briefly that morning. The encampment was now swarming with officers. They took me to see a general and several other high-ranking officers. I told them that Griffin had received five new letters from his wife in that morning's mail and that maybe I could reach him and bring him in safely by reading them to him. At first, the general balked and said that he could not jeopardize my life by asking me to do that. Furthermore, the general was reluctant to open private mail, but I was insistent.

However far gone Griffin was, I wanted to see if I could save his life; we all did. I argued that if I could read letters from his wife aloud to him that I might be able to have him reconnect to reality. In the end, the general acquiesced because they were in a standoff and there were no other good options.

It was pretty straightforward how the brass figured out who killed the colonel and his guard. That morning, Griffin was rambling around the campsite with his carbine on a shooting rampage. The Marines, acting quickly, neutralized and surrounded Griffin with a perimeter of probably one hundred yards. They shouted at him that if he raised his carbine one more time, they would shoot to kill. As I remember, he did indeed raise his rifle and randomly shot, aiming at nothing. The Marines, however, did not carry out their threat, realizing that if he hit anyone, it would be a freak accident since there did not appear to be any attempt on his part to aim at any particular target.

Nonetheless, Griffin was not going to escape alive. They were not in the mood to have any more colonels killed or allow him to take another innocent life. After receiving approval from the general, I approached Griffin. I moved closer and closer to him with the letters from his wife in my hand, taking one step at a time. I froze when he appeared to jump. At first, due to the distance, I was shouting at him. The entire time seemed like an eternity to me. As I closed within maybe fifty yards, I started reading aloud the letters from his wife. Everyone else inched forward to get better aim and to close the perimeter.

As I got within thirty feet, I could tell he had no idea who I was, nor did he recognize the letters from his wife. My life depended on him vaguely recognizing them or at least being curious about them. He stopped the random shooting as I started my long journey toward him; he seemed curious about me, or perhaps the letters perplexed him. Eventually, I got within ten feet of him. He seemed to be listening to the letters, but he was completely psychotic. I was the only one close to him. All the Marines were still thirty yards away, aiming their weapons at him, ready to take him out if he raised his carbine. Their objective now was to keep me alive. With me ten feet from him, and with the Marines so close, any hostile movement by Griffin would no longer be forgiven. If he raised his rifle in any direction, he was going to die.

He kept turning around in circles, looking at the Marines who had him encircled. I waited until his back was toward me to make my move. I rushed the ten feet as fast as my adrenaline-soaked legs allowed. As he turned to face me, he became startled and started to level his carbine in the direction of my chest. I was able to grab the barrel with my gloved hand, forcing it down before he could get off a shot. During the ensuing struggle, he emptied his weapon's clip between our feet. I held onto that muzzle for dear life, even as it severely burned my hand, my cotton gloves offering little protection from the red-hot barrel. As he was emptying his magazine, the Marines rushed forward and tackled him. As I had a death grip on Griffin's rifle, I ended up on the ground with Griffin under ten or so Marines.

They tied him up and held him at gunpoint. I was amazed that even after Griffin had killed their colonel and another Marine, the Marines did not mistreat him. There was no hitting him with rifle butts or rough handling. These Marines knew, by the grace of God, it could have been one of them who snapped. Everyone knew Griffin was crazy and not responsible for his actions. All of us had been through unbelievable hell, and the fact that more of us did not lapse into a psychotic state was a testament to the durability of the human mind. After he was placed under arrest, since he was a friend of mine, I offered to escort him, along with armed guards, back to the USS *Repose*. Once aboard the *Repose*, he was placed into a locked ward. I now knew beyond a shadow of a doubt that he was completely and utterly gone. He never came to recognize me.

I never shared with anyone that Griffin was a former Army captain and deserter. No, I was in a terribly difficult position. If the brass learned I knew he was a deserter, I could have been charged. We all have moments in our lives that we wish we could do over. That was one of those moments. My mistakes and poor decisions cost a colonel and a Marine their lives. What was ironic and hard to take were the many people who slapped me on the back, hugged me, and said I should receive a commendation for my actions. At the time, I did not even think about it; it was something I knew I had to do. There was mention of being awarded a brass ribbon for valor but, for some reason, it never materialized. Perhaps it was due to the ugliness of the situation involving a crazed warrior fragging an officer and his guard.

Afterward, I sent several cards to his wife, whom I had met before we left, and his mother-in-law, but they all went unanswered. I guess they did not want anything to do with him anymore. I never heard what became of him, but I assume he was found not guilty by reason of insanity and locked in a mental ward.

CHAPTER 14

Marriage

IN APRIL OF 1951, I disembarked in San Diego from the merchant marine ship USNS *Sylvester Antolak,* which was my ride home from Korea along with 1,350 other leathernecks. The mayor of San Diego was there, along with crowds reported to be 15,000 strong, cheering our arrival home. Fireboats in the harbor were shooting streams of water into the air from their water cannons. My brother George and his wife Lila Mae made their way through the large crowd to greet me. They took me back to their home in north Los Angeles, where I was able to get some much-needed rest and nourishment for two or three days.

After my short recuperative visit with George and Lila Mae, I headed to Denver to see Lois for our fifth in-person meeting.

I had lost a lot of weight during the war and was reduced to skin and bones. During the seventeen-day running battle and retreat from the Chosin Reservoir, I had become so undernourished that I looked like a concentration camp survivor, not a Navy corpsman. Supplies had constantly dropped from the skies, but we had little time to eat and absolutely no time to cook. We had eaten frozen rations by putting them in our mouths until they defrosted enough to swallow. When I returned home at twenty-two years old, my stomach was shrunken in, my skin was stretched tight against my skeleton, and you could count every rib and see both clavicles. As skinny as I was when I went to Korea, I returned emaciated. During my trip to Colorado, with my ill-fitting uniform hanging on a bag of bones, I was offered food by just about everyone. I was such a sad site that no waitress would take my money.

When I arrived in Denver, Lois was shocked and a bit frightened by my appearance. She and her family were very concerned that I was starving to death and constantly offered nourishment. Lois and I visited for a couple of days and discussed wedding plans before I headed home to Mannville for a quick visit with my family before reporting to my next duty station, the Memphis Naval Air Station in Tennessee. The plan was for me to return in May for our wedding.

While there were international headlines about the dire plight of the 1st Marine Division fighting for its survival, twenty-year-old Lois was ignorant of my circumstances at the time. It was ten or more years after my return from Korea before I spoke of the horrors I endured during that battle. I was sitting at the Durants' kitchen table alone on the first night of my visit when I started to sob uncontrollably. The rest of the family was there and heard their daughter's fiancé break down. I am sure it was uncomfortable for all present, but everyone pretended as though nothing happened. Lois said she kind of just ignored it at the time. She knew it had something to do with Korea. Her instincts guided her to ignore it, pretend it had not happened, and to not ask me about it. I guess she thought it might be an embarrassing episode for me, so she just let it be. It was very strange to Lois, who had never seen a man cry. I have often thought this uncontrollable emotional release happened because I finally felt safe sitting there at her kitchen table. The constant and unrelenting anxiety caused by not knowing whether each minute might be my last seemingly did not subside until that very moment. The uncontrollable sobbing was the "sigh of relief" that was long overdue.

Supposedly, veterans return home from war changed men. Was I changed? If I was, I was not aware of it. Lois could not have made that determination either because, up to that point, our entire courtship had basically consisted of four years of letter-writing. Unbelievably, before getting married, we had only spent a total of eight days together in person. She did not know me well enough to say if war had changed me. She might have asked me a couple of times about my battle experiences, but I always brushed her inquiries aside. She will tell you that she never heard me talk of my experiences until many years later when I would share just a tale or two from my combat experiences with the kids. I never told them the whole story, just selective bits and pieces, and only after many years had passed. It was only through eavesdropping on these sporadic conversations with the kids that Lois came to understand what I had been through.

We were married on May 16, 1951. The wedding was a small but fun affair. It was at the 7th Congregational Church at eight in the evening followed by a reception in the church basement with punch and cookies. Lois' baby sister and brother served as the flower girl and ring bearer. As no one from my family attended, Lois' brother Bill served as my best man while Lois' best friend, Blanche Johnson, served as her maid of honor. Betty Lynn, another close friend, and her sister Lucille served as bridesmaids.

After the reception, the family and some close friends went to a restaurant for dinner and drinks. Near the end of the dinner, the waiter came up to Lois and me and said that the chef wanted to speak with us in the back. Unknown to us, it was a ruse to get us out of the restaurant and into a waiting car which took us to a motel on the west end of Denver.

After arriving at the motel, I was busy attempting to undo the thousand little buttons on Lois' dress, when we suddenly got the feeling we were being watched. I looked out the window to see the entire wedding party, cheering us on from the parking lot. Once they knew they had been seen, they harassed us by yelling and knocking on the door and window. Thankfully, after a while, they gave up and left. The next morning, we returned to the Durants' and packed for our week-long honeymoon in Colorado Springs. We stayed at the Antler Inn, the town's largest and nicest hotel.

My new bride and I arrived by bus at my next duty assignment, the Memphis Naval Air Station, on June 8, 1951, about three weeks after our marriage. We lived in a private home for $7 a week with another couple and two spinsters, which meant six of us were sharing a kitchen and one bathroom. During the three months we were stationed in Memphis, we bought our first car, a small 1949 Chevy coupe with very little mileage. I remember being thrilled to pay a farmer $600 for it. During that time, the price of every automobile was going through the roof because servicemen returning from the war needed cars, creating a huge demand.

Being a Korean War veteran, I could name my next duty assignment. I chose the Naval Air Tactical and Training Command in Jacksonville, Florida to be close to my family and so I could work in the base hospital as a clinical lab technician. We left Memphis for Jacksonville in August, not quite three months after we arrived. In Jacksonville, we rented the upstairs of a huge house about thirty minutes from the base.

While living in Jacksonville, we traveled the sixty or so miles back to the farm to visit with my parents and siblings every weekend. This was when my family met my bride for the first time. Lois has always been a people person with lots of friends. In addition to being extremely attractive, she is sweet and humble. It is a very rare individual who does not instantly like her. My family was no exception.

Six months after arriving, we were visiting my sister Mary and her husband Dalton when I suddenly collapsed. After I came to, Lois, who did not have a driver's license, had to drive us home. After arriving home, my condition continued to worsen until Lois decided to call an ambulance. The ambulance crew took me out on a stretcher in a delirium.

I spent the next five months in the hospital. I was diagnosed with a ruptured amebic abscess on my liver and was, by all accounts, the first to have survived such an event. They continually flushed my torso with antibiotics, and, at one point, I lapsed into a coma for several months. Several doctors took a personal interest in my case since they knew me from the San Diego hospital. To this day, I believe that I picked up a bug in Korea.

While I was lying in a coma, Lois, lacking a driver's license, stayed home and was, for the most part, ignorant about my condition. She does not remember the hospital ever calling to give updates. She carried on as if nothing had happened, working at a local deli counter within walking distance of our apartment. She never doubted I was going to get better, and as the days stretched into weeks, and weeks stretched into months, she just assumed I would come home. Asked why she was not at the hospital worried about her new husband, she replied that she did not know what to do and assumed everything would work out in the end. Everyone who knows Lois knows she is the most optimistic person on the planet; one who sees only the good in everyone and every situation.

After getting discharged from the hospital in July of 1952, the Navy wanted to retire me as part of an overall shrinking of the armed services following World War II and the Korean War. I successfully fought the discharge, pointing to my status as a combat veteran.

In the Navy, every medical doctor has a requirement to train corpsman, and it is mandatory that all hospital corpsmen receive training in lab work. I was extremely fortunate that I had been mentored under an incredibly capable flight surgeon while stationed in Jacksonville. My technical laboratory abilities had progressed rapidly under him, qualifying me for independent duty early in my career. This meant I could be the chief medical personnel on a base or ship. Due to my newly-found lab competencies in Jacksonville, I was promoted to Hospital Corpsman 1st Class on April 16, 1952.

While in Jacksonville, Lois and I purchased a black Cadillac. How could a sailor afford a Cadillac? Well, I bought it ten months old. A brand-new Cadillac cost about $3,600 at the time. My brother Homer told me several times to get one, saying that they would increase in value. At the time, Homer was buying a new one every year. He got me a good deal on this used Cadillac for $2,600. Within a year or two, the value of Cadillacs did indeed increase 200 or 300 percent as the economy transitioned from a wartime footing to a consumer footing.

During our time in Jacksonville, our first son, Steven Allen, was born on February 25, 1953. At about 3 p.m. on that afternoon, I got a call from Lois, telling me it was time and I needed to come home and take her to the hospital. Steve was born at 10 p.m. that evening. What should have been a perfect family moment, the birth of our first child, turned into a bit of squabbling between us. I was not there at the time of my son's birth because I was out driving a couple of nurses to a party so I could show off my brand-new Cadillac. Lois was hurt and upset that I was, in her eyes, more concerned about showing off my new Cadillac than I was about the birth of our first child. She was further put off when, the morning after she had given birth, the head nurse told her she needed to make her own bed in preparation for the commander's inspection. Lois, exhausted from giving birth and not having had much sleep, was not too happy. When we got home three days later, I decided to walk to the garage across the street to shoot the bull with some mechanics while Lois went upstairs with a crying, fussy newborn. Again, she was pissed at me for my lack of sensitivity because she needed help.

The one positive memory Lois has of the birth of our first child was the comedic corpsman who brought "little Steven" into her room for the first time, wrapped in a blanket. When Lois pulled it back to look at her new child, she laughed out loud at the black baby the corpsman had brought instead.

CHAPTER 15

The USS Banner

ON MARCH 19, 1954, I reported to duty aboard the USS *Banner*, stationed out of Guam, an island on the southernmost tip of the Mariana chain of islands in the South Pacific. The USS *Banner* was a 177-foot AKL-25 class ship (light auxiliary cargo) and was the smallest vessel commissioned by the Navy to navigate the high seas without an escort. The *Banner* was a flat bottom boat with a five-foot draft when loaded with its full capacity of eighty tons of cargo. It had a lieutenant commanding officer, a warrant officer, and a junior grade lieutenant along with twenty-three enlisted men. I was to be its chief medical staff for the twenty-six-man crew.

When I departed for the *Banner*, Steve was eleven months old, and Lois was eight months pregnant with Sally Ann who was born on April 14, 1954, about a month after my deployment. Lois was now essentially a single mother with two small children. To get the help she needed, she moved to Denver to live with her parents. Lois' brothers were still young and living at home; her youngest brother Dave only being about eight years old at the time. While on board the *Banner*, I survived on $5 a month. I had the Navy send the rest of my pay to Lois who was helping her parents by paying rent. At the time, I think my annual salary was around $2,000 with allowances.

Lois' father died unexpectedly at the young age of fifty-two from lung cancer about seventeen months into my twenty-two-month tour at sea. This tragic turn of events left the Durants in dire straits. While Lois' dad left a $4,000 life insurance policy, there were now eight people to feed and no breadwinner. Thankfully, with Lois able to pay her mother rent, along with Social Security survivor benefits her mother received, the family was able to make it.

Upon my arrival in Guam, the corpsman I was relieving on the USS *Banner* took me to see the commanding officer. I found him ashore in a hut he shared with his concubine suffering from a hugely inflamed scrotum. The lieutenant's scrotum must have been eighteen to twenty-four inches across. The outgoing corpsman was desperate to get back to the States and his family and said he had tried everything he could think of, but the lieutenant was not improving and refused to go to the hospital. This was a very embarrassing issue for the lieutenant, and he was rightly concerned about losing his command if admitted to the naval hospital in Guam. The commanding officer allowed me to take over as corpsman so the other corpsman could leave.

My first act as a corpsman for the *Banner* was to call the chief medical officer in the Marianas, Captain Driscoll, who I knew quite well from the San Diego Naval Hospital where he trained me in emergency medical and surgical care. I explained that the ship's commanding officer was rightly concerned about being admitted to the hospital for fear of losing his command. Furthermore, if he were admitted to the hospital and did lose his command, it would be a big setback for the crew of the *Banner*. He instructed me to call the duty ambulance and have them transport the commanding officer to the dispensary right away. Captain Driscoll knew me to be a very capable corpsman and trusted me.

I followed his orders and had the lieutenant transferred to the shore dispensary over his strenuous objections. This turned out to be the right decision. My extensive experience working in emergency care at San Diego Naval Hospital and aboard the *Repose* hospital ship afforded me the knowledge to know when I could handle something and when a doctor was required. Most of the Navy's corpsmen did not possess the experience and knowledge that I had accumulated up to that point. I was uniquely well-qualified for the responsibilities I was to take on. The doctor lanced the lieutenant's scrotum to relieve the fluid buildup, drastically improving his condition within two days. Upon returning to duty, the commander made it a point to come by my quarters and personally thank me for overriding his protests and for knowing what had to be done.

The ship's mission was to tour and transport goods among the American Trust Islands in the Mariana Island chain. These islands were under the care of the Department of the Interior following World War II in a sort of Marshall Plan for the South Pacific. We had eight or so ports of call. Some of the islands were a couple of days apart, while others took over a week to reach. A few were so tiny that we were the only outsiders the twenty or thirty inhabitants would see all year. A couple of the smaller islands only required a single visit over twelve months, but most required multiple trips due to their large populations. Most of the time, there were no port facilities or docks. There might have been some old pilings left over from World War II that we could tie off on, but most of the time we anchored out at sea and rode tenders to shore. These were very large boats, equipped with inboard motors, and able to carry eight to ten people. They also doubled as the ship's two lifeboats.

Our arrival on these remote islands was always a source of great celebration for these Micronesians. We often brought them boxes of Kotex, pants, and basic medical supplies such as aspirin and antiseptics. With each arrival, the indigenous people would slaughter a pig and hold a luau in our honor. While it might sound nice to visit beautiful tropical islands and have pig roasts all the time, it got old in a hurry. Sometimes, depending on the route, we would have one or more luaus a week. We always stopped at each location for a day or so as not to be rude, and before each departure, we obtained a shopping list for our return trip. This was always challenging because each island had its own language, and we had to communicate mostly through hand gestures.

Occasionally, we had to pick up an entire island's population and "migrate" them to another island because they had eaten all their goats, chickens, and pigs and had no food left. On one occasion, we picked up tribes from two different islands. Unknown to us, these two tribes had been at war for who knows how long. Once out at sea, the two warring tribes started to attack each other with machetes. I immediately strapped on my .45 pistol for my own protection and as a precaution against the violence taking over the ship. In the end, we separated the two tribes as best we could on our small ship, and I spent the next several days suturing their wounds. Several natives had been thrown overboard during the melee. We had no idea how many we lost to sharks because no one knew how many we had originally taken on.

At each island, we usually picked up its only export, or form of currency, which was copra, the white meat from the inside of coconuts. Copra is used in various manufacturing processes such as soap and cosmetics. One of my many duties on this small vessel was to act as the purser or bookkeeper. I bagged and weighed the copra and then gave the inhabitants of the island credit for it, which I maintained in a set of books. We typically took on anywhere from twenty to thirty tons of copra on a round trip. Word would get out in Japan when the *Banner* was due in port, and copra buyers would meet us at the docks. As the ship's purser and bookkeeper, it was my duty to sell the copra to these buyers. I then deposited the proceeds into a Bank of America account we maintained in Japan. From the proceeds, we purchased the supplies for the natives, keeping a set of books for each island. It was a mixture of capitalism and socialism, as the more prosperous islands were subsidizing the more impoverished ones. Looking back, I realize that someone with fewer scruples could have easily absconded with a tremendous amount of cash belonging to the occupants of these islands. But at the time, as I was an honest farm boy, the thought never even occurred to me.

As a cargo ship, the *Banner* had a couple of cranes. Our cargo was normally household items and various bulk supplies. The ship had a freezer box in the forward hold for transporting perishables. We also carried a lot of tuna and live turtles, which were side businesses for the sailors onboard the ship. They purchased sea turtles from the indigenous people on Chichijima to take back to Guam; Guam's Filipino population considered them a delicacy. Sometimes we would transport anywhere from three to thirty of these 300-pound turtles. The inhabitants of these islands caught them by swimming out into the sea, grabbing them with their bare hands, and riding them back to shore, steering them with their hands.

Being an entrepreneur myself, I developed several side export businesses from which I made more than my Navy pay. One was buying thousands of fresh eggs in Japan and selling them to servicemen and their dependents on Guam. Another line of business was charging $22 for prescription glasses. At the time, if a serviceman or his dependents on Guam needed prescription glasses, the process took months, and the only style available was the big, bulky, ugly, black military-issued glasses. I collected 100 to 200 prescriptions per trip and dropped them off in Tokyo at an optometrist who charged $20 apiece; my cut was $2 a pair. Lobsters and prawns were another line of business for me. I'd buy them dirt cheap from the island natives and sell them to servicemen and their dependents on Guam and Japan. The extra cash was mostly sent home to Lois, or I purchased nice items for us at great prices, such as Noritake china.

I would say that half the sailors were doing what I was doing, and the other half were always broke. They took everything they earned and blew it on booze and whores. They were preyed upon by loan sharks (other sailors) who charged twenty to twenty-five percent. The biggest "banker" on board the *Banner* was named Hook. Even the commanding officer of the ship, one of the biggest boozing womanizers on board, was his customer. Hook was also the cook, so, of course, his nickname could be none other than "Hook the Cook." He made a fortune loan sharking, his biggest asset being how ugly he was. He was probably the ugliest man I have ever known. Because he was so hideous, the sailors feared him. Once, when Hook the Cook went on a month-long leave to Israel, he left me to collect on his debts. I did the first round but soon found that I did not have the personality for this line of business and could not do it anymore. You had to be a scary individual, one who people respected and would not dare screw over, and that was not me.

Another of my more interesting duties while aboard the *Banner* was interviewing and transporting prospective brides under the authority of the commanding officer. On each trip from Japan, we carried two to four young women to the island of Chichijima, one of our regular ports of call. I paid $400 to the parents of these Japanese brides, who had offered them up for sale.

Chichijima, located about 150 miles north of Iwo Jima, was where President George H. W. Bush had been shot down during World War II. It was also the basis of James Bradley's book *Flyboys: A True Story of Courage*. The book tells the story of U.S. servicemen who, during World War II, were shot down, executed, tortured, and, in some cases, eaten. The Japanese occupied these islands for years before and during World War II where they had a huge, top secret, underground naval facility used to manufacture destroyers and submarines. The Japanese decimated the local population during World War II, leaving practically no child-bearing women alive on the islands. The women left alive by the Japanese had been repeatedly raped and were infertile as a result of horrible cases of sexually transmitted diseases. The U.S. never captured the island because it was too heavily fortified, but after Japan surrendered, 25,000 Japanese soldiers were removed from the island, and dozens court-martialed and executed for war crimes. The Supreme Commander for the Allied Powers, General Douglas MacArthur, ordered the Japanese military infrastructure on the island destroyed and the island repopulated, hence my duty of bringing brides to this remote island ten years after the war.

Since the commanding officer knew I was the only farm boy in the crew, it became my duty to tend to two huge breeding Brahman bulls we took on board. I was responsible for feeding and monitoring the animals and hosing the manure off the deck. These bulls, prized specimens from King Ranch in Texas costing $5,000 apiece, were chosen because of their hardiness and resistance to disease, flies, hot temperatures, and the like. The bulls were to be transported to two of our ports of call to repopulate island cattle herds. I remember one was taken to Saipan, but I cannot recall the name of the island where the other was dropped off. When we returned to Saipan, the prized breeding bull had been killed and roasted to celebrate our return. We had a $5,000 luau courtesy of Uncle Sam.

It was not all lush tropical islands, luaus, and earning cash from side businesses. We were on a relatively small ship in the middle of the ocean, and that presented a constant danger. On one trip from Japan to Guam, while east of Japan, we were caught unprepared by a severe typhoon with waves rising thirty feet above the ship's deck. During the storm, the commander had to be strapped to the helm for three days straight because the rolling of the *Banner* was so violent he kept falling from his chair. His main concern was to keep the bow headed into the oncoming waves to keep us from being swamped. Navigation was only a secondary concern.

My quarters was a converted gun turret with five bunks in the fore, or front of the ship. It was accessible only by the open top deck; it was not connected to the rest of the boat below deck since the cargo hold was amidships. A former gun turret, the hatch was made of exceptionally thick steel weighing thousands of pounds. It was too heavy and dangerous to open during the storm due to the severe tossing and turning of the ship. I was trapped in that room for several days with two other sailors. We were forced to relieve ourselves in it since we could not get out. We had nothing to eat or drink, and with each passing day, we were becoming more and more desperate. We were in pretty bad shape and prayed the ship would not sink; if it did, this former gun turret would become our tomb. No one else could help us since everyone aboard ship was manning stations and otherwise preoccupied. Additionally, to reach us, they would have had to travel along the open deck to the fore. No one was to go on deck during a typhoon unless absolutely necessary. After three days, and knowing we were in a very precarious predicament, we became desperate enough to plan an escape.

Since I was the tallest of the three, I was voted to be the one who would hold the hatch open during a carefully timed roll so the other two could escape. Once they were safely out, it was up to me to extract myself. We had only seconds to execute our exit. If not timed right, the ship would roll back the other way, and the steel hatch would crush us. We eventually got up the nerve after mentally practicing the escape and timing the opening of the door with the rolling of the ship. I had hold of what is known as the "dog," or handle on the door, which rotated enough that it blocked what is known as the "knife edge," which keeps the door securely shut when the dog is locked in place. Because the knife edge was blocked by the handle, I only received a bad puncture wound to my hand during the escape as the ship started to roll the other way. One of the young sailors held on to the hatch a second too long in helping me to escape; his hand was cut completely off as the door slammed shut. Due to the extreme weight of the door pinching off his hand, there was very little blood as his blood vessels were, in effect, squeezed shut. The ship, once free of the storm, kept its heading for Guam. As soon as we were within range, the ship's captain called in a seaplane from Guam to evacuate the young sailor who lost his hand.

The *Banner* had not been aware of the oncoming storm, much less its expected severity. The ship notices, which would have warned us, were never read because each of the twenty-six men on board had multiple duties. The radio man, who would have received the weather reports, was also a helper in the engine room, so he never read the incoming messages warning of the approaching storm.

It appeared to me that the officers charged with navigating could not do so intelligently. To the east of Japan, a good way out to sea, lies a barrier reef, hundreds of miles long, that needed to be carefully navigated around, even in the best of weather. It was a perilous stretch of ocean, as evidenced by the many half-submerged rusted wrecks it had claimed. A junior grade lieutenant tried to tell the commander during the storm that we had already crossed the barrier reef. The commander, however, insisted that we had not. This led to a fistfight between the two on the bridge as soon as the storm subsided. I remember the junior lieutenant yelling at the commander that he had nearly killed all twenty-six men aboard with his incompetence. We sailors watched the fistfight unfold before our eyes. While both of their faces were bloodied and swollen in the end, the junior lieutenant, some twenty years younger, definitely kicked the commanding officer's ass.

The boatswain's mate and quartermaster, both petty officers first class, trained in navigation, determined they were better navigators after observing the commanding officer and junior lieutenant in action during the storm. They calculated we were indeed safely past the reef. Later it was confirmed we had passed over it during the storm, but only because the storm's low-pressure system had raised the level of the ocean. Otherwise, we would have run aground. Had that happened, I might have been entombed with two others inside that forward bunk. Because of the navigational skills of those two petty officers, the commander officer rewrote the ship's logs to cover up his own incompetence.

I finished my tour on the *Banner* after twenty-two months. When I got back to Denver, Sally was about twenty-one months old, and Steve was about three and a half. Steve did not have any problem with me coming home, even though he was too young to remember me. Steve was a great, easygoing kid. He knew he had a dad, and that dad was coming home, so he was sort of excited about my homecoming. Sally, on the other hand, really did not like me; she was very unhappy to see me. Every time I got near Lois, Sally would scream and carry on. I spanked her, which made my mother-in-law livid that I would strike a two-year-old child who did not know who I was. She had been calling my brother-in-law Ronnie "Daddy" up until this point.

Sally did not accept the new family arrangement until the day we were in the car with Denver in our rearview mirror. Sally was again screaming and carrying on. She kept crawling up to the front seat and getting in Lois' lap. While driving, I grabbed her, slapped her on the bottom, and forcibly threw her in the back seat. In that instant, Sally became a completely different child who got with the program, so to speak.

The *Banner* was just one of thousands of ordinary naval vessels in service during the time I served aboard her, but she was to become famous by association a few years later during the Cold War. She was selected for refitting as an intelligence platform and christened the USS Banner AGER-1 (AGER stood for "auxiliary general environmental research"). During intelligence-gathering operations in 1967 and 1968 off the coasts of the Soviet Union, China, and North Korea, the *Banner*'s intelligence gathering abilities were considered to be a success. The Navy granted authorization to convert two more AKLs into AGERs. These ships became the USS *Pueblo* AGER-2 and the USS *Palm Beach* AGER-3. The *Pueblo* would become the Banner's sister ship in the western Pacific while the *Palm Beach* would operate in the Atlantic. The USS Banner was eight hours away, steaming in route to the Sea of Japan off the coast of North Korea with the intent of relieving the USS *Pueblo,* when the North Koreans captured the Pueblo and its crew, creating an international incident.

CHAPTER 16

National Naval Medical Center

UPON COMPLETING MY TOUR OF duty aboard the USS *Banner*, I was ordered to the destroyer USS *Ingersoll*, whose home port was in San Diego. Lois and the kids, living the nomadic life of a sailor's family, joined me in San Diego while I waited for the destroyer to port again. Knowing it might be a month or two before the *Ingersoll* returned, I found a Quonset hut for us to call our home while we waited. The plan was for Lois to head back to Denver with the kids once I jumped aboard. When the Ingersoll finally arrived in port, I kissed Lois and the children goodbye and reported to duty. Once onboard, I did not even have a chance to unpack my sea bag before I was told that I had new orders to report to the admiral's command at the National Naval Medical Center (NNMC) in Bethesda, Maryland (now known as Walter Reed National Military Medical Center). I rushed back to our temporary living quarters, hoping Lois and the kids had not yet left for Denver. Luckily, she was still packing when I came running in out of breath, letting her know that we had a last-minute change of plans and a 3,000-mile journey ahead of us.

NNMC was the most pleasant duty station I had yet encountered in my eight years in the Navy. The sprawling medical center, surrounded by a golf course, had beautiful dogwoods, cherry trees, and azalea bushes everywhere. Located in the heart of upscale Bethesda, Maryland, just northwest of Washington D.C., it was the Navy's most prestigious medical facility for the care of military personnel, clinical research, technical training, and the teaching of Navy doctors and nurses. The president, as well as members of Congress and other dignitaries, receive their healthcare there. It was also the site of serious Cold War military research, which was to become my field. I arrived on December 2, 1955, after driving the 3,000 miles across the country with Lois, Steve, and Sally in our Cadillac.

Upon arrival, I followed my orders to report to the admiral's command. The command personnel greeted me with puzzled looks on their faces. I was met with "Who are you?" and "Where did you say you came from?" Not knowing what to do with me, they sent me away and told me to call them the next day. In short order, after calling different commands on the base, they determined I was to report for clinical training at the laboratory and hematology schools. The fourteen-month classes had begun a week earlier, but I was allowed to enroll late. The school administrators and teachers quickly determined I was overqualified for the lab courses because of my extensive lab training and experience at Jacksonville Naval Air Station, and because of my experience in emergency care at San Diego Naval Hospital and aboard the *Repose*. I was then enrolled in more advanced classes studying the physical sciences including biology, bacteriology, pathology, and hematology, among others.

On March 8, 1957, after completing my clinical studies, I was assigned to the Naval Medical Research Institute (NMRI), located on base and under the command of Captain Herschel Sudduth, an M.D. and Ph.D. The mission of NMRI was human biology and research with a major Cold War-related focus, centering on radiation sickness.

It had been ten years since I had dropped out of high school to join the Navy. I was now a 27-year-old enzyme-radiation biology technician detailed to the Biophysics Department within NMRI, headed by Captain Goldman. I did not know it at the time, but my rapid advancements in education and rank, not to mention my duty assignment in Cold War research here in Washington D.C., was unheard of for a farm boy who had only completed the eleventh grade.

My first assignment was under Dr. Morales in the Kinetics Lab where I quickly established myself as a first-rate lab technician. For two years, Dr. Morales had been working to prove the existence of a new enzyme. The big breakthrough in his research came one day when a fellow naval scientist suggested he had improperly reversed the polarity of one of the variables. With the assistance of one of his peers, Dr. Morales' research was in a state that should have proved this enzyme's presence. The problem was that the test designed to prove its existence required I perform multiple laboratory procedures using critical timing, all within one minute, using micro-quantities of enzymes and heat. This experiment drew so much attention that scientists gathered not only from NMRI but from other facilities around the nation to witness its execution. I needed to perform it in front of a half-dozen scientists, and I had to keep replicating it to make sure the results were valid.

As the birth of my third child drew near, I put in a request for six weeks of leave, which Dr. Morales denied, citing how crucial I was to his experiments. Chief William (Bill) Coles, an expert and author of much of the naval hospital regulations, came to my aid. He was a brilliant man with whom I was fortunate to work with during my time at NMRI. Bill Coles was an E-7 Chief, the highest enlisted rank at the time, and instrumental in writing the U.S. Navy's hospital regulations after World War II. It was a rare month when he was not called into dispute resolution regarding a hospital somewhere in the world. He became a major mentor to me. The knowledge of Naval hospital regulations he imparted upon me assisted me greatly throughout my naval career.

Chief Coles informed Captain Sudduth that Dr. Morales, a civilian, could not order me to continue working during my child's birth. In response, Dr. Morales argued that I could go on leave, but that I must be required to come in to perform the kinetic procedures when he had the enzymes ready. However, Chief Coles countered that I could not be on leave and be subject for duty simultaneously. Although Dr. Morales wanted me to continue running these experiments, Captain Sudduth told him to shut them down. According to Captain Sudduth, they had run their course. I was to be allowed to take the leave I had requested. Since I was the only technician capable of performing these delicate procedures, this effectively put an end to the experiments.

Our third child, William (Bill) Joseph, was born on October 3, 1957. He was named after Lois' father, Harry William, and my father, Homer Joseph. Upon returning to duty, I was assigned to the Biophysics Radiation Lab where Captain Goldman placed me in charge of categorizing and cataloging thousands of animal blood sample slides, which NMRI had in storage from the numerous experimental atomic blasts the U.S. government conducted in the Bikini Atoll. The animals, which included sheep, goats, dogs, and cows, were deposited on various salvage ships the Navy positioned around the blast zone so the U.S. could simultaneously test the effects of the blasts on these ships and the animals. The blood samples included both pre- and post-blast samples.

To study the effects of nuclear radiation on human cells, I also analyzed thousands of tissue and blood samples taken from the indigenous people living near the Bikini Atoll atomic bomb experiments. While the government moved the indigenous natives away from the direct blast zone so they would not be killed, they purposely left others in harm's way. The government publicly stated that they did not know the inhabitants were in the outer blast area. This, of course, was a bald-faced lie because I analyzed blood samples taken both before and after the atomic blasts. The U.S. exploded a total of twenty-three test bombs from 1946 to 1958. The public did not know that the tests were not only done to evaluate the weapons but also to conduct a tremendous amount of research regarding the survivability of humans in a nuclear war. If the West could develop a cure for radiation sickness, it meant a strategic advantage over the Soviet Union in the event of an exchange of nuclear weapons. Accordingly, our medical research went on for years after the explosions.

The Navy constructed the first laboratory-sized nuclear reactor at NMRI which was used to test exposure of radiation on mammals. NMRI was working with thousands of radiated animals a year, many of which went through my procedures. My subsequent duties within the Biophysics Radiation Lab included preparing tissue sections for histology and histochemical studies and preparing various special histology stains.

The preparation of tissue samples included performing all manner of tasks associated with biological studies, including autopsies of experimental animals, freeze-drying tissue for anti-radiation sickness studies, fixation, embedding, cutting, and staining with selective stains. My performance reviews at the time noted that my work was of superior quality and that I had developed a technique for cutting tissue sections exceedingly thin due to my "unusual mechanical abilities." I routinely cut high-quality frozen embedded tissue sections at two microns, whereas most good histopathological technicians could achieve no less than five microns. At one point, the Navy discussed whether to patent my technique and modifications to the slicing apparatus but, in the end, decided to keep it in the public domain for humanitarian reasons.

The resultant data from my advanced pathology studies of radiation exposure became the basis of published radiation mortality tables. No one else was performing this research, as there was no established discipline in nuclear medicine at the time. These mortality tables specified mortality as a function of time and exposure. For instance, my tables spelled out the dosage of radiation exposure that would kill every single mammal within two hours and the amount of exposure that would allow a fifty percent survival rate after thirty days.

The lab had some of the world's most famous scientists, including a German named Friedrich Philipp Ellinger, who was chief radiation biologist and head of pharmacology at NMRI. Dr. Ellinger, an M.D. and Ph.D., defected to the West from Germany during or shortly after World War II with the assistance of U.S. intelligence. His primary goal was to find enzymes or an agent that would help find a cure for radiation sickness.

The most eccentric scientist at NMRI was also a medical doctor and Ph.D. whom I will not name. This doctor was a true genius who had terrible difficulty interacting socially. When I was introduced to him, he nodded his head but did not bother to turn around. I worked with him in the same room for months, and I don't think we ever exchanged more than a dozen one-word sentences. Additionally, his hygiene left something to be desired: I don't think he bathed but once per week, and he wore the same clothes day in and day out. Someone found one of his paychecks in the trash and brought it to my attention. I subsequently discovered that he had not cashed over $2,000 in salary. Accordingly, I went to the commander and obtained permission to have his salary deposited into a bank account in his name.

In the Biology Department at NMRI, there were several other fields of research, usually with top-secret military applications. In addition to radiation sickness, another aspect of our clinical research included searching for a cure or prevention for malaria, which has taken a tremendous number of fighting men off the battlefield for centuries. Chief Coles was an expert in breeding mosquitoes. He bred several species in a lab with temperature and humidity controls for malaria research. This research included tests done on inmates at certain prisons. They were infected with malaria and became part of clinical drug trials. We also experimented on sexually transmitted diseases such as syphilis and gonorrhea, another affliction that affects the readiness of fighting forces overseas. Like the malaria research, these clinical tests were also conducted on prisoners, something the ACLU would undoubtedly have a heart attack over if they had known.

Another great scientist I worked with in the Biophysics Lab was Captain Barr, an aviation flight physiologist and inventor of the heart pump monitor. Captain Barr was conducting research on one of the first monkeys to return safely from space in preparation for human space flight. This monkey was a national treasure at the time, and his retirement home was NMRI.

It was while working in the Biophysics Lab at NMRI that I started taking several college classes. The Navy enrolled me in first-year English and Algebra III at George Washington University in DC. The classes were held at the National Institutes of Health across the street from the hospital. Being enrolled in these classes was, at first, very intimidating for this high-school dropout. I was gaining confidence in my academic abilities bit by bit, but enrolling in courses at a first-rate university was a big step for me. I felt I was at a disadvantage because my grade school was a one-room schoolhouse in the Deep South, and my county's high school had less than 200 or so students. I was not even a high school graduate. It was while taking these college courses that I first discovered just how good my boyhood education was.

While working at NMRI, I also volunteered to be a human guinea pig for many experiments to supplement my take-home pay. I was limited by Navy regulations to three a month at $30 each. It was a rare month that I was not able to make the extra $90, although doing so nearly cost me my life once.

This most harrowing test was for a new experimental breathing apparatus. I was submerged in frigid forty-degree water in a high-pressure steel tank outfitted with small Plexiglas portals that allowed the researchers to monitor me while I was inside. Before being submerged into this steel tank, I was dressed in a deep-sea diving rig with an iron helmet. With the lid on, they simulated an environment of 600 psi, the equivalent of being at a depth of over 1,300 feet. A short time into the experiment, the breathing tube separated, allowing the frigid water to start filling my helmet. I was thrashing around for what seemed an eternity before they realized my helmet was filling with water and that I was about to drown. I was not only holding my breath while inside the tank, but I nearly lost consciousness while the researchers, with fumbling fingers, struggled to detach the iron helmet before I drowned.

Nearly drowning was not the only danger. A diver at that depth would normally have to ascend at a slow pace to avoid the bends. I now had nitrogen in my bloodstream from being decompressed too rapidly. They immediately threw me into a decompression chamber and called medical personnel from the hospital to monitor my condition. Though I felt miserable for a few days, their emergency actions saved my life.

Dr. Kenneth Sell, a brilliant man possessing multiple degrees, including a Ph.D. from a European University, arrived at NMRI as one of the first three immunologists in the world. He was either the perfect anecdote for a bureaucratic Navy or a complete misfit for the armed services; I never did decide which. He was a type-A personality. It never occurred to him that he might not get his way. He was a "hard shell" kind of guy, a real tough bastard. He and I were part of the same personnel promotion ceremony on July 3, 1957. He was promoted to captain, and I, after ten years in the Navy, became a chief.

The first thing he did upon achieving the rank of captain was to complain to the commanding officer, Captain Sudduth, that it was an insult for him to share his ceremony with an enlisted man. The second thing he did was to sit down with me for about thirty minutes to size me up. After determining that I was what he was looking for, he went to Captain Sudduth and informed him—not asked him, but informed him—that he was taking "Chief Custead" over to the Tissue Bank and designating me as his chief lab administrator. The third thing he did was get rid of twenty professionals under his command who he considered dead weight. He then authorized me, as his new lab administrator, to hire twenty replacements, most of whom were mid-grade officers, civilians, and newly-graduated research scientists. This was completely unheard of, and no one at the time believed the captain had provided me with such authority. But here I was, a newly promoted chief hospital corpsman, interviewing and hiring research scientists. Dr. Sell did not have time to be bothered with such mundane administrative matters since he was regularly traveling the world attending symposiums and meeting with dignitaries.

Dr. Sell sure as hell did not care who, or for what reason, he threatened with a court-martial. It did not matter if the order was legal or even if he had the authority to order someone else who did not report to him. He stepped on a lot of toes, sometimes the wrong ones, but he never received any reprimands owing to his celebrity status. A couple of years later, he was given command of NMRI, but he only viewed that as a technicality because he had seen himself as the commanding officer all along. I probably carried out a thousand illegal orders for him. Once he threatened me with court-martial if I did not get a print job done by 5:00 p.m. There was a conference the next day, and handouts needed to be printed. The print shop said they could not get it done in the time allowed, but that did not stop Dr. Sell from threatening me, and everyone else involved, with court-martial. In the end, the handouts were available for his conference.

Dr. Sell had assumptive authorities no one else could get away with. I would say he invented the term "going rogue." At one time, he decided he was going to expand the Tissue Lab, going so far as to almost break ground for a new building when the upper echelon found out. The next thing I knew, he told me to find some land off base on which to build a satellite lab so the bureaucrats would not find out about it. I found a piece of land on Wisconsin Avenue across from a bar named Hank Deitle's Tavern, about five miles north of the base. After purchasing the lot on his behalf using Navy funds, I got his secret satellite lab built without the Navy finding out until it was too late.

CHAPTER 17

Noyes Drive

LOIS AND I FOUND A small house to rent upon our arrival in Washington D.C. It was on Noyes Drive in Silver Spring, Maryland, twenty minutes or so from the Bethesda hospital base. This house was to become our home for the next six years. Finding our home in Silver Spring was a lesson in the good that exists in strangers. In addition, we made a lifelong friend.

After driving across the county, we checked into the Colonial Inn Hotel at the corner of Nicholson and Rockville Pike in Rockville, Maryland. We then went out looking for dinner. It was late on a cold winter evening when we found Bish Thompson's Seafood Restaurant a few miles down the road in downtown Bethesda. Our waitress, Stephanie Gamble, took one look at us and decided we were the sorriest lot she had laid eyes on in a month of Sundays. Stephanie was a second-generation Ukrainian and quite a beautiful woman. Steve and Sally, who were three and two respectively, were falling asleep at the table and did not have winter jackets. We started up a conversation with Stephanie and told her we were looking for an affordable place to stay. Without hesitation, she insisted we go directly to her house that night, where she would help us find a new residence. Her husband Jack was a reserve warrant officer in the Navy, which, I guess, contributed to her taking us under her wing.

She was alone in the house with her little nine-year-old daughter Andrea, because her husband was away at engineering school in New England. Andrea was mature beyond her years. I remember being shocked when Stephanie sent her nine-year-old daughter out late at night to get a newspaper. That evening, after giving Steve and Sally a bath and putting them to bed, Stephanie went to work finding us a place to live. She started with the newspaper and recognized an address, saying she knew the owner from her second job as a cab driver. This gentleman had her pick up a fifth of whiskey and bring it to his house on a regular basis. She then took us out to look at the house and visit the owner sometime after midnight while her daughter looked after our sleeping children. Stephanie negotiated the rent down from $125 to $75 per month, which was affordable on my 1955 salary of $2,765. She told the owner, "You know that house is not worth the asking price. Don't insult my friends," as if we were old, lifelong friends.

When we came back well after midnight, we woke up the kids, went back to the hotel, and moved into the house the next day. Luckily, it was furnished, but it was in terrible shape, barely habitable. Stephanie also negotiated that any repairs I did could be deducted from the rent. One month, I paid rent of only $16 because I spent $59 on repairs. The owner never questioned a single receipt in the six years we lived there. He never came by to inspect anything, nor did he ever call or increase our rent. Occasionally, we caught him driving by very slowly in his yellow Mercury, checking the place out. Stephanie was a big-hearted person who found us a home and became a longtime friend.

Our third and fourth children, Bill and Clay respectively, were born while we lived on Noyes Drive. William (Bill) Joseph was born on October 3, 1957, and Clayton Bard on February 8, 1960. As mentioned, Bill was named after Lois' father, William Harry, and my father, Homer Joseph. The name Clayton was chosen for no other reason than it sounded like a Southern civil war general's name. As I mentioned earlier, Clay's middle name has been handed down father to son for 17 generations and can be traced back to Germany on my mother's side. We were now a family of six paying $75 per month for rent plus utilities on a monthly salary of less than $200 per month. Our house had only two bedrooms with an in-law suite in the walkout basement, which we rented to Jim and Nelly Davis and their little girl for half of 1957. Jim, who I first met while working at the Memphis Air Station, worked with me at the Naval Hospital. We charged them only $25 per month to help them out while Jim completed his optical training. Mrs. Davis also helped watch the kids while Lois worked waiting tables at Mrs. K's Toll House, a nearby five-star restaurant. After the Davis family was transferred to San Diego, Lois' mom lived with us for six months along with Lois' youngest siblings, David, Linda, and Larry.

Our first real scare with one of our children happened shortly after we moved into this home. One Sunday morning, Sally, a toddler at the time, fell down the three concrete steps on the front porch and fractured her skull. We were inside when Sally stumbled into the house, wobbling badly. She was non-responsive and clearly in a bad way. Lois and I quickly loaded the kids into the car and raced to the emergency room at the NNMC. Several Navy captains cared for Sally, many of whom had been called to duty from home due to the seriousness of Sally's injuries. She ended up being admitted for several days so they could observe her as she recovered from her serious head trauma. I went over to visit her several times a day while on duty.

The next child-related scare was also quite serious. In 1961, Clay, a one-year-old, was acting extremely lethargic and cranky one Sunday morning. He had a temperature of 105 degrees, so we knew he was quite ill. It was not until I was holding him at the breakfast table that I noticed he was not holding his bottle with his left hand. I felt up and down his arm and immediately noticed his shoulder was bright red and warm to the touch, flinching when I moved it. I was not overly concerned with his high temperature as a general symptom. Fevers are quite common in kids and are something every parent learns to monitor carefully and treat at home. However, when I felt how hot Clay's shoulder was, I immediately knew there was a severe infection. We loaded the kids in the car and headed to the emergency room at the NNMC, and again, we had the full attention of every specialist in the hospital as they probed in his shoulder to withdraw puss and fluids for analysis. This was done after taking Clay's clothes off and carrying him outside to the frigid winter temperatures in an attempt to cool his dangerously high fever. They eventually determined Clay had osteomyelitis in his shoulder, a bacterial infection of the bone marrow. It is extremely rare, affecting perhaps only two out of 10,000 people per year, and very difficult to diagnose, requiring a painful bone biopsy. The doctors told us it probably developed after he was picked up by the arms, his shoulder separated, and bacteria attacked the joint. Clay spent seven to ten days in the ICU while they continuously injected penicillin into this shoulder to flush the infection. We thanked God as he eventually recovered and went on to live the life of a normal boy, at least as far as we knew at the time.

It was not until many years later, when Clay was a teenager, that I first learned of the lasting repercussions from his bout with osteomyelitis. I was finishing the basement in our Parkwood Drive home, hanging the ceiling, when I requested his help holding up a long piece of wood that I was hammering into it. I told him to hold the wood up with both hands, but I noticed him struggling to lift his left arm over his head. He was looking for something to stand on and arching his back awkwardly. I asked him what was going on, and he said he could not reach his left arm up high enough, that he could not raise his elbow above his shoulder.

I stood in stunned silence for a moment, realizing the impact of what I had just seen and heard. Clay had always been an exceptional athlete, becoming the captain of his state championship high school soccer team, but he never once mentioned any problem with his shoulder. He simply accepted it as part of who he was and felt that saying something was not going to make it better.

It turned out that his shoulder was crippled and, what was worse, Lois and I did not know it until Clay was a teenager. The disease had left him with little to no cartilage, and his condition worsened as he aged. He dealt with his shoulder continually separating and inflaming all his adult life until the pain became so unbearable that he could not sleep through the night unless he tied his left arm down in a tight sling. When he reached his late forties, he had complete shoulder replacement surgery. Clay now says that after considerable recuperative pain and nine months of rehabilitation, his shoulder no longer bothers him, and he has a new, increased range of motion, though the range is still not what it should be.

Bill turned out to be a colicky baby for the first three months before turning into a child with the most wonderful disposition, one who almost always minded us and never got into trouble. He always seemed to take disappointing his parents more seriously than any of his siblings. Later in life, he took up smoking, but he would not smoke in front of his parents, even as an adult, up until he quit the habit in his thirties. Bill had a tough time in high school, and I spent a great deal of time with him and his schoolwork. Math, in particular, was one subject he hated. I spent entire weekends tutoring him.

Clay was always an above average student, getting mostly Bs on his report cards, with a few A's and C's mixed in. We never worried about him because he was always a self-starter. The one thing that set him apart was that he never asked permission to do anything, believing it was always better to ask for forgiveness. For example, when the family was living in Interlachen, Florida, while I was stationed in Antarctica, Lois woke up one morning and could not find Clay or his younger brother Phil anywhere in the house. Clay was about four years old, and Phil had just learned to walk and was still in diapers. Lois was in a panic, tearing the house apart looking for them, when she got a call from a neighbor who recognized our sons in town. It turned out Clay had taken his little brother, together with his piggy bank, to the old Brush Post Office and General Store four blocks away to buy candy. As they approached the house, Clay had one arm wrapped around his glass piggy bank and the other hand holding Phil's hand. Phil was using his free hand to hold up his falling diaper.

During our time at Noyes Drive, Steve and Sally thrived. They were two and three respectively when we moved there, and by the time we left, they were eight and ten, attending the third and fourth grades at Woodside Elementary. Sally took ballet, while Steve's obsessions were Zorro and playing with his best friend Winston Boor. Lois and I always took a very active role in their schooling. I went so far as to bring home radioactive material from the lab, which caused one of the neighbors to call the fire department thinking our house was on fire. I turned out all the lights in the house to demonstrate to the kids the energy that was in this speck of radioactive cesium by hooking it up to equipment that flashed a neon light. Of course, in the 1950s we did not know what we know now about certain radioactive materials. Since the 1990s, the largest application of the element has been as cesium formate solution, which is used by the oil industry for drilling fluids. It also has a range of applications in chemistry and the production of electricity and electronics. The radioactive isotope cesium-137 now has applications in medicine, industrial gauges, and hydrology. At the time, I did not know the element was mildly toxic. It is a hazardous material, and its radioisotopes present a high health risk. In hindsight, I can say that if we knew then what we now know about cesium, I would never have brought it home. I guess in the end, it was the multicolor flashing display that got the attention of the neighbors who called the fire department. I remember it being quite comical trying to explain to the fire chief that there was no fire and that we were "only playing with radioactive material." I guarantee that was the first and only time that fire chief heard that explanation.

★ ★ ★

John Welsh and his family were neighbors on Noyes Drive. John became another lifelong friend, and perhaps the best friend I was ever to have. Lois, while fond of John, was always confused as to why I valued his friendship so much. I think it was because he always made me feel needed. I always got a great sense of satisfaction from helping John and his family. John came from an impoverished background in New York City, growing up in a cold water flat (an apartment with no running hot water) with only one shared bathroom per floor. After high school, John joined the Air Force and, after a few years and after earning a couple of stripes, was stationed in NATO Headquarters in Turkey. There he met his wife Vedia, who went by the name Vy. Upon returning to the States with his bride, John was assigned to the Pentagon. He was spending half his income and two or three hours per day commuting from his home in Maryland to the Pentagon via bus because he did not own a car. When John transferred to D.C., he assumed the area had a subway like New York City, the only American city he was familiar with, which, of course, was not the case at the time. I assisted in helping him learn to drive and obtain a driver's license.

John and Vy were in a bad way financially, not having anything but perhaps a mattress on the floor when Vy was nine-months pregnant. John was never very smart about money; when he rented his house, he did not know that he not only had to pay rent, but also the utilities. Vy, being from Turkey, and John, knowing only the cold water flat in New York City, both insisted for some time that they did not have to pay the utilities. It was only after they were cut off and I paid to have the electricity turned back on that they came to believe me. John, to his credit, always paid me back.

Vy, who was raised a Turkish Muslim but converted to Catholicism as a teenager, felt deceived. I think she believed she was marrying a rich American, but she soon realized John did not have a pot to pee in. She was well-educated and had a high-paying job at the World Bank when she arrived in the United States. Unfortunately, she had to give that job up when she became pregnant and moved to Noyes Drive because she had no mode of transportation.

How Vy came to the Catholic faith is an interesting story. In the Islamic faith, all that is required for a divorce is for the man to state that he wants one. Vy's family was upper-crust in Turkish society. Her father fell in love with an English woman. By Islamic law, the children are automatically the property of the father in a divorce. Vy was sent to live with this new woman in England, and her father was to join them at a later date. After a couple of years, her father changed his mind and decided not to join the English girlfriend, and Vy was dropped off at a Catholic orphanage at age twelve, where she subsequently converted to Catholicism. In spite of this hardship, she somehow managed to attend college in England. She never saw her father again, but her mother later became a part of her married life, even visiting her in the States multiple times.

Seeing how desperately poor they were, I showed John how to get assistance from the military and civilian relief organizations, the first of many times I came to their aid. I don't think John owned any clothes at this time except his uniforms. After leaving the Air Force, he worked a string of minimum-wage jobs and eventually purchased a nice home in which they raised their four children.

John and Vy eventually divorced, and John spent every penny he made on child support for his four children. He was a wonderful father who loved his children with all his heart. I think the final straw for Vy was when John, poor as hell, purchased a dilapidated school bus for $350. He was very much into his kids' sports and thought the bus was going to be a team bus for the kids. The bus ran for only a little while before it broke down. John wanted me to work on it, but I refused. I knew there were a thousand regulations, certificates, and license requirements to own and operate a bus, especially for transporting children. Even if I did relent and spent my free time getting it operational, I knew John would be breaking a dozen laws if he used it to transport his son's team. Just getting it to the point of passing inspection would cost thousands. There was a limit to my generosity when rescuing John from his own foolishness. Eventually, he parked the bus in his backyard where it became a terrible eyesore. After the divorce, John was arrested several times for not paying child support. It was not for want of trying; he simply did not make enough to support his four children. The sheriff would arrest John at his place of employment, the Duron Paint store, where he worked for minimum wage. I bailed him out many times, and he always repaid me. I also served as John's mechanic, keeping his old wreck of a car on the road for years.

John was a very likable guy, and our children were extremely fond of him. Every time we visited with John, it seemed he wanted to spend more time talking sports with the kids than with Lois or me. Financially destitute, John came to live with us before finding a deserted, dilapidated farmhouse to live in with a homeless kid on the other side of town. I drove him home a couple of times but never did see his dwelling. He always had an excuse for me to drop him off at some place or another but never where he lived. I believe he was too embarrassed to let me see the dilapidated shack.

The homeless kid he lived with called us when John passed away. He explained that after one of my sons had dropped John off, he walked home, laid down, and died. I was not surprised by the news because John had been unable to eat on Christmas Eve, the last time he had had dinner with us. He had been living on cigarettes and coffee with about ten teaspoons of sugar per cup, and his bones had been sticking out. By the time I reached the place where John was living, his corpse had been taken by the state. His body was to be turned over to a teaching hospital in Baltimore for medical science since he was considered indigent with no known family. My kids were so fond of John that they became upset at the thought of his body being unclaimed. They wanted him to have a decent burial, so I hunted his body down to a morgue in Baltimore. The search was not easy since "John Welsh" was a pretty common name in Maryland.

Once I found John's corpse, they would not release the body to me unless I had some proof of who John was. I knew as an Air Force veteran he was due a proper burial at Arlington, so I drove the sixty or seventy miles back to the shack and was told by the owner that anything John owned would be in his broken-down car. I did not have a key, so the owner handed me a hammer and said, "Go at it. I am just going to have the car taken to the junkyard." In the trunk, I found a box of moldy, wet, stinking papers. I took the moldy pile home, spread all the papers out on the dining room table, and proceeded to dry them one by one with a hair dryer until I found his Air Force discharge papers.

In the end, I was able to get John the twenty-one-gun salute at Arlington instead of a pauper's grave or worse. Lois and I paid for his funeral ourselves even though, with seven children, we were struggling to get by. His children, Mike, Michelle, Karen, and Brian, were grateful for what I did for their dad. Michelle, who had graduated from college and become a teacher, sent us $100 to help pay for her dad's funeral. I was very touched by this act of kindness on her part. As a teacher, this was a lot of money for her at the time, but it helped us because we did not have any savings to spare.

In the end, I was happy to help John's family one final time after his death. I left Vy with some crucial financial advice. I told her that since they had never paid the court fees, their divorce was not legally finalized, thus making her a veteran's widow eligible for military survivors' benefits.

CHAPTER 18

Fort Belvoir

I WAS NOW THIRTY-THREE years old and had been in the Navy for fourteen years. I had seen combat duty in World War II and the Korean War. I knew I wanted to continue my career in an intellectual capacity while working in the beautiful scenery of Washington D.C. Accordingly, I decided to apply to the Nuclear Engineering School at Fort Belvoir in Virginia. Acceptance into this program was the first step to a specialized duty assignment monitoring the environment in and around the experimental nuclear power plant at McMurdo Station, Antarctica. I included the following letter of recommendation in my application to the Nuclear Engineering School:

To whom it may concern:

I have known the applicant, Elmer B. Custead, for the last four years. During this time, he was associated with the Division of Pharmacology and Radiobiology at the Naval Medical Research Institute, National Naval Medical Center, Bethesda, MD. This Division has been and is currently investigating the effects of a radiation protective agent, which is administered following exposure of the animals. Mr. Custead has a good basic knowledge of the use of ionizing radiation in biology and medicine and its implications. He is thoroughly familiar with many of the methods and techniques used in exploring this field of research. The initiative, foresight and skill of the applicant, as well as his dependability and unusual mechanical dexterity, assure him success in any work he may choose to undertake.

Dr. Thomas A. Strike

The Navy Department of Medicine wanted to create billets for nuclear health physics. There was a lot of discussion as to whether these newly-created billets should be commissioned or enlisted. Captain Sudduth spoke of commissioning me as a medical services officer, but I pushed back on this idea, even though it would have been an honor. After a great deal of deliberation, I declined. As a chief hospital corpsman, I was already performing duties above my pay grade and that of many junior officers. In most instances, junior officers relied on me to show them the ropes. The commanding officers knew I was a chief on whom they could rely. They valued me as their right-hand man. It was a rare day when Captain Sudduth did not stop by my office and close the door for informal conversations, conversations he did not have with his officers. He knew I was a fount of all scuttlebutt in the command, to which he would not otherwise be privy. Even after he retired, he called me regularly to chat and get caught up on the latest developments. I was proud that, as both an M.D. and a Ph.D., he sincerely regarded me as an intelligent friend.

Another reason I turned down a commission at that time was that as an officer, I would lose control over my career in nuclear medicine; it was standard operating procedure to rotate junior grade officers through several duty stations to gain experience. Additionally, the pay of an ensign, the starting rank of an officer, was lower than what I was making as chief because of proficiency pay I earned.

I should admit that there was a bit of snobbery at play as well. About fifty percent of the ensigns I dealt with in the Navy were like newly-walking infants. I had one ensign on the *Banner* who misspent a whole day arguing I should be on the watch rotations on that small vessel. I tried explaining to him until I was blue in the face that, as the hospital corpsman in charge of the medical wellbeing of the crew, I was effectively on watch twenty-four hours a day, seven days a week. At the end of this long day of arguing, I saw that I was not getting through to this young ensign and just ignored him. I found the best junior officers understood that their chiefs were usually a valuable resource, while the worst ignored our experience.

While I had pretty much made my mind up, I sought Lois' counsel on accepting a commission. In the end, she knew that I wanted to stay on my current career path as a chief, preferring highly specialized research in nuclear medicine and supported my decision to decline becoming an officer. I knew she was probably a little disappointed in my decision since officers' wives enjoyed a higher social status in the Navy. In the end, the Navy decided to send me, as an enlisted man, to acquire this new specialty due to my extensive background and experience in radiation research. Accordingly, I received orders on July 22, 1961, to attend nuclear engineering school at the Army Engineering Center at Fort Belvoir. Several years later, the Navy determined that this specialty should be a commissioned medical service corps billet, but this was not until after I had returned from duty in Antarctica.

Nuclear medicine was an emerging field for which there was no established degree at the time. Because of this, I was required to take selected classes at universities around the nation. A lot of my coursework was done at the University of Virginia, University of Cincinnati, and the University of Connecticut. Additionally, I was included in top secret training at Kodak Labs in Rochester, New York. There I received instruction on the use of a highly-specialized crystal to be inserted into classified machinery. This machinery would be transported to Antarctica ahead of my arrival. All in all, my training in nuclear engineering and medicine with the Navy was the equivalent of a bachelor's of science in nuclear engineering. Just before I completed this training, the University of Florida admitted its first two students into its brand-new curriculum in nuclear health physics, the first university in the nation to do so.

Upon completing all the required coursework, I earned certification as a nuclear power plant operator specializing in health physics from the U.S. Naval Nuclear Power Unit. The core fifteen-month courses ran from July of 1961 until October of 1962, which were followed by "duty under instruction" in an operations phase running the reactor. The nuclear plant, the first of its kind in America, was geared toward not only providing electricity to surrounding jurisdictions but to national defense and Cold War research. Part of our training was hooking up the reactor to electrical grids from Baltimore to Richmond. The final phase of my training was in environmental monitoring in preparation for my upcoming assignment in Antarctica. I completed all my training in a little over two years and, by September of 1963, I was ready for my first assignment in the newly created billet of nuclear health at McMurdo Station, Antarctica.

I was the oldest student in the training classes. Seventy-five percent of the students were Navy, three or four were Air Force, and the remaining were Army. Paul Feltner, who was to relieve me in Antarctica, and I were the only corpsmen in the class. Most of the Navy students were Seabees (construction). I was not well liked by most of the instructors because I had a great deal more experience in nuclear health than many of them. I pointed out to teachers that some of their measurement equipment was not even operational. They did not appreciate my perceived one-upmanship. My grades were constantly marked downward, placing my class standing officially as last in a class of forty-four. Furthermore, negative comments were written in my personnel files such as "Chief Custead has problems following instruction." I tried not to take offense at these petty politics. My personnel reviews started very favorably, noting that I was helping others in the class, and went downhill from there. I just laughed it off, knowing that despite the grades they were giving me, I was being assigned to Antarctica, one of the most demanding duty rotations of all.

★ ★ ★

Upon my acceptance into the nuclear school, Lois and I moved out of our rented home on Noyes Drive and into a new three-bedroom duplex on Soldier Road on Fort Belvoir in Fairfax, Virginia. This was to be our temporary living quarters while I attended nuclear schooling in preparation for Antarctica.

Lois and I experienced a bit of culture shock living on an Army base for the first time. We had never lived on a base, much less an Army base, so we did not have anything to compare it to. While we enjoyed our time there, the neighbors seemed to be of a different caliber. We got the impression there were inordinately many alcoholics among the population. Whether correctly or incorrectly, I attributed this to the culture of the Army. Due to its size, it trains their personnel to perform one specific task day in and day out. The Navy, being a tiny fraction in size of the Army, trains its sailors in a much broader capacity, making their jobs more challenging.

Every Saturday night we enjoyed a good social life going to the club while we left little Bill and Clay under the care of Sally and Steve. Our fifth child, Phillip J (no middle name, just an initial), arrived on April 9, 1962 while at Fort Belvoir. People often ask why we gave Phil the middle name of just the letter "J" instead of the name "Jay." We thought we were being cute.

Overall, the kids enjoyed their stay at Fort Belvoir. There were so many children around that finding a playmate was as easy as walking out the front door. Sally developed her first crush in the second grade, and Steve had his first encounter with a bully at age ten. He came home crying one day after being bullied by the kid across the street who was a little older and a lot bigger. I took Steve outside and told him to go across the street and give the kid a licking.

To my surprise, and making me proud, Steve showed a great deal of courage by walking across the street and giving the bully a dose of his own medicine. I was there encouraging him to stand up for himself. Amazingly, after that, Steve and this kid became best buddies.

We experienced a frightening incident when my brother Homer, his wife Fern, and their children Ricky and Patricia visited us at Fort Belvoir. Our kids had all been warned time and time again not to ride their bikes down the nearby, aptly named, Graves Hill Road. It was so steep that we knew the kids would not be able to control a bike on it. I had just arrived home one morning after working the night shift at the reactor. I was standing beside the car when Lois came rushing out of the house screaming that Patricia, about eleven at the time, was lying at the foot of the hill and needed help. As I looked down the hill, I could see a small body lying motionless on the pavement. Lois had come out to get the newspaper and saw Patricia head down the hill, lose control, and slide headfirst into the curb. Lois ran inside to alert Homer and Fern and to call an ambulance just moments before I arrived. I sprinted down the hill with Homer and Fern in close pursuit. We found their daughter's face torn off from the top of her right ear to over and around her chin to the bottom of the left ear. The EMTs arrived from the base hospital within minutes. I assisted them in loading her into the ambulance. I jumped in the back with Patricia, and the ambulance screamed off for the emergency room. Her injuries were so grave that her father fainted.

As soon as we arrived at the emergency room, I took the lead in pulling the gurney into an operating room. Wearing scrubs from the prior night's duty at the reactor, combined with my experienced demeanor, gave everyone in the emergency room the impression that I was a doctor. After scrubbing in, I immediately started to work on her before the doctors on duty arrived. As the actual doctors entered the operating room, I was already in the process of going through the wound and pinching shut the blood vessels to stem the bleeding. After I got the bleeding under control, I removed the plastic headband she was wearing, piece by little piece, as it was embedded in her flesh. At this point, I had four Army doctors and two nurses in the room assisting me. Because of my confidence in what I was doing, they also assumed I was a doctor. They had no idea that they were watching a naval chief hospital corpsman, drawing on his extensive experience. They assisted as I started to stitch Patricia's face back together. I started with heavy stitching to stretch the skin back into place; then I cut edges on both sides of the torn skin to get a clean joint to aid healing with minimal scarring. There was no need for anesthesia since she was in a coma, a state she stayed in for three days. We started working on Patricia early in the morning and did not finish until late into the afternoon, operating for eight hours straight without a break. The doctors in the operating room let me lead the effort while Homer and Fern were waiting anxiously outside in the waiting room.

This was not the first time I had performed surgery of this kind. While in San Diego I had once put over 170 sutures into the face of an enlisted man who had his face severely lacerated in a knife fight. It was not until after Patricia's operation was finished and we were standing in the corridor discussing the past eight hours, that one of the Army doctors said, "Dr. Custead, that was great work you performed in there." At this point I corrected him, explaining that I was a Navy hospital corpsman. Needless to say, they were shocked. They wanted to know if it was typical of Navy corpsmen to possess such advanced medical skills. I told them that with my extensive experience, I was not a "typical" naval corpsman.

Patricia's parents took her straight home to Florida as soon as she was capable of traveling. She grew up to be an attractive young woman like her mother. The only visible scars were at her hairline, easily hidden by her hair. The last time I saw Patricia was at her parents' fiftieth wedding anniversary. She may have been in her mid-fifties by then and was still very attractive. I always felt a special fondness for my niece Patricia because of the special bond we had from this accident. Lois believed she looked to me as her hero.

CHAPTER 19

Antarctica

UPON COMPLETION OF MY NUCLEAR training, I received orders to McMurdo Station, Antarctica, for a tour of duty that would last from October 1963 to October 1964. This meant leaving Lois, who was pregnant with our sixth child Paul and caring for our five children, on her own for over a year. The two logical choices for my growing family were either Denver, Colorado, or Palatka, Florida, so Lois could be near one of our families for the support she was surely going to need. In the end, we chose Interlachen, Florida, a small community near my parents' farm, for financial reasons. A friend of my parents offered a newly refurbished house rent-free in exchange for keeping up the yard and paying the utilities. Also, because the Cadillac was getting old and unreliable, I purchased a brand-new GMC Carryall, a precursor to the SUV. I did not want to leave Lois with the added burden of a car that could break down.

My parents were in their seventies at the time and therefore could not be of much help to Lois. Lois' mom, who was then only fifty-five, twenty years older than Lois, came to help shortly after I left for Antarctica. Lois' brother David, still in high school at the time, arrived shortly afterward at the start of summer break. Both Lois' mom and brother stayed until the end of the summer. My brother Paul stepped up and was very good about looking after Lois and the kids. I was grateful for the way he watched over my family in my absence. He often took them sightseeing or to the beach, usually bringing his children Rosemary and Oliver along as well. Once he even rushed over to shoot a rattlesnake that Lois found on the road in front of the house, thus making sure his nephews and niece were safe. At the time, I had a hard time reconciling his devotion to my family with how badly he had treated me as his kid brother.

The house was a wonderful, comfortable home on a one or two-acre corner lot. The neighborhood was well off the two-lane highway, with hard clay streets. Wood-sided and painted white with a front porch, the house, like most Florida homes, stood atop pilings a few feet off the ground. Spanish moss hung from the trees. A feral dog lived under the house, though we rarely saw it. In the back was a combined shop and garage, where, after running an electrical line, we placed our washer and dryer. Nearby was a paper mill, but luckily, the trade winds typically blew the smell away. However, a couple of times a year, when the wind was right, it could smell to high hell. Train tracks ran along the back side of the property. It was a very safe and ideal Southern town for the kids because there was no worry about traffic and it had a kind of Andy Griffith/Mayberry feel to it. One drawback, though, was the twenty-five mile trip to the grocery store. Another downside was the lack of central heating, as the oil furnace in the dining room was the only source of heat. Lois, who is from Denver, said the coldest night she ever spent on this planet was while living in that house. The temperature got down to seventeen degrees one night. Lois had Steve bring all the mattresses downstairs so they could sleep in the dining room next to the furnace.

In October of 1963, after spending about a month getting Lois and the children settled into their temporary home, my brother Paul drove the family and me to the Palatka train station. Everyone came to see me off, including my parents. I took the train north to Rhode Island where the gigantic C-130s, specially outfitted for South Pole travel, were based. About fifty of us prepared here before taking off on the ten-day, 9,000-mile flight to Antarctica. I was handed the expensive, specialized crystal from Kodak Labs, needed for the top-secret equipment at McMurdo. I was instructed to wear it around my neck to keep it at body temperature. If I remember correctly, we refueled four times: in California, Honolulu, Hawaii, and Christchurch, New Zealand. At each stop, we were handed a bagged meal. Once in Christchurch, the Navy issued each of us a locker to store our uniforms, civilian clothes, and personal items that we were not to take to the Antarctic. In addition to survival gear, the Navy also issued us specially designed underwear, shirts, and pants. In the Antarctic, the only evidence of rank was the insignias sewn to our clothing and hats.

The last 1,100-mile leg of the journey from Christchurch was the most dangerous. Every plane going out of Christchurch picked up a Marine sergeant who was the expert on navigating every flight in and out of McMurdo. When my group left Christchurch for McMurdo Station, a winter flight had never yet been attempted. The summer flights, of which we were one, were dangerous enough. A vast majority of the journey was over water, and the distance was so great that the flights reached a point of no return. After passing the point of no return, the plane would be forced to ditch somewhere on the Antarctic continent if the crew could not find the ice field because it would not have enough fuel to make it back. It was not uncommon for flights to turn back several times before making a successful trip.

About two hours before arrival, the pilots turned down the heat in the plane and instructed us to don our winter gear to get acclimated to the cold. Someone brought a bag of fresh onions, which promptly froze into rocks. When I debarked from the plane at the bottom of the earth on October 17, 1963, it was the start of the Antarctic summer, a balmy day at twenty degrees. The days were almost twenty-four hours long in the summer, but the sun was never more than a few degrees above the horizon, giving the impression that it was perpetually dusk. Caterpillars (transports on tank-like tracks) were brought out to Williams Field to transport us the six or seven miles to the base. However, the public health officer I was relieving was at the airfield to greet me and invited me to walk with him back to the base. I was glad to do so after being in a plane for over ten hours. I was also anxious to try out my new survival gear, which came in handy on our trek since we had to struggle the last mile or so when the winds kicked up, reaching thirty to forty miles per hour.

McMurdo was the principal logistics base for four other United States Deep Freeze stations in the Antarctic. It was the focal point for air and ship cargo arriving from New Zealand and America, and the base from which support for the U.S. Antarctic research program emanated. Arriving as a radiation specialist and just promoted to Senior Chief Hospital Corpsman, I joined the ranks of glaciologists, biologists, aerologists, and bacteriologists, among others. All these scientific specialists were officers, while I was the only enlisted man among them. While primarily a naval scientific base, McMurdo also hosted independent researchers.

Interestingly, the Russians had a base in Antarctica and were allowed to use Williams Field. In November of 1963, two planeloads of Russians landed in route to their Antarctic base. Despite the Cold War, we gave them fuel and supplies and helped them put the skis on their big planes.

The Russian dress uniform, a matched black plastic trouser and jacket, both cotton-lined, looked very odd to our Western eyes. No insignia crest or other sign of rank was evident. They all wore the high, black riding-type boot with their britches pegged slim to go inside of them. The Americans and the Russians were each intrigued about being so close to each other's sworn enemy. It was quite humorous and interesting to see the Americans filming the Russians and the Russians filming the Americans simultaneously. I saw several men pointing cameras at each other at the same time.

The Russians were well-received and mixed well within the camp while I was there. They proved a humble people. More than anything, they enjoyed our mess. Several made themselves sick by eating too much of our overly-rich food.

The saddest, most embarrassing thing happened while they were with us, however. About twenty Russians were in one of our enlisted barracks. Of a half-dozen musical instruments lying around, each of the Russians could play several. As the evening wore on, the Russians played and sang their national anthem at our request. At their request, no American would admit to even knowing how to play our national anthem.

My primary *stated* duty at McMurdo Station was to ensure personnel were kept safe from the Navy's three-year-old experimental nuclear reactor. This included monitoring radioactivity in the environment multiple times per day by collecting air, water, and snow samples using three different measurement labs. I bunked alone and lived in my office, which also served as my main lab. The other two labs, which were small huts, were each a mile or two away from the main base and each other. My secondary, *unstated* mission was to allow the State Department to spy on the Russians through my research. While I did not have firsthand knowledge, I suspected

I was really reporting to the CIA through the State Department; it uses the State Department for cover. This aspect of my job was so top secret that I was taken out of the military chain of command. Instead, I reported my research measurements, in code, to an officer in the State Department. The requirement to take hourly measurements meant that my secondary and unstated reason for being in Antarctica was the more important of the two, at least to the State Department. The first, while important, was a cover for spying on the Russians.

The experimental nuclear power plant in Antarctica was built for the dual purposes of testing nuclear power under adverse conditions while also providing power for McMurdo. The power plant was located about a mile away from the base and placed on the far side of a hill which was intended to act as a buffer between the base and the reactor. I worked entirely on the base, but made daily rounds measuring environmental radiation. When I first arrived, it was common knowledge that there was a leak in the reactor, the source of which had yet to be determined. This caused a great deal of concern and was being investigated at the highest levels at the power plant. All that was known was high levels of radiation existed in the environment around the reactor. I was chosen for this assignment because of my advanced understanding of what was then the very young field of nuclear science. Within six months of my arrival, the commander of the reactor, Lieutenant Flagler, became furious with me. I recorded radioactive levels not only around the reactor as previous technicians had done, but also at sites dozens of miles around the reactor's perimeter. I found no difference in radiation levels outside the reactor versus twenty miles away and concluded the radioactivity around the reactor was naturally occurring, and not the result of a leak. My mistake was to report these findings directly up my civilian chain of command at the State Department instead of first notifying Lieutenant Flagler. It was not intentional, but I embarrassed the reactor's commander, as he was the last to find out.

The reactor was online for a total of twelve years before a real leak appeared in its cooling system in 1972. The reactor was disassembled bolt by bolt and removed from the environment. This task also included removing 12,000 tons of crushed rock from the site and moving it to California under a 1959 treaty which mandated the removal of any radioactive waste material.

One of my three labs was named the Cosmic Ray Laboratory. My research measurements at that lab were designed to test for global radiation levels. Measuring global radiation levels is best done at the South Pole because radiation from all over the world drifts to the South Pole due to the polarity of the region. During the winter, my daily measurements showed a definitive spike, indicating the existence of high-altitude nuclear explosions. I quickly deduced that the Soviets were the culprits based upon the characteristics of the radiation. I could tell by analyzing the isotopes that it was not ours. Shortly after winter, travel restrictions were lifted, and after my data had reached the State Department, a dozen "men in black" showed up from the State Department and confiscated my lab logs. The minute they showed up, I knew exactly why they were there, but they treated me like a dumb farm boy nonetheless. Part of the explanation of my treatment was the top-secret nature of the data I had sent to them, so I knew not to take it personally. That aside, there was still an air of arrogance and an insulting demeanor about them that left me feeling rather disrespected.

I received two letters of commendation for my findings of Soviet mischief after I returned to NMRI in Bethesda. The White House issued one, signed by President Lyndon Johnson. It was a one-page letter using a lot of words that said nothing because of the highly secretive nature of my work. It quickly became quite popular and was passed around as all the brass at the National Naval Medical Center wanted to read it. Everyone marveled at how vague it was, which only served to increase their curiosity. They all wanted to know what I had been reporting to the State Department while stationed in McMurdo. Yet they knew that they could not ask, nor would they expect an answer. Because this letter traveled to so many offices and through so many sets of eyes on base, I never did get it back.

The second letter of commendation was issued from the Department of the Navy. My commanding officer showed it to me, but I never possessed it because he was ordered to have it destroyed after showing it to me. It was a little more specific, alluding to the highly-classified nature of my findings.

One of the reasons I was selected for duty in Antarctica was my personality. The job was tough, unrelenting, and involved extreme isolation. I was chosen for this assignment only after extensive psychological evaluations determined that I could handle the isolation. I never suffered from loneliness or depression while sequestered in my labs. Besides this, I was one of the select few in the Navy trained in nuclear health physics and highly capable of conducting this research.

My training in this new field saved a sailor's life. On November 30, 1963, after three hours of sleep, I was called to make a radiation contamination evaluation of Chief Holmes. The chief was badly wounded from a "procedure that ran amuck" and heavily contaminated when he was brought into camp. I reverted to a hospital corpsman, as dispensary personnel had no concept of how to cope with radiation. A doctor visiting from one of the icebreaker ships wanted to operate right away. I tried to persuade him to delay the surgery until I could decontaminate his wounds, but he would have none of it; he was going to proceed. It was not until I convinced our own Dr. Bates to side with me that, at last, the visiting doctor allowed us to clean the wounds of radioactivity first. Without my intervention, the idiot doctor would have sewn shut radioactive wounds, sentencing the chief to death. I performed six and a half hours of surgical washing to clean the radioactive contamination from the wounds before the surgeons could start the surgical repairs.

During the summer, almost every flag officer and captain came through Antarctica so that they could get a ribbon to pin on their chests. It seemed like every week we had people coming down for ribbons. We called them "tourists." During the summer months, the base housed about 250 men, while in the winter, it was whittled down to a hardcore sixty or seventy people. The summer weather was mild enough by comparison that I would typically walk to do my measurement rounds. If the weather was bad, I would take one of the caterpillars. One time I hitched a ride in a motor toboggan (a train-like tractor vehicle that pulled individual cars) on a return trip from Scott Base to my Cosmic Ray Lab. I found myself in the crowded company of a couple of these "tourists." There was a congressman, a couple of Navy captains from Washington D.C., plus others I did not know. I overheard the congressman joke to one of the captains, "I hear Kennedy hired a real brilliant young man, doctorate degrees in several fields, put him to work at the Treasury. Things were going great the first year. Things were really humming in his department. Then, for some unknown reason, he becomes moody and despondent. He just upped and blew his brains out. Kennedy then transferred him to the State Department."

Those of us who overstayed the winter received a special "Winter Over" ribbon. Flights and icebreaker ships stopped coming in the winter, when an average day's temperature could reach fifty degrees below zero and winds could blow between twenty and eighty miles per hour. The coldest day recorded while I was there was eighty-three degrees below zero on June 14, 1964. Communications were blacked out during the winter, so we were truly isolated and on our own.

In that cold air, we were placed on a diet of 6,200 calories per day. It took several thousand calories just to heat the air we breathed. The mess hall faced special problems in that some items had to be maintained at temperatures higher than the outside temperature. Meat was stored cold, but not frozen.

I explored Antarctica by airplane, helicopter, motor toboggan, and dogsled. The last and most primitive mode of transportation, was more of a hobby, as motor toboggans were warm, fast, and safe. The dogs were bred from two main lines which I believe originated from Captain Robert Scott and Sir Ernest Shackleton's dogs. Besides their use for sledding, the dogs also served as companions. While they spent most of their time outdoors, including sleeping, the dogs were allowed inside the huts on occasion. The men got a laugh watching the dogs on movie nights when they begged for candy. One dog named Boots liked to sit in a chair and watch.

Flying on the gigantic C-130s, I traveled as far inland as the underground Byrd Station (1,300 miles) and the South Pole (850 miles). Hitching rides on helicopters around Ross Island, I traveled to Cape Royds (fourteen miles) and Cape Crozier (thirty-one miles) to see penguin rookeries. I was fortunate that one of the helicopter pilots, Captain Stallings, was a nephew of my brother-in-law, Dalton Sanders.

My second and most memorable helo flight with Captain Stallings was in November of 1963. I enthusiastically accepted an invitation to join a party going to Cape Royds. The trip was beautiful. We saw an icebreaker at work from the air. We followed the shoreline of Ross Island, where McMurdo is, northward through the Dellbridge Islands, a chain of four islands named Tent Island, Inaccessible

Island, Big Razorback Island, and Little Razorback Island. We flew by the leading edge of the Barne Glacier and past Cape Evans. We flew over Scott's Hut at Cape Evans and put down at Shackleton's Hut at Cape Royds. The Shackleton Hut was used in 1908, and remaining from that expedition were bales of grain, corn, oats at the stables, and several tons of food tins behind the hut. Inside were the rudiments of life: cooking utensils, magazines, houseware, furniture, etc. We also visited the Adélie penguins which were sitting on their eggs by the thousands.

On our return trip from Cape Royds, we set a course for a couple of miles offshore and followed in the crushed ice wake of the three icebreakers: USS Atka, USCGC Burton Island, and USS Glacier. As we circled toward the wake, we could see twelve to fifteen miles of open sea.

The crushed ice wake of the icebreakers turned into a stream of life. We must have seen fifty to seventy killer whales playing. The ice bank was lined with thousands of seals and dozens and dozens of emperor penguins.

We set down on the ice twice on the return trip, once near some seals and again near penguins. The seals weren't afraid of humans at all and would just lie and look at us. The penguins, on the other hand, were a source of laughter as they would try and walk away from us as fast as they could. When their fast walk wasn't fast enough, they flopped down on their bellies and flapped wildly with all fours. It was quite interesting and cute to watch as they moved about, always in a formation, playing follow the leader like a school of fish.

After leaving the seals and penguins, we headed toward the icebreakers again. While in the air, we had the most beautiful view of 12,448-foot Mount Erebus stacked between cloud layers. With the black volcanic rock, Erebus was appropriately named. In Greek mythology, Erebus was a primordial deity, representing the personification of darkness.

We set down on the ice in front of the icebreaker USS *Glacier*. We watched as she cut a wedge first to the right, then to the left, then, after backing off as far as possible, to full power straight ahead. I had been in the Navy sixteen years, and given my Navy background, that was a powerful sight to behold. I had seen a film of this, but film doesn't quite put you halfway between the camera and the ship, standing on ice twelve to twenty feet thick. Dead ahead she came, half her length out of the water so that I could have walked under the keel at the bow. And there she stayed until she backed off. She would have to take a smaller bite next time, as nothing gave. Twenty miles and weeks of work.

There was one character in Antarctica I will never forget. He had been living and doing research there in his own government-sponsored lab for seven or eight years and was by far the most experienced iceman on the continent. He escaped from the Soviet Union during

World War II as a German POW by walking from Siberia over the Arctic to freedom during the winter while it was frozen over. Equipped with crampons and an ice pick, he took me out on expeditions over treacherous ice. He taught me how to cross the ice safely and showed me the danger signs to look for and how to tap the ice with my ice pick to listen for the sounds of potentially hidden crevasses. He taught me what to do in case one of us fell through and how to keep the fifty-foot rope between us taught at all times. A common danger was windswept ice that would cover a crevasse which might be tens or hundreds of feet deep. Should one of us fall into a crevasse, the other would act as the brake on the fall and be there to rescue the other. Of the half dozen expeditions, we experienced only one close call. I had the wits scared out me when my expert companion, who was leading the way, fell through up to his armpits.

We explored wonderful, beautiful ice caves made from what appeared to be frozen blue sky. We explored crevasses that were hundreds of feet below the surface ice. One of these was perhaps the most beautiful place I had ever been or would ever be, heaven included. It was made of the most beautiful white and blue ice crystals.

★ ★ ★

We had many visitors at McMurdo Station. Typically, they were VIPs who mostly socialized with the officers. One was Cardinal Francis Spellman, who at the time was vicar apostolic to the Armed Forces and later became one of the eight cardinals in the U.S.

He came down every year to get away and to visit the troops. One day he came into the lab where I was engrossed in *War and Peace.* It was my second time reading it, the first being with Commander Brown while on the *Repose* in China. Cardinal Spellman and I immediately forged a relationship over this book. It was one of his favorites, and he said he would teach me a strategy to help me gain the most pleasure and understanding from this novel. For the next three weeks, he spent much of his time with me in the lab. He placed large pieces of paper on the wall and drew grids outlining the main characters. He made me spell and pronounce each of the Russian characters' names and memorize their titles, quizzing me every day. He said I was not going to be any smarter after "pretending" to read this book. The amount of time he spent with me, one sailor, over his three-week stay left the officers perplexed. With his tireless help and friendship, I finished the book shortly after he departed, appreciating this magnificent novel on a new level.

While I grew up in a churchgoing family and believe in God, I don't think that God and the military mix. For seventeen years now, I had refused to salute a chaplain as I believe a military man cannot be both an officer and a man of God.

After visiting the South Pole, Cardinal Spellman arrived back at McMurdo in time for Christmas. We had a lovely dinner, but the day seemed long, with me spending most of it in my laboratory. Only two men showed up for Cardinal Spellman's first Christmas Mass, perhaps because the military is not an environment that enthusiastically accepts and encourages men's religious needs. The day before, Christmas Eve, as I was stepping into my lab, I noticed Chaplain Fuller standing in front of the chapel. When a young sailor seeking spiritual counsel started to enter, Commander Fuller barked, "Don't you go in there with those muddy boots!" I watched the young sailor turn, look at the chaplain, try to clean the mud from his boots, give up, and walk away. He walked right past me and, and as he did, I saw a hurt and bewildered face. I doubt that sailor ever attempted to talk himself into going into that chapel again. What were the feelings, the spiritual requirements, the possible spiritual reward of this man had he been allowed to enter the chapel with muddy boots? I guess we will never know. I just don't believe the military and religion are compatible. While the Navy has never asked me for my opinion, I think the military should make the chaplain an enlisted billet to allow him to better relate to those of his flock.

★ ★ ★

As summer was coming to an end in March of 1964, we enjoyed watching the most unusual two-hour outdoor volleyball game ever played. Everyone was wearing Antarctic survival gear, including ski masks, as the temperature at the time was twenty-five degrees below zero. March marked the beginning of winter, which meant the "tourists" left along with all the planes and icebreakers. We were stranded and on our own until spring.

On March 6, 1964, I received a message from the Red Cross announcing the birth of my sixth child, Paul Durant, whose middle name came from Lois' maiden name. He had been born the day before. Lois was not able to get through, but somehow, she was able to have the Red Cross deliver the message. Paul's birth was announced to the base over the loudspeaker, mentioning that he was my sixth child and what a good Catholic I must be, which gave me quite a good laugh. Ham radios were the only way to communicate during the winter, if at all. I tried reaching Lois through a ham radio operator in New Zealand, who then patched me through to a radio operator in Washington, who then patched me through to Florida. The last leg of this relay was a pastor and ham radio hobbyist in Interlachen, who then called Lois and patched me through the phone line. Unfortunately, the static was so bad that we could not understand each other. With the start of winter, communications would be blacked out. I did not hear from Lois or any further news of my new baby again for six months.

One of the annual duties I performed was to travel by helicopter sixty-five miles south of Ross Island to supervise the locating and recovery of an experimental nuclear-powered weather station. It had been placed out there by a large defense contractor, and it was the military's duty to monitor it over the years. The flight afforded us breathtaking views. The beauty of the ice and the ice destruction south of Ross, Black, and White islands is beyond my ability to describe in words. Entire islands were being gouged out by the landlocked ice flows. The crevasses were miles long and hundreds of feet deep. As the ice crushed between the islands, it was stacked up into the air and splintered like emerald blue Empire State Buildings leaning every which way. The ice to the south was glacier ice, rough with weird patterns which contrasted with the smooth, new ice around McMurdo.

When the nine of us arrived at the weather station on November 26 of 1963, it took an hour and a half to locate it under eight feet of ice. After digging it out, we called in another helicopter to lift it out and set it down. Two electronic instrument men among our crew did the actual work. The weather station weighed several tons and there was an ongoing concern that it might become damaged and leak radiation, which was the reason for my presence. We spent several days out there, sleeping on the ice in specially-designed sleeping bags. When the helo was there, we climbed inside to get warm. The helicopters came and went as they were needed elsewhere.

Helicopters were the most dangerous mode of transportation due to the extreme weather conditions. While we had a pretty good safety record, the large helicopters were still the source of most transportation incidents. The base had three helos, but always struggled just to keep one flying. Two brand new Army helos were brought in, uncrated, and set up. Right afterwards, winds of ninety miles per hour beat them to death. They then had to be sent back to the States for salvage. A helo from one of the icebreakers crashed on the ice below camp, resulting in injuries. A helo from the Jacksonville Air Base arrived fully overhauled and was put into service while the Russians were there. While taking ten Russians out to Williams Field, the entire tail rotor and prop assembly separated from the craft. All on board walked away from the crash after feathering down from 300 feet to a very hard landing, with the Russians laughing about it afterwards.

Even in the middle of summer, it was highly dangerous to get a plane into the Williams Field ice runways. In December of 1963, about two months after I arrived, we were all anxiously awaiting the next C-130, which was bringing Christmas letters and packages. A lucky few were looking forward to some rest and relaxation in Christchurch on the return flight. The first attempted flight was turned back by fire. The weather at Williams Field caused another three to turn back. At last, we had a fifth attempted flight on the way. We were all praying they were beyond the point of no return, forcing their arrival. Personally, I was anxious for a letter that I knew was aboard from Lois and the family.

Unfortunately, the fifth attempted flight did not go well. Williams Field became socked in by whiteout conditions from an unexpected squall that hit after the plane had passed the point of no return. It started on December 12, when we experienced a very long twenty-four hours without sleep. All hands on base were called to Williams Field, including all firefighting and medical personnel. With whiteout conditions, we knew that our long-anticipated plane carrying Christmas gifts and letters was in trouble. The C-130, past the point of no return, was forced to continue to Williams even though they knew the conditions there were bad. They were stranded above us, unable to land, and running out of fuel. With gale-force winds blowing so much ice and snow, the ground control approach (GCA) radar in the controllers' tower, which was used to guide the plane in, became useless. The bottom could no longer be defined, meaning that with the whiteout conditions on the ground, the pilot could not determine via instruments if he was flying at ten feet or 1,000 feet.

With the gale-force winds, we could not keep the ice runway free of snow. We realized that when she set down, it might make little difference if she did so with or without wheels. Williams also had a snow runway for planes equipped with skis, used for landings and takeoffs between here and the other Antarctic stations where there was no equipment to clear the snow.

As the hours dragged by, radar fixes kept the plane in our general vicinity. We hoped that if they could fly long enough, they might outlast the weather and the GCA could bring them in. After five and a half hours of flying in circles, and with the fuel nearly exhausted, the decision was made to dump the cargo to lighten the plane in case of a crash landing and to stretch a few more minutes of flying time out of the remaining fuel. The cargo included 7,100 pounds of Christmas mail and packages.

With the engines running on fumes, cargo dumped, and all passengers tightly strapped down, four attempts at landing were made and aborted. With each failed attempt, her engines would scream as she went by, gaining altitude for another attempt. She came so close to the deck before aborting each time that we could have hit her with snowballs. The landing was made on the fifth attempt. When they crawled out, they found themselves some two miles away from the runway in the snow. No one had been hurt and there was not much obvious damage to the plane other than the landing gear was crushed from the plane sliding to a stop on its belly. The men were strained but happy to have come out of this adventure alive. One of the men I knew on board said to a friend, "I wasn't really scared until I saw a crew member take a cross hanging around his neck, kiss it, and cross himself with it."

The mail recovery operation started the same day. Of the bags of mail that burst open upon hitting the ground, only a few individual letters were found due to the gale force winds. First recovered were two bags located several hundred feet apart. As the recovery operation went on, several hundred pounds of mail were found. The mail had been hand-thrown during two passes over a calculated recovery zone. I looked at dozens of packages, many in Christmas wrappings. Of these, the paper wrapping was fragmented like cracked glass. I saw a box that contained pecans and became excited because my mother had sent me pecans from our farm every year since I left home sixteen years prior. While the address label was destroyed, I was sure they had to be from Mom. Unfortunately, my excitement dissipated when I opened it up to find what looked like ground coffee. I had to stick my nose in the remains to confirm that it was indeed smashed pecans. I investigated another busted crate ironically marked "Fragile—Do not drop." I couldn't make out what its contents had been until someone pointed out it had once been a 16-mm movie projector.

Mail was found for days; however, not one card from home was found. Lois' letters were lost to the howling winds of the Antarctic wilderness. This was not the first time I missed out on Christmas mail; that had been in Korea, when we set fire to a ten-foot-tall pile of mail when the Chosin Reservoir Battle broke out.

A life-and-death medical emergency during my tour led to the first-ever winter flight to Antarctica. A Seabee suffered a severe head injury, broken ribs, and broken vertebrae from a headfirst fall from sixteen feet. The Navy launched a historic rescue operation in the dead of winter that put many men's lives at risk, not to mention a multi-million-dollar plane. They launched a C-130, outfitted with extra fuel tanks, from the Quonset Point Air Base in Rhode Island to Washington D.C., where they picked up a special medical team from NNMC in Bethesda. From there, the pilots flew around the clock to Christchurch, New Zealand to pick up the Marine sergeant considered the Navy's best Antarctic navigator. From there, and this is where unbelievable courage was required, they set a dead reckoning flight path to McMurdo Station. Flying by dead reckoning means that you point the plane in the right direction and then fly using time and math because you do not have a beacon or radio signal to guide you. They had to calculate air speed, winds, wind direction, and time elapsed to target the plane toward its destination. After eleven hours aloft, if their calculations were correct, they would find themselves over Williams Field. If their calculations were off, then they would be ditching in either the ocean or somewhere in the Antarctic wilderness in the dead of winter. Survival under either of these two scenarios would be a long shot.

Upon the plane's departure from Christchurch, all available men, myself included, were ordered to Williams Field. Close to two miles of fifty-five gallon drums of diesel fuel had been laid out in an effort to guide the pilots to the 10,000-foot ice runway. The temperature was at zero degrees, so cold that we could not get these drums lit, or if we did, they wouldn't stay lit. We were using acetylene torches on the drums, trying to get them to ignite. We worked around the clock from Friday evening until Sunday morning getting all the barrels lit. Once lit, the barrels would burn for approximately six hours. As they burned out, we had to replace them. The men were also in the grading equipment, bulldozers, and road graders, at least the ones they could get started. As the plane approached, they were grading the ice runway. The blessing was that the weather was clear, as a storm had just ended, but another was expected. The pilots had to hit this eye in the weather or it would mean near certain death.

Our miles of lit oil drums worked. In addition, all lights at nearby Scott Base were lit up in hopes of aiding the pilot. Jubilation erupted when the control tower received a scratchy voice over the radio from the pilot, 164 miles away. When the commander of the aircraft was seventy-three miles away, he radioed that he could see the runway lights—our burning diesel canisters. When the plane landed, it was kept running so that its hydraulics would not freeze. Every couple of minutes, the pilots gunned the engines, breaking the skis free from the ice by moving the plane a few feet forward.

They loaded the patient, along with a medical team from the base, and, as soon as they topped off their tanks, they were back in the air. I don't know what happened to those brave pilots who risked their lives to save one of their own, but I sure hope they were awarded medals. We received the following telegram from the man's parents, forwarded to us from the Chief of Navy Personnel in Washington D.C.: "We wish to extend our eternal gratitude to the Navy for its all-out effort in saving the life of our son Bethel Lee McMullen and to the gallant men who risked their lives in the evacuation attempt at Antarctica. Your heroic performance should bring comfort to all parents in the Navy. Thank you for keeping us advised of his progress. Signed: Ruby and Richard Salz."

The next winter, the Navy started making test flights to hone their winter flying skills after proving it was possible.

★ ★ ★

As my tour ended, I reflected on how I had been an important asset to the base and to the cause of Antarctic research. I had solved the mystery of the "leaking" nuclear reactor and discovered the existence of high-altitude Soviet nuclear testing. Additionally, I was much appreciated by the sailors. I will never forget the sailor who came up to me in the mess during the winter and said, "Chief, I want to thank you. You're the best chief in this camp. You take the time to talk and associate with us sailors. We appreciate you treating us as human beings and individuals capable of intelligent conversation. You're the only chief in camp who knows we are alive."

In October 1964, about five months after that memorable conversation with that young man, my tour ended. I decompressed in New Zealand for two months before heading home. Having spent the past year outside of the naval chain of command, I knew I did not have to report in until I returned. As far as the Navy was concerned, I was "off the grid." Even though I had a newborn son I had not seen and wanted to spend Christmas with the family, I decided not to head home right away. I had always enjoyed and taken advantage of the opportunities the Navy provided to see more of the world.

When I got to Christchurch, I stayed on the naval base where I had been issued a bunk. Most of my time was spent taking buses everywhere and having meals with natives wherever I went, as they were very friendly to Americans. They always wanted to take us home, give us dinner, and have a conversation. After two months of enjoying New Zealand, I left on a military transport headed for the States. An American civilian couple with their two small children and I were the only passengers on board the gigantic C-130. In the same way we had arrived, we were provided bagged meals for the long flight home to America, bringing my trip full circle.

CHAPTER 20

Return to National Naval Medical Center

AFTER EXPLORING NEW ZEALAND, I arrived back in Interlachen in December of 1965. I brought with me a large tin can of Mann's Potato Chips as a treat for the children. Just as when I returned from duty on the *Banner*, I was not well received by the smaller ones who were too young to remember me as their father. Lois loves to tell the tale of me spanking Clay, four at the time, who promptly told her that he had had enough of me and that she should tell "that man" to go!

Since I had been reporting to the State Department, I had been unaccounted for until this point. The Navy did not know when to expect me, so I continued to enjoy a couple weeks "off the grid" with my family. However, I knew my free time was coming to an end, as the Navy would soon be expecting me to "come back in from the cold," as it were. After a few weeks, I took the GMC north to find a home near my duty station at The National Naval Medical Center. I stayed with our friends and former neighbors, the Welshes, the first night or two until Dr. Tom Strike, who I was good friends with from my command at NNMC, and who knew I was back in the area looking for a house, phoned me with some good news. He told me of a house located in his own Parkwood community in Bethesda, located just minutes from the naval hospital. I knew Lois would love the community which had both elementary and junior high schools within walking distance and was situated along beautiful Rock Creek Park.

Unfortunately, the house had been a rental for twenty years and was in horrible shape. The lawn consisted of hard-packed dirt with an occasional weed. The house had not been painted in years, the wood trim was rotting, and shutters were either falling off or were missing. In fact, the home was the scourge of this beautiful, tree-lined neighborhood adorned with azaleas the size of Pontiacs.

Dr. Strike and I knocked on the door to find a naval medical doctor and his family readying themselves to move out that day. The tenant gave me the address of the property management company to which I should send the monthly rent of $130. The tenants left the house in a filthy state, so that night, John Welsh met me at the house to assist in the difficult task of readying the home for my family. John concentrated on the single, filthy bathroom while I spent hours cleaning the kitchen, where I discovered it was infested with roaches.

The next day, I was in the GMC again driving back to Florida. The moving company was called before my return trip so the Interlachen house was just about empty upon my arrival. I loaded the family of eight into the three bench seats in the GMC Carryall and headed back north again. I will never forget how excited Lois was when she saw the beautiful neighborhood. She was perhaps a little disappointed when she saw how run-down the house was, but she knew I could make it a beautiful home on par with the rest of the neighborhood in time.

Finding this dilapidated rental in such a beautiful neighborhood was a stroke of luck. To put my luck into perspective, on my 1965 salary of $5,363 per year, I would have only qualified for an $18,000 mortgage. Typical yearly salaries of the neighborhood residents were two to four times what I made, ranging from a low of $10,000 to maybe as high as $20,000. Furthermore, the houses in the neighborhood were selling for about $48,000. Even when I retired from the Navy, I was still only making $14,500, while the average salary in the neighborhood was around $45,000. I was an enlisted man with a family of eight living amongst doctors, lawyers, vice presidents, and deputy undersecretaries of government agencies in a beautiful neighborhood less than two miles from the hospital. Furthermore, I moved the family into the house without obtaining anyone's permission or even signing a lease. Once we settled in, I just started sending the monthly check to the property management firm.

After about a year of living in this decrepit rental, Lois and I decided it was time to buy our first home. We had just welcomed our seventh and final baby, Becky Lynn, who was born on September 26, 1965. We first explored nearby neighborhoods for which my salary could qualify us. Unfortunately, I made so little that the houses we looked at were just too small for such a large family. Discouraged, I then decided to attempt to buy our rental, hoping to make a lowball offer due to its unbelievably bad condition.

The first problem with this strategy was that I had no idea who the owner was, as the house was held in trust. I spent months researching the owner of the house through the Rockville, Maryland courthouse land records. I found out that the landlord had paid $18,500 for the property eighteen years earlier, but I was not able to determine the owner, who clearly did not want to be found.

Finally, I stumbled upon some old shipping crate boards in the attic. All the boards were crumbled and deteriorated, but on one I found a shipping label with the name and address of "Major Abbot" on it. My research traced the name *Abbot* back to Texas, where he was now a general at Brooks Air Force Base. When I first tried to contact Mrs. Abbot, she denied being the owner because she knew the terrible condition of the house and did not want to take calls from disgruntled tenants. After I informed her that I was interested in buying the house, she admitted she was indeed the owner and was planning to sell it. I also learned the reason she was selling the house. General Abbot had been kicked in the head by a horse a year before we moved in and was in a coma.

She said lawyers were already telling her the property was going to be a loss due to its horrible condition. I confirmed what her lawyers had told her by describing in detail the problems with the house, including a leaking roof, plaster damage, water damage, and roach infestation. While negotiating with her, I told her that I did not want to keep my family in the house because it was barely habitable, but would be interested in buying it if the price was affordable on my Navy salary. I added that I would rather purchase the house than go through the cost and aggravation of moving the family. Near the end of our conversation, I offered to purchase it from her for what she had paid, $18,500, adding that I was taking a huge risk due to its dreadful condition.

Soon after, in January of 1966, we had the title to our first home. When the home became too much for us to keep up years later in our retirement, we sold for it $425,000. In hindsight, our sale was poorly timed, as the housing market became white-hot shortly thereafter. At the time, though, because of its immaculate condition and stunning landscaping, it was the highest-priced house ever sold in Parkwood. The next owners sold it three years later for $725,000, and the owners after that sold it for $900,000.

The transformation of the house from a barely habitable dump to one of the best homes in the neighborhood did not happen overnight. A military salary meant limited funds, so all the improvements were done by my own hands with the help of my five boys over many years.

In addition to being surrounded by neighbors with salaries double and triple what I made, I was also outgunned when it came to educational credentials and titles. These neighbors were attorneys, prominent professors, renowned doctors, and employees of the World Bank and the CIA. Directly across the street were the Bonners. Walter Bonner was a Watergate attorney. To the right of the Bonners lived a couple from New Zealand, the Woodwards. Mr. Woodward worked for the World Bank. After the Woodwards moved out, the Cohens moved in. Dr. Cohen was a medical doctor specializing in arthritis, received an honorary degree from an Italian university, and was a renowned specialist. His wife was a former colonel with the Israeli army.

Living in the scourge of the neighborhood presented its challenges. The house had never housed long-term residents and was an embarrassment to the neighborhood. Most, but not all the neighbors were downright hostile to the existence of the house and its transient tenants. They would not even acknowledge our family's existence at first.

Very slowly, however, the neighbors grew to accept us; they saw that I was putting some care into the house after years of it being an eyesore. However, I believe the real catalyst to our eventual acceptance amongst the neighbors was our seven children. I believe they came to admire our children who were being raised with very strict discipline. The children were exceptionally polite and very respectful to adults. Furthermore, my boys mowed the neighbors' yards, raked their leaves, and delivered their newspapers while Sally babysat their children. It probably also did not hurt that the neighbors came to understand that I could fix anything from cars to hot water heaters, and that I was always willing to spend an afternoon lending a hand. I will always be especially grateful to Mr. Bonner and his family, who were the first neighbors to be welcoming to us, taking Steve and Sally sightseeing in Washington D.C. with his kids.

We had moved into our Parkwood home during the middle of the school year. Maryland had been teaching "new math" for several years, and the statewide exam on this new math was to be given the day after our children were enrolled in Parkwood Elementary School. With unpacked boxes everywhere, I found some table space and chairs for our two oldest children, Sally, a fifth grader, and Steve, a sixth grader. I studied their book with them until I learned what this new math was: a simple log system. Soon my two darlings grasped it as I illustrated the concepts to them by playing with beans on the table top.

The next day, Steve and Sally took the statewide exam and earned the highest scores in the county. One child answered every question correctly, the other missed only one. The school principal called and asked, "What school did the children attend before arriving at Parkwood? It is obvious they came from a very well-funded and progressive school system with excellent teachers." The principal's sails collapsed when I told her the children had last been in a very poor community in the Deep South, and that neither of the children nor I had ever heard of Maryland's new math system before the prior evening. I told her the three of us had learned it the night before playing with beans on the dining room table.

Education was paramount in our home. The older kids had it rough, as Parkwood was to be their fourth elementary school. In fact, Sally recounts that in her earlier elementary school in the South, there was talk of what it would mean if black people were allowed into their schools. Sally, who later became a CPA for Price Waterhouse, credits me with being her greatest teacher, giving her determination and a very strong belief in the value of education. I always helped all the children with their homework and drilled them with flashcards as a fun exercise in our home life. Additionally, I spent precious leisure time playing Monopoly and dominoes with them. Sally said that as a child she always hesitated to ask me any homework question because she knew there would never be a short response. I always made my kids discover the answer; never giving it to them. Over summer breaks during their middle school years, I made Sally and Steve write two summary reports from *National Geographic* articles each week before they were allowed to play. Additionally, discussing current events and interesting articles from *Time* Magazine was a common practice at the dinner table.

★ ★ ★

As soon as I got the family situated in the new home, I reported back to duty as chief administrator of the Tissue Bank at NMRI on New Year's Day 1965. Captain Sudduth was still in charge. My records indicated that I had finally gained some weight but was still in pretty good shape at 182 pounds.

Being the administrator for the Tissue Bank meant that my office was in the main building facing Wisconsin Avenue and directly below the Presidential Suite. In September of 1965, President Lyndon Johnson arrived for a gallbladder operation, so security tightened up drastically, as it always does when the president is staying at the hospital. One day, while I was standing outside of my office conversing with someone, President Johnson, accompanied by several Secret Service agents, came strolling by wearing a bathrobe over his pajamas. He stopped and asked me what I did in the hospital.

I told him that I was the Chief Administrator for the Tissue Bank and that I had been, up to this point, heavily involved in nuclear medicine, specifically radiation sickness research. I also told him I had just returned from Antarctica and recounted to him my role monitoring radiation down there. He was fascinated with the work we were doing, so he came into my office, along with his armed Secret Service agents, took a seat, and talked with me for a couple of hours. He was really interested in my findings of Soviet atmospheric nuclear testing. I relayed to him how the men from the State Department all showed up as soon as winter broke and confiscated all my logs. At one point, I remember him saying, "Wow, I am the president, and they have not told me any of this." Of course, I did not bring up the letter of commendation he had signed knowing that the President doesn't actually sign most of what goes out of the White House under his signature.

For the next few days, he came by to see me daily to further his understanding of the nuclear research projects in which I had assisted. He was a very charming Southern gentleman despite his reputation as a ruthless, cutthroat politician. I also met his two young adult daughters during that time.

Eventually, the Secret Service deemed me to be harmless and stopped following the President into my office; they seemed more interested in the pretty young women who worked there. They were so interested in these women that they often snuck down to my floor by themselves, stopping to prop up their shotguns and automatic weapons in the corner of my office before either going to the mess for a bite to eat or out to flirt with the women. At times, I had so many weapons in the corner of my office that someone could have mistaken it for the hospital arsenal.

In 1968, I had the pleasure of working with Brigadier General Charles Lindbergh, who conducted research at NMRI as a civilian for several six-month periods. Most famous for the first solo flight across the Atlantic in the *Spirit of St. Louis*, he was also an explorer, inventor, and social activist. He had been a colonel in the Army Air Corps until he resigned his commission in 1941 in protest of the U.S. becoming involved in World War II. However, after the Japanese bombed Pearl Harbor, he had a change of heart and flew combat missions in the South Pacific as a civilian when President Roosevelt refused to restore his commission. President Dwight D. Eisenhower later restored Lindbergh's assignment with the U.S. Army Air Corps and made him a Brigadier General in 1954.

Lucky Lindy, as he had been called in his earlier years, was working at NMRI in the Tissue Bank on studies to keep heart tissue alive in a nutrient solution, the precursor research to heart transplants. The director of the Tissue Bank, Lt. Vernon Perry, introduced the general to both Dr. Sell and me.

Sometimes we had the press fishing around for Lindbergh after hearing rumors that he was there. We went to great lengths to keep his presence a secret, going so far as to assign a code name for him. Lt. Perry, Chuck Brodein, a captain in the Medical Corps, Dr. Sell, and I were the only ones at the hospital who knew he was there. Captain Brodein was his sole contact at NMRI. No mail came to or from Lindbergh except through me, and his arrivals and departures were kept top secret. We were only made aware of their approximate times.

The general was an eccentric sixty-six-year-old at the time. I would describe his appearance as a little rough but not woolly. He was so introverted that he would not eat with other people, requiring Dr. Sell or Captain Brodein to bring him food. Captain Brodein fixed a place for Lindbergh to sleep in the basement of the Tissue Lab by removing shelving from a large double-door closet, while I was charged with supplying clean bedding. Captain Brodein would sometimes take him home for a dinner and a shower while his wife did Lindbergh's laundry. Captain Brodein said that on the day of his arrival to town, the general would show up at the Captain's house several hours prior to his family waking and would hide in the bushes until they woke. On one such arrival, Captain Brodein said he found Lindbergh asleep in his bushes. Lindbergh kept his life so private that he never even took a cab. He would walk most places, sometimes for hours to and from downtown D.C. On probably four occasions, he allowed me to drive him downtown, but I was never allowed to know his destination. He always instructed me to drop him off on a street corner. Knowing that he had been the most famous person in the world after his transatlantic flight, I understood his reclusiveness.

★ ★ ★

I believe it was in 1969 when the Nuclear Regulatory Commission issued an order that all facilities in the nation that possessed nuclear materials had to have a designated individual in charge and answerable to the Commission. The admiral of the base selected me for this role since I was the only one with the required knowledge and expertise.

Stepping into this role elevated my stature within the Navy, which led Admiral Rickover's staff to summon me to their offices in Arlington, Virginia, for a two-week series of meetings. Admiral Rickover, the legendary "Father of the Nuclear Navy," was personally aware of and interested in my role as a nuclear engineer at Fort Belvoir and in the Antarctic, as well as my radiation sickness research at NNMRI. This made me incredibly proud. He and his staff asked me a lot of questions about my nuclear work. True to his reputation, I found him very straitlaced.

With the addition of my new role as administrator of the base radioactive inventory, I now reported to two commanding officers, Dr. Sell of the Tissue Bank and Rear Admiral Ballenger, the base commander. My new role placed me in charge of all the purchasing, inventorying, and issuance of nuclear material to scientists.

One doctor at the hospital opened a private clinic in Bethesda for a newly developed radioactive treatment of cancer. This was one of the first, if not the first, nuclear health clinic in the world. He was planning on expanding his clinic with two new locations when I put an end to his naval career.

I became aware of worldwide press covering this NMRI doctor's clinic and, being an expert in nuclear materials, I knew this doctor could not buy the radioactive isotopes that he was using in his private practice on the open market. That made me go back over my inventory records, which, in turn, made me realize that he had been checking out more radioactive material than he could have possibly used in research. I kept my inventory not by counting quantities, but by measuring available half-lives. Once I put two and two together and documented the missing isotopes, I went to Admiral Ballenger's office and requested a meeting with him right away. As soon as I presented the evidence against this doctor, the admiral sent two officers to escort the doctor back to his office.

Upon his arrival, the admiral's first question was, "Why are you in civilian clothes?" This was a most unfortunate time to be called to the admiral's office because being in civilian clothes was evidence that he was working at his private practice while on duty. The admiral presented my findings to the doctor with me present. He concluded: "I know Chief Custead, and I know he is very knowledgeable in this area, so I have no reason not to believe his charges against you. What do you have to say in your defense?"

The doctor came clean to the Admiral and admitted everything.

After hearing him out, the admiral told the officer that he was stripped of his commission and to vacate the base that day. Afterward, Admiral Ballenger turned to me and said, "I wish that bastard were in uniform. I would really have enjoyed publicly ripping the stripes off his sleeve right then and there."

That was not the only naval career I ended. In addition to purchasing nuclear materials, I also purchased laboratory supplies and equipment. I started to notice a certain lab was purchasing unusual items. This was not the first time I had been acquainted with embezzlement from the federal government. When I was stationed on the *Banner*, I heard stories of men who ordered huge $25,000 generators shipped to Japan and later sold privately for profit. In this current instance of purchasing discrepancies, I traced several of these requisitions to the lab for which they were supposedly purchased. I visited the lab and asked to see the purchased items, but there was no evidence the items were present. I knew the lieutenant in charge of the lab had a brother who owned a hardware store in Bethesda, so the next step in my detective work was to visit the hardware store, where I snooped around and found the tools that matched the NMRI purchases. Having completed my investigation, I provided my commanding officer, Captain Goldman, with the evidence, and the crooked lieutenant was gone that same week. I was not present when Captain Goldman confronted the man, but the fact that he abruptly disappeared indicated that Goldman gave him an option of resigning his commission that day or facing trial.

★ ★ ★

On December 23, 1968, I received a Christmas present from Uncle Sam, a letter from the Department of the Navy informing me that I had been "nominated" for duty in Vietnam. Unbelievably, it concluded, "It is hoped that you will enjoy a pleasant and rewarding experience in your new assignment." My tour was to start in June of the following year.

CHAPTER 21

The Vietnam War

Take a man, then put him alone
Put him 12,000 miles from home
Empty his heart of all its blood
Make him sweat and live in the mud
This is the life we have to live
And why my soul to the devil I'll give
You "peace boys" from your easy chair
Don't really know what it's like over here
You have your call without really trying
While over here the boys are dying
You burn your draft cards, march at dawn,
Plant your flags on the Whitehouse lawn
You all want to ban the bomb
"There is not war in Viet Nam"
Use your drugs, have your fun
Then refuse to take a gun
There's nothing else for you to do
And I'm supposed to die for you?
I'll hate you till the day I die
You made me hear my buddy cry

I saw his arm, a bloody spread
I heard them say, "This one is dead"
It's a large price he had to pay
Not to live, no, not another day
He had the guts to fight and die
He paid the price....What did he buy?

*Written by a Marine in Mike Company,
Da Nang, Vietnam*

The young Marine who composed the above was received at the Station Hospital on 30 July 1969 after suffering bilateral amputations of both legs above the knees. At 1000 hours, 31 July 1969, he expired due to excessive loss of blood.

The above poem and descriptive note were posted on a bulletin board outside one of the surgical units at the Da Nang Station Hospital (Station Hospital). I stood in the broiling heat under an awning and copied it down verbatim.

The Navy needed a master chief to relieve the one currently assigned to the Station Hospital in Da Nang and offered me a deal after performing a Navy-wide candidate search. I was told if I accepted the assignment, I would be promoted to master chief, the highest possible enlisted rank. Since I had already served in two other wars, I was also presented the option of riding this one out in the safety of Bethesda at my current rank. While I served during World War II from the relative security of a hospital ship, Korea was as bad as it got for a soldier.

The decision to accept the assignment to Vietnam was not all that difficult. I was not overly concerned about going because I figured it would be more like a repeat of my service in World War II. I would be stationed in a well-protected combat hospital despite it being located 100 miles or so south of the North Vietnamese border in a designated war zone. I would have declined the promotion if I thought I was going to face another combat situation like Korea. I am sure I would have ended up like those veterans of World War II—too battle-fatigued to get off the landing craft at Inchon. In hindsight, Vietnam turned out to be its own special kind of hell. A hell that took its toll on me and my beloved family. Later in life, I experienced major battles with post-traumatic stress disorder, otherwise known as PTSD. I now know that mental issues caused by my war experiences were there all along, just buried very deep.

Da Nang is a large city at the mouth of the Han River near what was then North Vietnam and the home of the U.S. Army's I Corps headquarters. In civilian terms, my duty assignment was to be the general administrator of the largest combat receiving hospital in Vietnam, located in an area classified as a "forward combat area." The hospital was known by its acronym NSAH, for Naval Support Activity Hospital. I was to oversee almost 500 corpsmen, fifty nurses, and 175 support personnel for 600 beds and was to report directly to the officer-in-charge, a captain. My arrival was seventeen months after the infamous Tet Offensive, which had taken place from January to February of 1968. During this Communist offensive, the hospital admitted 2,175 wounded Marines and Allied troops and received the Navy Unit Commendation for its heroic actions in saving countless lives. At the height of the battle, seventeen layers of helicopters hovered over the landing pads waiting to land and offload casualties. The base was so large that somewhere between fourteen and sixteen helicopters could be accommodated on the ground at once.

Under the operational control of 3rd Marine Amphibious Force (III MAF)/I Corps, Station Hospital was part of the largest naval support activity in history. The primary function of the hospital was to provide medical treatment to the United States Marines Corps and the other free-world armed forces fighting in I Corps, including US Marine Corps, US Navy, US Army, US Air Force, US Coast Guard, Republic of Korea Marines, Australian troops, and Vietnamese civilians. Station Hospital also treated North Vietnamese Army (NVA) and Viet Cong POWs in its POW ward. I Corps ranged from the demilitarized zone to all Da Nang and Quảng Nam Provinces. The Navy's treatment of the combat wounded, with this incredibly large, centralized hospital, was in direct contrast to the Army's medical system, which utilized numerous small hospitals, one of which was about a mile away.

According to Stars & Stripes[1], Station Hospital Da Nang was the largest casualty-receiving hospital in Vietnam. It was constructed in 1965 near the Marble Mountains. The mountains were filled with tunnels providing a path for the NVA and Viet Cong to move undetected in the area. Situated on a large river sandbar, the hospital had no local source of potable water, requiring water to be trucked in every day from another base ten miles away. At its height, the year before I arrived, Station Hospital had 700 hospital corpsmen working with 45 physicians, six dentists, and 30 nurses, and was designed primarily for the care of Marines in the I Corps sector, treating about 24,000 patients. By the time I arrived a year later, I had 485 corpsmen under my charge. Patients came by helicopter from the front lines and were taken immediately to the triage receiving area for determination of treatment. Over fifty percent of our casualties were either South Vietnamese soldiers or civilians. Station Hospital was a place of hope for the wounded. The hospital was subjected to almost daily rocket and mortar attacks, usually at night. Located directly across from Station Hospital was Marine Aircraft Group 16 (MAG-16). This air base had the capability of launching a fighter aircraft every thirty seconds, twenty-four hours a day if needed.

I arrived in Da Nang in late June 1969 as a freshly promoted master chief, one of only four such promotions in the Navy that year. Making master chief was an honor of which I was very proud. Only a handful of men are promoted to this rank in the Navy each year. No hospital corpsmen had achieved that rank the previous two years, and only three had done so in 1969.

A Continental Airlines commercial aircraft took me from Dulles International to a very large commercial airport in Da Nang, converted to military use. Most arrivals took military transport buses to where they needed to go, but not me. As the new master chief, I rated being picked up by a private jeep. The jeep ride was a non-eventful five miles or so to the hospital over what was considered a rural highway. It was called a highway only because it was paved; however, it was only as wide as the jeep. I remember taking in the sights and noticing that it was not too hot or humid even though it was summer. I attributed the balminess to the fact that Da Nang was a coastal city with a breeze.

When I arrived, I was driven directly to my quarters which were across from the helo pads at the front of the hospital base. The captain's and nurses' quarters were in the row of Quonset huts directly behind me. The hospital was composed of mostly Quonset huts with either concrete or wood floors. My quarters had the more comfortable wood floors and were among the best on the base, save for the captain's. In Antarctica, there would have been eight men living in the quarters that I had all to myself. I had stuffed wingback chairs, a sofa, a coffee table, my bed, and a desk. My hut was air-conditioned, as were most buildings except for the mess hall. Along each wall were two long windows allowing for plenty of natural light, and toward the back was my shower and head. There was considerable current reading material in the quarters as well. As far as clothing, the first thing I asked Lois to send was my black dress shoes. Everyone wore the standard issued high top boots, but I found them too heavy and hot.

My first week was spent learning my way around the huge base and getting to know the division chiefs who would report to me. Fortunately, I knew three from Bethesda and, overall, I knew about a fourth of the chiefs. The Navy is not that large, and after many years, I had come to know a great number of men from all over the world. Three or four other corpsmen I knew were brought in either as patients or in body bags from the bush.

While lying in my bunk my first night, I heard heavy fighting in the distance. I just laid there and listened. I was told the next morning that some of the men regularly climbed on top of the huts to watch the nightly fireworks. The next night I joined them. My first time watching left me in awe. The sky all around us was lit up like the grand finale on the Fourth of July, except it lasted for hours and stretched from very high in the sky down to the horizon. Helicopter gunships, C-130s, and fighter jets flew constantly, dropping munitions and firing their guns with tracers. It was quite a sight to behold.

I quickly learned that the two most dangerous things in this hospital, besides the random nightly rocket and mortar attacks, were dogs and mosquitoes. Rabid dogs were very common. The other danger was "the plague," our term for malaria. We received dozens of infected men every week from the bush, constantly reminding us that it was all around us. I became terrified of mosquitos, spraying my quarters religiously.

One thousand or so Vietnamese laborers and translators worked on the hospital base. I had a "mamasan" who was assigned solely to my quarters. For $3 a month she provided maid service six days a week including cleaning, making my bed, and shining my shoes. Unable to pronounce their names, we gave them American names. The woman assigned to my quarters was affectionately named "Patty."

Among my duties and titles was senior enlisted advisor to the officer in charge, and master chief for nursing services. I also counseled the men in just about every area that affected their military and civilian lives. For instance, I had one young man who was up on disciplinary charges for impersonating an officer to gain admittance to the officer's club. He obtained a GED to enlist and could barely write. I helped him craft a letter to his senator, Senator Joseph Tydings of Maryland, from whom he was seeking help. These young enlisted men often wrote their congressmen and senators when they thought the military was mistreating them, and it was not uncommon for the senators and congressmen to enthusiastically write dozens of letters back. I received many letters each week from state and federal politicians who felt they were doing their part protesting the war by siding with the enlisted men against their officers.

Station Hospital received its patients from medivac helicopters. The chopper pilots were some of the bravest heroes I witnessed in the three wars I served. I know of three times during my tour when a pilot, shot during his rescue mission, died from his gunshot wounds as soon as he landed his patients safely at the hospital. The crews would rush out to the helicopter to unload the wounded and tap the cockpit door to let the pilot know he could take off. When nothing happened, they would look closely to find the pilot slumped over in his seat, dead from loss of blood. The pilots were subject to small arms fire as they flew into these hot zones in the middle of firefights to rescue the injured. Somehow, they would make it to the hospital. I believed they flew on pure adrenaline, refusing to die until they got their wounded comrades to safety. As for the wounded, corpsmen gave initial life-saving medical treatment in the field and onboard the choppers while en route to us.

The helicopter pilots were not the only heroes. Working at this hospital wasn't for those with weak stomachs as it was a twenty-four-hour-a-day, seven-days-a-week combat wounded operation saving most of those who arrived with a pulse. Doctors, nurses, and corpsmen gave it all they had to send our troops back home alive. The hardest task I had to perform was double-checking identification procedures in the morgue as a guard against identification mistakes. Almost every day, I had to perform these procedures, sometimes on a metal pan with a single body part in it. The Marines themselves were often the reason we could not identify the dead. Often they would remove the dog tags, thinking they would be of help when, in fact, they should have left the tags on their dead comrades. The bodies, or what remained of them, arrived in body bags.

The hospital had been on a sandbar for five years. Nothing grew for quite a distance around the hospital's perimeter due to the constant use of Agent Orange, thus restricting the enemy's ability to sneak up on us. Frequently during downtime, we would sunbathe on top of the chief's club. We did not use suntan oil because we accumulated a shiny coat of orange oil on us after a couple of hours. As the planes came back from spraying the defoliant in the countryside, they emptied their tanks as they circled overhead awaiting clearance to land, thus creating a fine mist of Agent Orange in the air. Little did I know at the time how this oily substance soaking into my skin would drastically affect my health later in life.

Rear Admiral Zumwalt was a daily visitor at the hospital and a remarkable man whom the men loved. He would arrive every day with a list of patients to whom he wanted to award medals. Most of the time, the Marines were awarded a Purple Heart, but occasionally medals were awarded for gallantry and bravery as well. The admiral would arrive at 8 a.m., and it was my duty and honor to escort him and his photographer around the hospital. The admiral was one of the most likable men I ever met while serving my country. He was truly a caring, down-to-earth individual. He often stopped by dozens of beds that were not on his list to chat and to lift the soldiers' spirits. This man took the injuries to his young men to heart in a way that I greatly admired.

Admiral Zumwalt was the polar opposite of the officer-in-charge of the hospital and my direct supervisor, who was already there when I arrived in country. The captain was a real son of a bitch who regularly and intentionally jabbed at the morale of the hospital staff. From what I could see, he had a politician's desire for self-promotion. I can't think of a single instance that he ever visited with any of the patients unless, of course, they were the son of a VIP or a camera was present. The captain had a big press staff, and if anything good happened, you could be sure he took credit for it. He was flying back and forth to Saigon regularly, and he flew back to the States several times as well. His efforts at politicking paid off in the end because he was promoted from captain to rear admiral in 1972 and placed in charge of the Bethesda Naval Hospital and then to Surgeon General of the Navy in 1973, just three years after he left Vietnam.

As the base master chief, I should have been his right-hand man, but instead, we had a very tense relationship based upon mutual mistrust. He almost completely ignored me, instead relying on his junior officers to manage his hospital administrator. He was that detached. Instead of using me as his senior enlisted advisor, the captain ordered his departing senior personnel chief to remain in Da Nang by his side until he was transferred back to the States. I came to appreciate that I did not report directly to him because he did not care at all for the men who worked for him or their families. He was first and foremost a political animal, so those around him were either insiders or outsiders not to be trusted.

The captain did not want to deal with the nurses. He considered them a waste of his time and a pain in his ass. The captain, therefore, ordered they be placed under me, which infuriated them to no end. They were all officers, and reporting to an enlisted man insulted them gravely. It seemed the captain felt he did not have time to deal with such mundane tasks as detailing nurses, but I believe the real reason he put me in charge of them was that he knew the nurses had never been accountable or controlled by anyone. They had become accustomed to complete independence. As the only females at the hospital, they were experts at creating drama and strife, which the typical Navy man did not know how to handle. The chief nurse, a commander, wrote a lot of letters up the chain of command objecting to having to report to a master chief. She never gave up this fight.

The biggest run-in I had with the captain occurred over a fraternization charge which was the talk of the hospital. It came to his attention that a lieutenant nurse and an enlisted corpsman were in love and engaged. They were a committed couple who had been together since before they arrived in Vietnam. The captain illegally ordered they not have any contact with one another. I went to see him about it because the entire hospital was in an uproar over his insensitivity. I voiced my concerns, and after I was done, he said in an extremely rude, abrupt, and condescending manner, "Thank you for your thoughts. You are dismissed!" I had never been so rudely treated by a senior officer in my entire naval career.

The next morning, his executive officer called me into his office and threatened me with being placed on report (a military action very detrimental to one's career) if I did not name names and tell them who was saying what. I told them in no uncertain terms that, as the senior advisor, my communications with the enlisted were privileged, and that I would not cooperate in their witch hunt, thus effectively calling their bluff. This infuriated the Captain.

Shortly after that exchange, the captain called an all-hands meeting. I was standing in the front row with my staff of several hundred behind me. In that meeting, he said he did not care how the Army did things and that fraternization was against regulations. He said this because it was common knowledge that the Army often broke protocol and found quarters for couples. He then looked right at me and dressed me down publicly in front of the whole base. "Master Chief Custead had better get his priorities straight if he thinks this is an issue that warrants any more consideration. Maybe Master Chief Custead is not fit to be the Master Chief of this hospital."

He then announced that he was ordering the young corpsman to be transferred to the bush. A couple of days later, that young corpsman came back to the hospital in a body bag. The young nurse had a nervous breakdown and had to be transferred to a mental facility for care back in the States. I am not sure she ever recovered, nor could I ever, for the life of me, understand how that bastard captain could live with himself.

Shortly after I arrived in Da Nang, ten male Navy nurses I had known earlier arrived from NMRI with orders reading "Attention: Master Chief Custead." They were sent to the hospital under experimental instruction to see how male and female nurses could adapt to a working war environment. A petty officer first class assisted in observing and making notations for me. I was surprised that the male nurses appeared in Da Nang because I knew they had been designated for a hospital in the States. Somebody realized that I was familiar with their protocol of instruction and knew I had participated in this project, so I was placed in charge of them. The male nurses lasted only eight weeks because the female nurses went berserk, treating the males cruelly.

Anyone arriving into the hospital's war environment took a couple of weeks to adjust. Even accomplished surgeons from private practice would be physically pushed aside by experienced corpsmen and nurses who knew that every second counted with the horrible traumas before them. Ordinarily, everyone understood this and gave those newly-arrived a brief time to get used to the situation. But these female nurses did not extend this courtesy to the newly arrived male nurses. They used the situation to publicly humiliate and berate the male nurses in front of everyone by yelling at them, "Why are you here if you are so incompetent?" The war that erupted between them was bigger than the war outside of our gates. The men, in my estimation, were gentlemen. They arrived with written protocols they followed religiously and tolerated the extreme rudeness of the female nurses. Up until this point, the female nurses had only singled out corpsmen and ganged up on them with rumors and rude behavior. In the end, the female nurses' treatment of these male nurses was so beyond the pale that I determined that they were a real and chronic problem at the hospital. I lost a couple of good men who refused to work under these circumstances.

The head nurse was my biggest antagonist. She felt the need to argue with me over every trivial detail. She could not control her nurses, nor did she want to. Having her nurses cause constant havoc was her way of protesting the embarrassment of having to report to me, and the situation did not improve the entire time I was there. Most of the nurses were lieutenants and did not seem bothered by the chain of command; they just enjoyed causing disharmony. While we always remained professional toward one another, the head nurse was very vocal about the grave injustice and insult of having to report to me. As her boss, I ended up giving her a lower award for her Vietnam service than she thought she deserved. I believe any objective reading of the situation would lead any supervisor to conclude that she purposely fostered a difficult working environment. She was incompetent in managing her nurses and the award I gave her for her Vietnam service objectively reflected that. She ended up contesting the award once we both got back to the States, and I found out later that she was eventually successful in obtaining the higher award.

Another Navy experiment that I had the misfortune to supervise was a group of about 100 convicts who were in Da Nang as part of a plea bargain to either join the Navy or go to prison. These men were part of a 1960s social science project that failed miserably. I had to complete hundreds of hours of paperwork to court-martial every single one of them because they would simply refuse to work or follow an order.

As president of the Chiefs Club, it was my duty to make an accounting of all funds and inventory. Our booze and beer money came from selling popcorn at the movies. Just like in previous wars, the military provided movies for patients who were not restricted to bed to boost morale. The hospital was constructed on beach sand and a platform of plywood, painted white, with wooden benches made a makeshift outdoor theater. Often, the "incoming alarm" sounded and interrupted the movie, making everyone head for their bunker. Once the "all clear" sounded, the patients returned to watch the rest of the film.

Once we had a near disaster when three 100-pound sacks of popcorn we ordered never arrived. No popcorn meant no funds for the Chiefs Club, and no funds for the Chiefs Club meant no beer or booze. The popcorn was always a personal order bought and paid for from the funds of the club. After weeks of tracing the chain of custody of this popcorn from a private company in California through fifteen signatures, I found it led back to the officer in charge of the personnel center in Da Nang. When I confronted him, he admitted to stealing the money and wrote me a check for $300. However, by the time I recovered the funds, the hospital was about to close. Since the hospital was in the process of winding down operations, I gave the funds to the nearby orphanage.

As master chief, I also had to keep an eye on the enlisted club. One night, a particularly tough group of leathernecks came in from the bush and were getting out of hand in the club. Though I always carried a .45 pistol on my hip, I armed myself with a carbine and proceeded to walk into the club with M.P.'s and close it down early at 10:30 p.m. I lingered until I was sure this group of troublemakers had left before I went back to my quarters. I was extremely nervous, but I knew that if these men were allowed to continue to drink, something much worse was going to happen.

It was a rare night when we were not under mortar attack. Some nights it would be a single round while other nights we suffered multiple shellings. Since the base was the biggest hospital in the world at the time, the enemy hitting something was a matter of chance, but they were successful at hitting Quonset huts and killing or further injuring patients several times. We had around-the-clock security on our perimeter, but Charlie, our slang term for the Communist forces, was successful in getting through the lines to launch these attacks. Because the hospital was located on a sand bar near one bank of the river, we had to have swift boats patrol our backside as well as the area on the far shore. In this nightly game of cat and mouse, the Marines patrolled the perimeter on foot, and as soon as an attack was launched, the Marines would close in on the enemy forces who fled back into the jungle.

Being master chief meant I received monthly top-secret briefings. In one, I was told of ninety-seven deserters hiding in area villages. Those on the list were eligible to walk into our hospital anytime for medical treatment. Some had been out there for years, often with families. We frequently delivered their wives' babies. To this day, I believe a lot of the missing in action took up Vietnamese wives and melted into the countryside. Alternatively, if we caught them fighting against us, they would end up in Leavenworth. I was briefed on thirteen such deserters who had been captured fighting for the Viet Cong.

Another dirty secret of the war was the murder of Americans by Americans. Again, my access to top-secret information meant that I knew the truth behind the stories in the newspapers, especially *Stars and Stripes*, a military propaganda tool. If the military was forced to acknowledge an incident, they put a spin on it. For example, when the military told *Washington Post* reporters about an accident that occurred from a Marine playing with a grenade while drinking in the club, I knew that it was either a black-on-white racial incident or a case of an officer being fragged (the deliberate killing by a soldier of a fellow soldier, usually the murder of an officer). Because of the knowledge that this was going on all the time in Vietnam, I wore a sidearm around the clock for protection against fragging. At times, I felt I had just as much chance of being murdered as being killed in action. Most of the fragging occurred at night, which is why I locked my door and kept my sidearm locked and loaded, always within easy reach.

In addition to treating POWs and civilians, the hospital also sponsored a nearby orphanage which had received international attention. The orphanage was within walking distance of our hospital, next to China Beach, a favorite relaxation destination. Despite its proximity, it required a jeep ride since it was against regulations to walk anywhere outside of our gates, as it was just too dangerous. I regularly visited the orphanage with different chiefs a couple of times a month. Rather heartening and quite an operation, it housed hundreds of children. The Sisters of Saint Paul de Chartres ran the place. They sold scrap and grew vegetables in their attempt to feed these unfortunate children. One room was filled with small wooden cribs and contained babies as young as two weeks old. The room had fifty-seven babies, some without diapers, and no mothers in sight. Another section of the orphanage had 263 children up to high school age. Once the children became too old, they had to go out into the village to fend for themselves. I noticed lots of GI babies; very fair or with black curly hair. I noticed one GI baby dead in a crib. A sister in her sixties tried to cover the baby before I could see it. She told me she buried about fifteen babies each week. The chiefs and I would typically take the orphanage a large case of candy that we purchased in the PX.

Prisoners of war who were being treated at the hospital were kept under lock and key in a high-security section that always contained eight to ten North Vietnamese wounded prisoners. It was a constant reminder that our civilized society provided the best medical care and diet to these POWs while the Communists inflicted pain and torture on captured Americans.

Christmas was a break from the war. In December and January, it took twenty men working full-time in a warehouse to process the Christmas presents for the patients sent from good-hearted Americans, family members, churches, the Girl Scouts, and others. Unfortunately, most packages were addressed to specific Marines, and with the average stay of a patient being just three days before being evacuated, the vast majority had to be forwarded or returned.

Those with no return address or items that could not otherwise be forwarded went to churches and the local orphanage. Several of the packages were given to the mamasans who worked so hard keeping our quarters livable. While the Christmas care packages were well-meaning, they created quite an administrative burden on an otherwise busy hospital. Nonetheless, we felt it was our duty to track down the addressees and get the packages forwarded.

Occasionally, I took a jeep out to the bush to visit troops on morale-boosting missions with one or two of my corpsmen. I always did this on weekends, as it was important that I was at the base from Monday to Friday for Admiral Zumwalt's visits. As master chief, I made these trips to the bush one of my priorities to show the troops that we were there supporting them. These excursions were mostly day trips, but we sometimes bunked down with them overnight.

On these trips, we occasionally experienced firefights, but for the most part, the "gooks," as the peasant fighters were known, were not good soldiers. They did not aim at anything but simply shot in your direction. I always carried a .45 in a holster and brought a carbine in my Jeep. Sometimes, we would arrive in a village, and men would scatter. The corpsmen with me would fire over their heads as they escaped into the jungle. I felt safe in the bush with these fellow corpsmen as all of them had, like me, been attached to fighting Marine units. Corpsmen such as these were every bit as good of fighting men as the Marines they fought alongside. We corpsmen wear a Marine uniform with Navy insignia when attached to a Marine unit. It takes a trained eye to spot the corpsmen since they blend in so well with the Marines they fight alongside. In fact, I was married in a green Marine uniform because I had lost my sea bag for the third time and that uniform was all I had to wear.

I also went out to sightsee some of Vietnam's most beautiful and historic sites six or seven times, always traveling with a contingent of well-armed corpsmen. One place we visited was the Marble Mountains overlooking China Beach, located about ten miles to the south of Da Nang. This group of five limestone and marble hills went hundreds of feet straight up out of the earth and were a high holy site. Steps were carved out of the side as well as the inside of the mountains. We climbed one of these mountains called Thuy Son, the only one that could be climbed. There were so many trails that it was necessary to follow chalk markings to find our way to the top. As we climbed the stairs, we saw thousands of small Buddhist temples and figurines. Most of them were made of gold and had been placed there over hundreds of years. On the top of the mountain was a forest with a huge temple and a gold Buddha statue three times life-size. We could tell we were not welcome there. It was obvious that the locals had weapons under their baggy clothes. They drew closer as we neared the top. I had no doubt they would kill us if we were stupid enough to take souvenirs or otherwise disrespect this holy site. They were hiding all around us in the jungle on top of this mountain to guard their temple against being defiled or disrespected.

Years later, in 2013, my son Phil, while on assignment with the Defense Intelligence Agency, stayed at an oceanfront tourist villa on China Beach and visited the Marble Mountains, retracing his father's footsteps. The mountains, although still Buddhist holy sites, were filled with hundreds of tourists from around the world. One of his tourist guides was the daughter of a Viet Cong fighter.

★ ★ ★

My tour was supposed to last until June 1970, but as Da Nang started to fall to the enemy, the Navy decided to abandon the hospital and turn it over to the Army. In April 1970, I was placed in charge of winding down the base and handing the keys to the Army. In the end, I had three medical officers left with me on this huge, fifty-acre base. One day I awoke to find they had disappeared without notice. It did not surprise me they got cold feet and ran due to the rapidly deteriorating security situation in Da Nang. I was already uneasy with it being the four of us; I was so nervous that I was barely sleeping. I was now the last American at Station Hospital when an Army master sergeant arrived with forty or fifty staff in preparation of taking possession of the hospital. The transfer plan was abandoned within days. As the situation deteriorated further, the Army master sergeant and his staff received orders to leave. The plan was changed to transfer the hospital to the South Vietnamese, so South Vietnamese officers arrived in the U.S. Army's place. The South Vietnamese looked at me menacingly. I could tell there was a feeling on their part that the U.S. was abandoning them. With open hostility toward me, I knew the time had come to hightail it out of there, orders be damned.

By this time, Da Nang was chaos; the entire area was like an anthill. Before the evacuation began, there were 100,000 U.S. personnel and 800 different commands and organizations. The few still left in the area were all scrambling to leave. I couldn't tell you if the people evacuating were doing so because they were following orders or not. In the end, there was no formal transfer of the hospital to the South Vietnamese because, like those three medical service officers, I decided, orders or no orders, it was time to leave or I was going to be killed or captured. I was so scared that my pulse rate was through the roof nonstop.

My plan to get out was well thought-out, despite the chaos. First, I called the central HQ in Da Nang. The personnel chief, the same guy who had stolen our popcorn, told me that he was arranging for a small plane to arrive at the airport the next day and that I could grab a seat on it. I was so anxious to get out of there that I immediately proceeded to load my jeep with boxes of important hospital papers as well as my seabag so that I would be ready the next morning.

I was left with a single jeep and, since they were being stolen by both the South Vietnamese and other American servicemen, I chained it to a large block of concrete. I was now surrounded by South Vietnamese at the hospital and could tell the mood was quickly changing for the worse. They looked upon the Americans leaving

Da Nang as abandoning them to the mercy of the Communists who were slowly taking control of the area. The South Vietnamese Army's attitude toward Americans was deteriorating rapidly. Their open hostility toward me scared me to no end. For those last couple of days, I lived in constant fear for my life and could not sleep. Americans were starting to get shot by their South Vietnamese allies. Their hostility was warranted because they knew that any South Vietnamese who had collaborated with the Americans, even our maids, were going to be murdered by the Communists.

The jeep was my only way to the airport, about five miles distant through territory that was growing more hostile by the hour. By the time I decided to abandon the hospital, my heart was continuously racing. My hands were shaking as I unchained the jeep I had loaded the day before. I scanned my environment 360 degrees around for danger. I strapped on my .45 and placed a carbine next to me in the front seat along with enough ammunition for a prolonged firefight in case I came under attack on my way to the airfield. As I started the jeep, I felt as though the popcorn-stealing personnel chief and I were the last two Americans left in Da Nang. As I approached the airfield, my panic worsened—it appeared to be abandoned.

The popcorn stealer had said that he was arranging evacuation for not only me but three or four others still in the area. My heart was jumping out of my chest thinking I had been left behind. My thoughts quickly changed to proactive planning on what to do if I ran into Charlie. Should I fight? Should I surrender? I quickly decided that the option with the highest probability of survival was to surrender. I figured that as a master chief, I might be of value in a prisoner swap. Until then, however, my strategy was going to be hiding and evading the enemy until I could find other Americans. Unfortunately for me, the enemy was everyone, North and South Vietnamese. As I approached the gates of the airport in the midmorning and my fears of being left behind were seemingly confirmed, my heart raced out of control.

I parked the jeep sideways within six inches of a building in a manner that would make it less noticeable. I began to wait it out in the vehicle with my carbine across my lap and my .45 on the seat next to me. I felt I could get to the pistol easier that way from a sitting position than if it was in its holster. I decided I would wait twenty-four hours, and if no plane showed, then I would attempt to make it through hostile territory to another base the following day. I desperately tried to stay awake, knowing my life depended upon it, but after days of very little rest, I dozed off a couple of times only to awake in a panic, scanning all around me for danger.

Early in the next morning, and to my great relief, a small plane arrived. The plane seated about twenty, and those on board assisted me with my belongings as well as my important hospital papers. Finally, after a couple of weeks of non-stop nerves, I felt safe and collapsed into a prolonged sleep borne of exhaustion. I don't remember a single thing about getting home until a stewardess woke me at Dulles International Airport in Virginia. To this day, I don't know how I arrived there, nor do I know what happened to all my important papers.

This nerve-wracking escape from Da Nang became the basis of what would later become one of my worst war-related violent nightmares. I would experience it over and over for the rest of my life. In it, I would wake to find my jeep stolen, leaving me helpless as the last American in South Vietnam. It is a nightmare that causes me to awake violently, gasping for air, and with my heart pounding out of my chest. One time I thrashed about in bed so violently that I kicked Lois hard in the small of her back, sending her flying to the hard, wooden floor.

CHAPTER 22

Letters to Home

IN WRITING THESE MEMOIRS, I took the opportunity to reread all the letters I sent home, not only during the three wars I served in but other duty stations as well. What struck me most was that in World War II and Korea, my letters never mentioned the war I was fighting. However, in reexamining the letters from Vietnam, I became starkly aware that a new element had surfaced in my writings. That new element was fear.

04 Jul 1969—"I spent most of the afternoon going through the back row of huts and buildings meeting people, familiarizing myself with the lay of this huge base and giving the ward men a chance to meet me. I inspected the galley, POW ward, and several labs. I want the men to feel that they can come to me and that I am interested in them. I've already run into several personnel problems. I had a kid this morning come and see me that 'just could not do his work.' He's been here two weeks, and he is expecting too much of himself. No one had gotten on him, nor had he asked for help. He is just scared. He says we are too close to Charlie and hears the fighting all the time. I assured him that there is a Marine airfield across the road from us, that there are several planes patrolling over us 24/7.

Darling, there is no need to worry about me. Something could happen of course, but Charlie would have to overrun several military installations before he could get to us."

08 Jul 1969—"The men here need me. I am the "Dad" that they can talk to. I help them understand the whys, how's, and when. In the past, they did not have a division chief they could turn to."

12 Jul 1969—"After writing you last night I went to the head, then up on the sun deck to watch the fireworks. God, every night since I've been here. The fighting last night was taking place about a mile behind our back fence. Special planes with fixed, radio controlled guided missiles and C-130 specially outfitted with large caliber, multiple barrel machine guns circle around and around. A burst from one of these guns is supposed to lay a network of hot lead down over every foot over an area the size of a football field. Not one Charlie could be missed from these guns. They are devastating. They really pounded the island in the river. He is after the fuel ammo dumps. Charlie will sacrifice thousands of men to try and get close enough to lob a mortar into the prime target areas."

15 Jul 1969—"So far, I'm batting a thousand with the men. They are sending their buddies in to see me!"

21 Jul 1969—"There is a young Australian woman in our morgue. Seems she was shot last night a few miles from here as she was entertaining on stage. No word yet as to whether it was friendly or hostile fire."

27 Jul 1969—"Gee, it's sure wonderful making over a grand per month now. Take home pay of over $900!"

Saturday Night—Date uncertain—"God! I saw a man this morning, the first one that really affected me. I prayed that he would not live. He did die 2 hours later in surgery. Every day, Marines wounded. Blackened flesh from powder burns. Looks unreal, like a B&W picture. This poor fellow had his entire backside, including his buttocks, both legs and one arm blown away. Another group came in, 5 men from 5" gun explosions. Severely burned and torn to pieces. I was in the ICU unit today. It is unbelievable how bodies are put back together and then start healing. We have been saving several from death every day. The helos land outside my office. I get tired of seeing them."

July 1969—"We are losing the war on both fronts here. Eleven o'clock—Boom! Base next to us. Four murdered. The building was blown with dynamite. Black vs white? Enlisted vs. Officer? We don't know yet. We have had about 60 people murdered here this year."

13 Aug 1969—"You asked about the boys being in trouble. Drunkenness, disobeying orders, smoking pot, being out on the road (on foot). Many of the men must go to various elements of our command, which is stretched out over 30 to 40 square miles. Interspersed with villages, which are off limits. To enforce them being off limits, the roads of [sic]are off limits except when traveling in a vehicle. The other day we had a man walk from the air station gate to our gate, which is a few hundred yards. The Captain fined him $650.00. It was in the middle of the AM, yet a $650.00 fine! If they were allowed to walk, then pot would be given to them by the natives. Charlie is always nearby as several deaths here today proved. Yet we have an average of 25 to 30 VD cases a month. Men will blow themselves up walking through land mines trying to get to diseased, stinking, rotten whores. I can go up to the Marine's camp, go to the club, etc. and be home before nightfall. But I am supposed to be on official business if I am traveling the roads. Of course, chiefs are always on official business. I have been to see my friend at the Marine camp twice and traveling that short distance (about a mile or less) makes me extremely nervous. We have not been able to make a single village safe after five years and thousands of lives. This is a crazy thing here Darling."

19 Aug 1969—"Almost no sleep last night. Didn't get to bed until about 2:00 AM, up an hour or so later when the rockets started coming in. They hit the dispensary directly across the road, killed five."

26 Aug 1969—"All hell broke loose here last night. We received 100 casualties and had to turn away several choppers to the Army hospital or to Marine medical units. We could not handle them all. Almost 200 died last week here at the hospital."

03 Sep 1969—"No, I have not been sick. Not really sick. Just sick of spirit. I wish at times that I hadn't come to this God-forsaken asshole place."

Sunday Evening—Date uncertain—"Hi Sweetheart. We had a rough crowd in from the bush country in our club tonight. I had to order the club closed early and I stayed longer than I ever have in the evening until I was sure they all went their respective ways."

05 Sep 1969—"We are on a sand bar at the mouth of the Han River. The river is about 5 miles wide. Mostly small villages in the area. From the hospital to the mountains on the mainland it is about 20 miles. The next valley over the mountains is the main supply route into the area. Ships fire over us into the delta. The entire delta is lighted up with flares every night. No big movement could move into the delta unobserved but, as coolies, one at a time, there are a few there every night to try to get to the fuel dumps two or three miles down the beach from us. Sometimes Charlie makes a good hit. The 3rd Marines are deployed along the inner edge of the sand bar and the hospital supports a detachment of them. We have had small arms fire about once a week. Out in the delta we spot with helicopters any activity and lay it on them heavy. Almost every night there is noise, lights, flares, and explosions. Still, that delta must be home to at least a million Vietnamese people. In addition to our closest mortar hits, the air station across the street was hit killing five hospital men. Almost every night mortar hits someplace around. Charlie only has to fire once. They do it quick and try to move before the Marines get to them. About 10 days ago one of our boys in the hospital was killed. No, it's not really bad Darling. We are not in the brush chasing them. The probability of being hit is one in a million. There is a lot of square yards here that I am on. We have been sitting here on this sand bar for 5 years now letting Charlie hit away at us whenever he is able. What you read about is fighting in the main valleys that lead to this area."

08 Sep 1969—"I can't turn around anymore without there being three people waiting to see me. Some of the problems are so childish

that I would like to give them some harsh orders or boot a few people in the ass. But alas, that is not the way that we do things these days.

Boy this place really gets on my nerves. We had the holy shit kicked out of us Friday night. I wrote you that last letter, mailed it, crawled into bed and before I even realized when or what, I was picking myself up off the floor. The good Lord was with us that night. Only one killed plus several wounded here at the hospital. Seems Charlie was really celebrating Ho's death and ceasefire by damn-near blowing several installations right off this sand bar. Nothing close by the last two nights, but again, every evening, guns and flashes in the delta. No one can tell Charlie from our friends (ha, ha). So here we sit and wait. Again and again.

Since I have been here, I estimate we have taken about 40 to 60 mortar rounds. Two have been killed and 30 wounded. Five or six buildings have taken direct hits. My office was hit by shrapnel. Luckily, it was at night when I was in my quarters."

13 Sep 1969—"Today I had to re-assign men. I had to take men to the captain to investigate a charge of homosexuality by one of my night shift men. A Marine corporal patient charged that the corpsman gave him extra shots, which made him fall asleep. When he awoke, the corpsman was masturbating his penis for him. In addition, I had arguments all day with the chief nurse. It's been a hell of a day."

01 Oct 1969—"Good God, Hell! But I have had two busy days. We have another large morale problem within the command. A young HM3 (corpsman) and nurse became engaged. The captain is making a decree that she either transfers to the hospital ship or he gets transferred. He ordered him to stay out of the nurse lounge. According to Navy Regs: 1). No males in nurse's quarters, 2). Guests may be permitted in lounge, patio, or other suitable areas. The captain says (wrongly) he is not allowed near her period. Every man in the compound knows he is wrong. He ended up transferring the young man to the bush. This couple was the only single rose in this bed of thorns here. They abuse the only young innocent couple here.

Seventy percent of the nurses that marry, marry corpsmen.

I went to the captain and tried to warn him about morale in the command. The girl is threatening a letter to her congressman citing Navy regulations. Everyone says it is 1969, not 1949. Now get this! I asked to see the captain privately and unofficially. This morning I was called in and ordered to name names of who said what, etc. He said if I didn't, someone was going to be placed on report. I called their bluff. I told them that I was their Senior Enlisted Advisor and that information was privileged communication and that would stand. I told them they might embarrass someone, but not me, nor were they going to frighten me. In the end, I tried to help the captain restore some morale and all they wanted to do was hang people. All they accomplished was to add to their long list of leadership problems.

Damn it. I am so mad. I have laid here for three hours trying to relax before I started to write to you again. Damn it, but could I write a book about this place. I wish that I had about three spiral notebooks. Ha, and I have another fight with the nurses tomorrow! If I am crazy when I get home, you just have to love me until I recover. I have got to try making it clear to them that they ask or suggest transfers to me—that I am doing the detailing! They want to transfer a man because he embarrassed a nurse. A label did not read as a nurse had wanted it to and he gave it to a second nurse, embarrassing nurse number one. God, isn't a man allowed a mistake, even if he made one? These old maids will ruin a man, no if, buts, or maybes.

What about the congressman's letter? Honey, I get these every week almost. This one happened to be about me. When I mail my next letter, I will enclose a copy of my response to the congressman. My duty is to detail, discipline and assist as their division chief. Believe me, I will handle them in a military way—all the way, which is generally anti-nurse. In this case, I had to break up a 'group,' types I have seen before. The group preyed on others and they needed to be broken up for the good of the command. Individually, they just do their jobs, but as a group, they gang up on those they perceive as weak."

03 Oct 1969—"If I were to retire now, I would make $457.20 per month."

15 Oct 1969—"Sgt Sky has spent five years here in special forces. I bought him a drink and asked him to confirm the story I read about in the 10 Oct 1969 Asian edition of *Time* Magazine [the killing of 100 South Vietnamese agents].

He told me about his involvement in the Saigon Berets case. He said it was completely General Abrams' fault due to professional jealousy. He was trying to bring Berets under his control. Did the Berets work for the CIA? Kill? His answer was 'God yes, at least 20 per week.'

He talked of his personal experience in the killings. He said 'We killed the three that betrayed us. Took them up in the helo over the sea and kicked them out. One each day. The last one talked, but we tossed him into the sea nonetheless. Had to, no choice. We first tied him to a tire and urinated on him for three days. He was Monayada (hill people). They never touch their head nor point to toes. I have shot more than I can count—hundreds—so have all of our officers.'" [sic]

18 Oct 1969—"A month ago a visiting chief from intelligence told me that there are 97 deserters hiding in a nearby village. Thirteen of them have been captured in combat fighting against us. We just got another. Well we will be filling Kansas [Leavenworth] with them. The news on the radio stated that troops reported fighting a unit of Charlie led by a Caucasian."

21 Oct 1969—"You ask how does everyone over here feel about the war? It's quite unique I am sure. To start with, they come and go from the battlefield being babied by the airlines, first class all the way. Once here, the year goes pretty fast for the youngster. They get two government paid vacations at some of the world's best tourist spots. All during a year of….what? Risking their lives for what? The old men such as myself remember Korea. We were fighting these commies up until the last. We had good morale and the men felt that they were accomplishing something for a cause. However, with no education base

in these people, a dozen hating religious practice between themselves, the men know it is impossible to accomplish anything, ever, for any American cause. American interests? Rubber exploitation perhaps? For whatever reason, these people cannot be made self-motivating. Why are we even here? The men here wish that they knew. To most, the risk is not that great, usually, and they look forward to going on R&R. As for the blacks, they seem completely angry; seem willing to give up everything so they have nothing. So they can pity themselves. Nine out of ten of their faces display an expression of constant hate. We are (in the states) offering them everything. For the last few years they have had more opportunity than common white folks. Everyone is trying to help, if it is accepted. But they want to refuse, bitch, and feel sorry for themselves, demonstrate, etc. I don't know what they want but sooner or later responsible leadership for them must emerge or else lots of people are apt to be killed."

01 Nov 1969—"You ask about my troubles and my making friends with the nurses. I'm arguing with every nurse here, protecting, running interference, re-educating, etc. Every time one bitches about a man I spend considerable time investigating and then either agree or disagree. They're not accustomed ever to having anyone, anywhere ever question them. Collectively, they create problems for me and give me challenges. The two senior nurses won't even stay in the same room with me! I walk in, they walk out. Yet, they have the girls in the ward argue with me. There are men here that were here before the nurses came. One chief and two 1st class managed all the wards. If a doctor was unhappy he spoke to the chief. Now we have 35 or more old bitches to frustrate everyone beyond belief. They tire me out and they create 80% (or more) of my work. The paperwork is generally very little. About two hours a day. I did speak to the young nurse whose boyfriend was transferred. Evidently, things are dying down in the command."

29 Nov 1969—"We had a regular western-style shoot out here this morning. Four shot and two dead—all Americans!"

02 Dec 1969—"I sure could not sleep last night. It must have been at least 3:00 AM before I finally fell asleep. I close my eyes and see such horrible things. I never had such experiences before in my life. It must be the constant fear of death. Also, there are poisonous snakes everywhere, not to mention mosquitoes with the plague [malaria]. I don't know what all. I'm thankful that I have a private, closed room. I spray every few days under the bunk, behind the locker, etc. just to be safe. I have had about 3 mosquito bites since I have been here and they scare me to death."

14 Jan 1970—"Hi…… that is as far as I got last night in this letter before our 'condition red' alert sounded around supper time. It was about midnight before I got to bed. Our intelligence tells us to expect an attack on our medical warehouse. They want our medical supplies. We expect an attack at any time regardless of the condition red status. They could hit us any place, anytime. I feel pretty safe though because we have Marines on three sides of us and the river behind us. On February 15th, unless we are expecting a large, prolonged Tet offensive, I'll transfer 157 of my men and close to 200 beds bringing the hospital down to 400 beds. "

31 Jan 1970—"Saw some sights today that I won't forget any time soon. Our place was medevac'ing patients out to other hospitals. Our 400 bed hospital could not accommodate all the wounded coming in. We are beginning to realize that we are in the middle of a Tet. A hospital corpsman came in—head, shoulder, part of one arm that was all that was left of him. Charlie led our men into his mine field. They went through it so we gave chase. Received 37 injured plus the dead from that one misadventure! So goes this stupid war."

8 Feb 1970—"Still, I hate this place. It is making me nervous darling. I've started locking my door from the inside. And even so, tired as I was last night, I was too afraid to go to sleep. I realized last night that I was really, consciously, afraid for the 1st time in my life. Oh, I've done exciting things before and I have had at times, looking back, I got a little faint, etc. But this is hell here darling. Fifty

Americans a month being killed by Americans! A couple of nights ago 24 injured, 2 dead from these negro Marines tossing grenades into a club. Not a single negro in the club at the time even though the club usually has a high percentage of negros in it at any given time. In the official report, a Marine was guilty of taking a grenade into the club and was playing with it drunk! Child psychology. Trying to keep the men from learning the truth in order to keep other idiots throughout the Marines from copycat crimes."

14 Feb 1970—"Remember Coffman from the tissue bank at NAMRI [sic]? Young, tall, blonde kid that used to come over to our house because he was interested in Sally? He came over to our house a few times. An artist. He made you and the family an Easter tree made from a tree branch he painted white and attached beautiful hand-painted eggs. There for a few months. Left for the Marines several months before I transferred. Well, I saw him today—before he died. I prayed that he would die darling. He lived several hours, died in the OR. A mine took off one leg and hip. The other leg had only a muscle and some skin still connected. One arm off, half his head and one eye gone. God, I have been upset all day! Funny, but I felt better after they told me that he had died. I walked around the hospital for a few hours trying to forget him. Wondering if I would have to go to ICU tomorrow to visit him. Jim was upset. He has been out in the bush for 8 months. Says he has seen too many friends go."

16 Feb 1970—"The captain has received death threats. The club that was blown up? They arrested three negros."

22 Feb 1970—"We had a problem here at the hospital for two days earlier in the week. For god's sake, don't say anything to anyone or else I could be in much hot water. We received a Marine, alone, with a live grenade inside his skull. After taking x-rays we realized that we could not do anything for him without endangering the lives of the surgical team. We put the Marine back in an ambulance and parked it out on the far corner of the helo pad beside a pile of sand bags. We watched and waited 12 hours for the man to die. Then we

waited another 14 hours until 11 o'clock at night. We cleared the area of sightseers and others in the vicinity of the ambulance. We then placed a (blasting) cap next to his head and used it to detonate the grenade. We protected as much of the body as possible with sandbags out of respect for the Marine and his family. The family must never know what happened to their Marine. There just wasn't anything else to be done! Unfortunately, it was not the first impregnated grenade this hospital has received. We have received 2 others before my tour. One was inside the pelvic area of a Marine. He was successfully operated on by a corpsman. The third one was just before I arrived. The surgical team removed it from inside the shoulder blade. The award nominations are still here hanging on the walls. Things like this happen when a Marine is hit directly by a grenade launcher. At any rate, there is no logic in expending a doctor for an effort to save a man that if saved, would probably have been severely brain damaged. So, because of how bad this was, I really did not feel like writing honey."

[I was against this course of action and considered it murder but I understood that this was the surgeon's call. Some patients came in booby-trapped, but the hospital operated at such a breakneck pace that no procedures were in place to screen for these deadly traps. It was a miracle that we did not lose surgeons this way during my stay. We were lucky.]

25 Feb 1970—"Had a flare-up in one of the wards yesterday. A young man and the nurse commander were going at it. She screamed at me for 10 minutes on the phone. I went to the ward to direct her anger from the young man to myself and probably saved her from putting him on report. Turns out, the kid wanted off of nursing service and thought a fight with the commander would do the trick. Evidently, he pissed her off by telling her that he reported to me and not her etc."

4 Apr 1970—"Only a few more weeks and we will be over this nightmare. I usually try not to listen to or think about the guns

blasting away almost every night. But last night they scared me again. I just lie in bed and realize I am scared. I guess only a fool wouldn't be. We have been receiving rockets again. I have told myself all year long that it would be a 1 in a billion chance of being hit. Have not yet and not too many Americans here have been. What the hell, I'll be home in a few weeks. I think a lot of people get nervous near the end of their tour."

5 May 1970—"From Da Nang, Vietnam—Gads, the stateside news! What a pity that we have not shot many more demonstrators before this. I really feel that the police should shoot back. And every person that can be identified should get a $5,000 fine and jailed until their parents bail them out. This is getting out of hand" [I think this refers to the May 4, 1970 Kent State shooting of thirteen students, four of whom died.]

10 May 1970—"I died last night. Even before I went to bed, I watched for an hour a huge firefight over near the river behind us. This entire situation is so stupid. We just sit and try to keep them off our backs."

21 May 1970—"I had the scare of my life last night. I got knocked out of my bed by a rocket. The closest one yet. This one hit the building nearest me. Fortunately, it was only full of beer. No one hurt. Probably only 80 to 100 feet away."

CHAPTER 23

Retirement

I ARRIVED BACK FROM VIETNAM to serve what would become my third and final tour of duty at Bethesda Naval Hospital. The difference was that I was returning as the command master chief of NMRI. My time at this prestigious military facility would end up spanning a total of twelve years. This "home base" of mine, to which I kept returning, was another remarkable aspect of my military career as it is nearly unheard of for a sailor to spend twelve years at one duty station. Typically, the sailor is required to spend three years at sea for every two years ashore. To my great fortune, the officers at NMRI established me as a man they wanted to keep, and I spent the final four years of my twenty-eight-year military career in the peace and quiet of Bethesda, Maryland.

The NMRI command knew that I intended to run out my final enlistment and retire at the ripe old age of forty-five. As a reward for a great career, they placed me in an office next to the commanding officer and assigned me extremely light duties.

Being a veteran of three wars, not to mention being one of the Chosin Few, provided me with low-level celebrity status, the kind someone might attain if they had been born in the late 1800s and lived to see the new millennium.

As word got around that this master chief had just returned from duty in his third war, I started to receive visitors from around the base. I had all manner of curious people show up in my doorway, from young seamen to fellow veterans and officers. I spent the final stretch of my naval career regaling visitors with stories of my unique time in the Navy. The one aspect of my career I was probably proudest of was how I uncovered Soviet nuclear mischief while working in a top-secret capacity for the State Department in Antarctica. To my utter consternation, this information was still classified at the time, so talking about it was forbidden. I had not even told my wife about it at this point.

As the day of my retirement, April 1, 1974, approached, I received a letter from my old nemesis in Vietnam, the captain. He was now the Surgeon General of the Navy. All his politicking had finally paid off. He had been promoted from the commanding officer of Bethesda Naval Hospital to the Surgeon General of the Navy. In the letter, he mentioned several highlights of my career, including my monitoring of the environment at McMurdo, a veiled reference to my top secret findings of Soviet nuclear explosions. To my shock, he also mentioned it was his pleasure to have me serve as senior enlisted advisor at the Da Nang Station Hospital during his command there.

I was the first master chief to be stationed at Bethesda Naval Hospital and able to retire with the equivalent of thirty years of service due to my repetitive early re-enlistments, each of which gave me an extra three months of service for computing retirement. As I approached my retirement date, I was repeatedly queried by medical service officers about whether I wanted to place my name in the hat for an opportunity to be named the Master Chief of the Navy, a ceremonial position held by a single man and the highest ranking non-commissioned officer in the Navy. There are seven master chiefs of different disciplines that report to the Master Chief of the Navy. As a master chief, I resided under one of those seven on the naval organization chart, the Master Chief of Hospital Corpsmen. I was encouraged by Admiral Zumwalt, now the Chief of Naval Operations, that I should put my name in for this prestigious position. With his support, I felt there was no way I would be denied the position. At the time, I had amassed an unheard of five years of combat and seven years of sea duty. I was still young at forty-five and felt that it was time to start a new career. The Master Chief of the Navy was ceremonial and would require constant travel for presentations, dinners, and so forth. I was emphatic that I did not want this nonstop traveling at this point in my life. Also, I did not think it was worth it because, while it would have been a great honor, the actual compensation would have only been a couple thousand more per year and I felt, at that time, that I could do better in the private sector.

I took a year off and fiddled around the house while sending out resumes whenever I found something that interested me. I received several offers for hospital administration positions, some from out of state that I immediately dismissed and some very well paying. In the end, I decided that I'd had enough of hospitals and working with doctors (and definitely nurses). I was not sure what I wanted to do, and while I decided, I had Lois take a basic typing course which enabled her to secure a clerical job at the National Institutes of Health. The plan was for her to have a paycheck for six months until I could decide what I wanted to do. She ended up making a career at the NIH for twenty-two years, telling everyone that she had to work as long as her husband was sitting at home all day.

Having dropped out of high school to join the Navy, and despite the college-level courses I took during my career, I still did not have a degree from an accredited university. My plans turned from finding a job to enrolling in college and earning a degree to open up my options in the private sector. I enrolled in the local community college and then transferred to the University of Maryland. Luckily, the college coursework I took while in the Navy counted toward my degree, shortening my journey considerably. After graduating with a degree in business administration, I went on to earn a master's in personnel administration, also from the University of Maryland.

The economy was in the tank by the time I graduated in 1983. Even Harvard graduates were having a difficult time finding jobs. While fruitlessly sending out resumes, I spent a great deal of time reading. I had so much time on my hands that I found myself becoming obsessed with researching the cult of the Church of Scientology.

Not one to give up, I turned my attention to becoming a real estate agent, which turned out to be a rewarding career that I continued well into my sixties. I believe I received my license in 1985 at age fifty-seven or thereabouts. We did not get rich and still needed Lois' paycheck, but with my military retirement, we lived comfortably and were able to do some traveling. It was also around this time that I joined the Masons while Lois joined the Order of the Eastern Star a few years later.

In 2000, when I was seventy-two, we sold our beloved Parkwood home and moved to the Leisure World retirement community, purchasing a nice two-bedroom, fifth-floor condo. By this time, Lois had retired from NIH and my real estate activities had all but come to an end. We enjoyed our newfound leisure time, especially our travels abroad to Spain, Canada, and Australia, where we were able to visit our daughter Sally. Lois kept active with weekly luncheons with her "girls" from NIH while I had two garden plots where I grew beautiful flowers and produce. Additionally, we attended the annual Antarctic reunion held in a different city each year, always finding extra time to sightsee while on these trips.

CHAPTER 24

Three Wars Later

LOIS WILL TELL YOU THAT I came home from my third war an angry man. She really did not know me before I went off to World War II or became one of the "Chosin Few" in Korea, and I certainly could not tell you if I was any different. I would argue to this day that I did not change one bit. However, I must give credence to what Lois and others have said. Not only did she notice a change, but my mom also noticed that I became very short-tempered and curt. She said her dear sweet boy who left the farm twenty-eight years ago was indeed much changed.

This time, instead of barely knowing one another, Lois and I had been married for quite some time before I departed for Vietnam. After Vietnam, it was indeed different. What effects did the nightly shelling and the unrelenting fear have on my personality, my subconscious? Lois said I came home with anger issues, that I would boil over in an instant with her or any of our seven children. My son Clay insists that I showed early warning signs of post-traumatic stress disorder, jumping out of my skin every time the screen door in the back of the house slammed shut.

My son Clay once asked me during our Saturday morning writing sessions which war had the most effect on me. I told him it was beyond a doubt the last, Vietnam. The number one recurring nightmare I suffer from is about escaping that country alive, about my jeep being stolen, about feeling as though I am the last Caucasian in the country and not knowing who I can trust or who would slit my throat.

According to folklore, soldiers coming home from war have flashbacks and are sometimes incapacitated by their war experiences. I am highly offended every time I see a bum begging on the street corner with a sign in his hand that says "veteran." It was not until the Vietnam War this became part of our popular culture. The overwhelming vast majority of veterans are hardworking, self-sufficient Americans. I believe the people begging for money on roadsides are simply alcoholics and drug addicts who also happen to be veterans. Being a veteran did not make them drug addicts or alcoholics. In my estimation, veterans are a step above the average American.

I was able to compartmentalize my war experiences along with all its bloody, gruesome maiming and death. I saw things that no human should ever see. Things that would incapacitate you if they were in the forefront of your mind. I believe the human brain instinctively knows to store these memories in locked file cabinets where you cannot easily get. This is the reason men do not speak of their combat experiences. I had successfully kept these memories locked away and was as normal as any other citizen of our nation.

It was not until I reached my seventies and underwent my first general anesthesia that my first psychological problems surfaced. The first sign of PTSD occurred while coming out of that anesthesia. I panicked and started to tear the tube out of my throat, the IV lines from my arms, and began yelling at the top of my lungs. I awoke in an utter panic, believing I was a prisoner of war. The hospital had to station two large orderlies, one on each side of my bed, to restrain me since they did not want to put me in restraints. I was delirious and hallucinating that the walls were moving and had crawling creatures on them. The hospital staff immediately came to the wrong conclusion, that I was suffering from alcohol withdrawal and experiencing delirium tremens. To them, it seemed logical that a man who had spent nearly thirty years in the Navy would be an alcoholic. They seemed hell-bent on attributing my behavior to alcoholism, despite Lois' unrelenting protestations to the contrary.

My health declined noticeably after this first surgery to fix a major aneurysm just below my heart. It was the first time I had ever experienced general anesthesia, and I was never the same after that. I believe that somehow that anesthesia opened locked files in my mind, files that had been put away because they contained memories so frightening and gruesome that a person could not function with them being open. My PTSD really started to get bad from this point forward and became progressively worse with each passing year. I had shown subtle signs of "shell shock," as they called it in World War I, after returning from Vietnam. Any loud bang would make me jump. As mentioned before, my son Clay reminds me that my worst tormentor was the back-screen door.

Lois fought for me while I was in recovery, knowing I needed help. She was finally able to convince the doctors I was a teetotaler and a psychologist was called in. As Lois filled the psychologist in on my naval career, the psychologist became amazed that the man before her had survived combat in three major wars. She then proceeded to treat me as a case study to advance her career. She brought in colleagues who were also intrigued by my amazing war history. In her treatment, she proceeded to force out memories that were better left locked away, memories that had been safely stored in the deepest recesses of my mind. In hindsight, what she did to me was selfish, incompetent, and immoral. Subsequent psychologists agreed with this assessment, including Dr. George, who became my subsequent long-term psychiatrist. He thought I was one of the most normal men he knew and led Lois and me to conclude that the psychologist could have been sued for malpractice.

Unfortunately, I had to have other surgeries that required general anesthesia, and each time I got progressively worse. I could not leave our fifth-story condominium without taking medication to calm my nerves. Once, in 2010, I was standing in line at the bank when two pneumatic tubes came to a stop next to where I was standing with two simultaneous loud popping noises. The noise, reminding me of incoming mortars, so frightened and incapacitated me that I fell to the floor in a twisted heap trembling. Two kind bank employees ran from behind the counter and, after making sure I was not injured, helped me to my feet. They walked me to the car where Lois was waiting for me. Lois drove me home, gave me medication, and put me to bed where I slept for several hours to recuperate from what was, for me, a severe trauma.

As the years went by, my PTSD increased so that just the sound of a fork hitting a dinner plate would make me jump violently and wince. It started with loud bangs but steadily digressed to lower level noises. All that was required to set me off was for the noise to be unexpected. Of course, the effects of Agent Orange had already been taking its toll on me years before the surgeries. This herbicide that had coated my skin with an orange glow in Da Nang caused nerve neuropathy, making my legs buckle out from under me many times a day.

Besides the sensitivity to noise, my PTSD also included flashbacks. As I was recuperating at home after my first surgery, Lois found me sitting in a chair in front of the television, sobbing loudly and uncontrollably. She said I was not responsive to her increasingly worried, repeated questions: "Elmer? Elmer, are you all right?" With each query, she became more and more alarmed. She said it was clear that I was not even in the room with her, and, in fact, I wasn't; I was experiencing my first "flashback."

We had been watching a television documentary about a Marine field ambulance emblazoned with the international symbol of the Red Cross on its side that had been riddled with machine gun fire. I recognized the damned ambulance. I saw that ambulance at the Chosin Reservoir in Korea. I had just tapped on the back doors letting the driver know that I had finished loading my six patients and that he could head south to evacuate the wounded men. I witnessed the ambulance being ambushed with heavy machine gun fire about 100 yards away from me. I immediately called for help and started running toward the ambulance. I remember to this day counting ninety-one bullet holes. I know they were from a heavy machine gun, most likely fifty-caliber. Most of the rounds had gone completely through both sides of the ambulance, chopping the patients and driver into a bloody stew. Afterward, the Graves Registry Unit cleaned the ambulance and invited the press to see it. The U.S. saved this ambulance as a propaganda tool to be used against the Communists to show that our Cold War enemies had no conscience. A *Time* reporter filmed the ambulance, and the pictures were published worldwide. This ambulance was a big news item at the time and became an international incident.

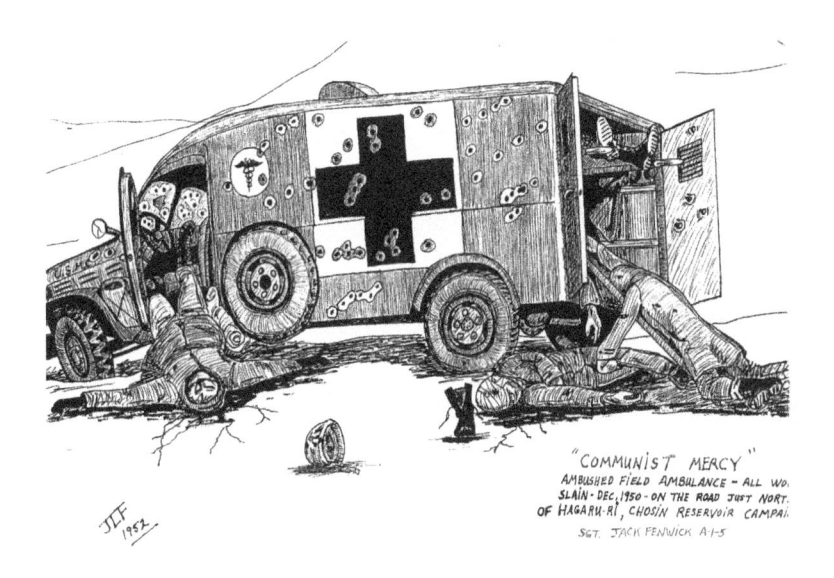

"COMMUNIST MERCY"
AMBUSHED FIELD AMBULANCE – ALL WO. SLAIN · DEC. 1950 · ON THE ROAD JUST NORT. OF HAGARU-RI, CHOSIN RESERVOIR CAMPAI. SGT. JACK FENWICK A-1-5

In my flashback, I am standing outside the bullet-riddled ambulance looking inside at a gruesome blend of brains, body parts, bone fragments, and blood. But this time, instead of thinking to myself, *Well, there is nothing more to do here,* like I did when it originally happened, I behaved not like a battle-hardened Marine but like a human being. I cried like a baby, shaking uncontrollably and screaming out in agony and hurt. Amazingly, the emotions I suppressed in the winter of 1950 came flooding out of me more than 50 years later.

What I cannot put into words is that in these flashbacks I feel I am there. My mind and body have both traveled back in time to that moment, and I am reliving it all over again in real time. I am once again a young man, and I can feel how bad my feet hurt from the cold. The hallucination of a flashback is like time travel. I lose all awareness that I am an old man sitting on a couch in a retirement community. As I cry, sob, and shake wildly, I am completely unaware that my wife is watching in horror, desperately attempting to call me back out of my daytime nightmare to come back to her from Korea one more time.

CHAPTER 25

My Legacy

AS MY FIRSTBORN APPROACHED college age, I decided upon a plan that would allow me to support each of my children's college aspirations while being fair to all of them. I could not afford college for seven children on a master chief's pay, so I let each of my children know that I would provide free room and board as well as auto insurance if the kids purchased their own jalopies if they were enrolled in college.

Steven opted to join the Army upon graduating from high school. His decision was based upon college not being the right path, coupled with a desire to see the world. He was trained as a medic and ended up stationed in Heidelberg, Germany. He came back briefly to marry his high school sweetheart, Missy (Carleen) Cooley, before heading back together to finish his tour. Missy obtained a job as a civilian working for the Department of the Army while there. The two enjoyed vacations all over Western Europe including visiting France twice, touring West Germany (as it was then called), Switzerland, Spain, Morocco, Austria, Northern Italy, and their favorite destination, the Netherlands; visiting Amsterdam no less than four times. When Steve's enlistment was up, he came back and worked nights at Holy Cross Hospital in Silver Spring, Maryland, while earning his business management degree from the University of Maryland. Upon graduation, he passed the CPA exam on his first sitting (a very rare feat accomplished by approximately 10 percent). Steve developed and has run an accounting and tax practice for many years. He and Missy have three children, Matthew, Michelle, and Michael. Matthew and Michael have stayed close to home, living and working in Frederick, Maryland. Michelle is now living in Wisconsin where she practices as a veterinary oncologist.

Sally started college at Frostburg State University, thinking about a teaching career. Unable to find sustainable employment in the small Alleghany mountain town of Frostburg, she transferred her second year to the University of Maryland, where she, like her brother Steve, also earned a degree in business administration. Sally had exceptional grades and was recruited out of college by Price Waterhouse. She, like Steve, also passed the CPA exam in full on the first sitting. While working on K Street in Washington D.C., she met her Australian husband, Peter Maiden, who was also employed by Price Waterhouse. Together, they toured the world, living in Singapore, Indonesia, and finally settling in Sydney, Australia. Sally and Peter have two children, Thomas and Anna. Thomas works in hospitality, consulting on the wine list at a prestigious Melbourne restaurant. He lives with his partner, Lisa Frankland, and daughter, Isabella, in Brunswick. Anna, having completed a commerce degree and having worked at one of Australia's largest banks, decided the corporate world was not for her. She is currently working on a second degree in health sciences, majoring in nutrition.

Bill, the next in line and a unique and independent soul, was perhaps the biggest surprise. He moved out when he turned eighteen and never returned. Not academically inclined at that age, Bill worked construction for several years after completing high school and attended the Diesel Institute of Mechanics at night to become a heavy construction equipment mechanic. After one too many miserable freezing January days out in the mud, he decided to try his hand at college. From being a reluctant student in high school, he succeeded in earning a computer science degree from the University of Maryland, Baltimore. Boy, did he surprise us and make us exceedingly proud! To say that we were pleasantly shocked at Bill's success in college would be a huge understatement. In high school, Principal Riddick told us, "Bill will never be a student; you should enroll him in a trade school." I never gave up on him, knowing that he always had it in him even if he did not know it himself. As a parent, I would like to think that it was my faith in him and my riding him hard to do his schoolwork that turned him into a successful college graduate. I wish I could tell his high school principal that Bill turned out to be a great success by any measurement. Bill has enjoyed a very lucrative career in construction management and is now the executive vice president of the largest utility contractor in Washington, D.C. As parents, you never know the answers, only the problems you face.

Bill has now been married to Robin Wright, a dedicated and talented primary school teacher, for almost thirty years. He adopted Robin's son Ben from a previous marriage, and they had twins of their own, Nick and Drew. Ben possesses a bachelor's in computer science from the University of Maryland and a master's in civil engineering from George Mason University. Nick joined the Air Force at age eighteen and has a degree in computer science/IT from the University of Maryland. Nick has a son named Jason. Drew completed three years of college before going to work full-time for the Air National Guard as a cybersecurity specialist.

Clayton, our fourth child, also became a CPA. Kind-hearted and generous, Clayton is perhaps my most jovial son. He always kidded that his decision to study accounting was because he had free used books from his older brother and sister. His decision was actually born of practicality. He was slated to graduate during the horrible economic times of the Carter administration, and an accounting degree was one of the few four-year degrees that guaranteed a job upon graduation. Initially working in a public accounting practice, Clay has spent most of his career in positions of financial management within private enterprises culminating his career as a Chief Financial Officer. Clay was married to Elaine House for over 35 years, now a dedicated Montgomery County EMS leutenant sergeant, and they had two sons, Joe and Sean. As of this time, Joe is a graduate, also from the University of Maryland, with a degree in criminal justice, and his ambition is to become a U.S. Federal Marshal. Sean is studying at Towson University and has expressed an interest in physical therapy.

My next son Phil, perhaps the smartest of my children, went on the most circuitous route to success. Starting out studying engineering at the local community college, he joined the Navy and was admitted to the Defense Language Institute, where he specialized in Russian language studies in preparation for a career in naval intelligence. After four years of life in the Navy, he decided to quit and go back to school. He graduated from the University of Maryland with a degree in Russian area studies and then enrolled in, but did not complete, a Juris Doctorate program at the University of Baltimore's School of Law. He became a Frederick City, Maryland, police officer and detective, remaining on the force for seven years, where he became an expert in the administration of polygraph exams. He has worked as a contractor for the Central Intelligence Agency (CIA), and as a government employee for the National Security Agency (NSA) and the Defense Intelligence Agency (DIA). His job as a special agent at DIA takes him to far corners of the world, "interviewing persons of interest to the U.S. Government," as he says.

With his first wife of sixteen years, Connie, Phil had two daughters, Nicole and Samantha. His oldest daughter, Nicole, is in her senior year of college and will graduate with a psychology degree, while his younger daughter, Samantha, has obtained an accounting degree from Salisbury University and is now working for the Department of Defense. Phil remarried ten years ago, bringing Kristen Anderson, a former police chief, child protection advocate, and lover of horses, into the family. Phil and Kristen have recently purchased Mount Welby, a twenty-three-acre Virginia estate that they have turned into a bed-and-breakfast.

Paul, the youngest son, graduated from Montgomery Community College with an associates of arts degree in business administration. Paul excelled in soccer, earning all-county, all-state and all-mid-Atlantic honors in college and was headed to play at the next collegiate level before a knee injury ended his athletic career. Paul is currently the docketing and operations manager for a prestigious patent law firm. He was married to Terry Payne for about seven years and had two sons, Tyler and Aaron. Good-looking and tall like his father, Tyler graduated from Towson University with a degree in finance. Aaron, also a handsome young man, enlisted in the Navy and recently graduated as a master-at-arms (security specialist) from San Antonio, Texas. He is currently off to his first overseas assignment in Bahrain in the Persian Gulf. Paul has now been married almost eighteen years to his second wife, Andrea Ladestro. Andrea grew up two miles from our Parkwood house in Garret Park. Paul and Andrea met at a law firm in Washington, D.C. in the mid-1980s, where they both worked at the time. Andrea has been a paralegal/legal assistant for approximately thirty years. Andrea brought her son Bryce into the family. Bryce is a wonderful young man who graduated from the University of Maryland with a degree in political science and served his country as a Secret Service agent at the White House before going to work for a government contractor. Paul and Andrea had a fourth son together, Kevin, who is presently in high school. Kevin is already over six feet tall and may end up being the tallest of all the grandchildren. Kevin loves basketball and has been on a couple of championship teams.

The baby of the family, Becky, became a registered nurse with two degrees. The first was in nursing from the University of Maryland, Baltimore County, and the second was a degree in social work from Marymount University. Becky has been married to a devoted husband and father, Ken Uhl, a self-employed IT consultant, for nearly twenty years. They live in the Manor Country Club community in Rockville, Maryland, in a beautiful home backing up to the golf course with their two wonderful children. Jack is in high school and is a black belt in karate as well as a promising musician who plays several instruments. Asnakech is a beautiful young lady in elementary school and is quite a gifted athlete, especially in soccer and basketball.

Epilogue

ELMER'S STORY IS IMPORTANT TO understanding the American experience, from the Great Depression through three major wars. His generation fought back the evils of Nazi Germany, Imperial Japan, and the enslavement of communism around the world at the unthinkable cost of tens of millions of lives, both military and civilian. To hear his story is to help ourselves understand his generation and an America that was much different than it is today. As a member of Tom Brokaw's "Greatest Generation," his life and dedication to the defense of our country helped transform America and its place in the world for the better. His is a story of a courageous fight against hunger and social injustices during the Great Depression on a farm in the racist South. His story, like the stories of all men of his generation, includes rushing to join America's fighting forces after the attack on Pearl Harbor. Young men, teenagers really, often dropped out of high school and lied about their age in their eagerness to defend America against Japan's unprovoked aggression. Our father's generation placed their lives at risk in their pursuit to join America's fight against Japan and Germany's mad tyrants, who were hell-bent on taking over the world. Dad never realized his boyhood dream of "licking the Japs"; instead, his fight in World War II was against the Communists in China and later against the same foe in Korea and Vietnam.

Elmer wanted to record his participation in history, not only to preserve his memories for his children but also to inform his grandchildren about a time when America was a much different place than it is today. They do not fully comprehend the history of the Cold War and how the Soviet Union's stated goal was to "bury" the U.S. and spread Communism throughout the world. His grandchildren did not grow up hearing the testing of neighborhood civil defense sirens sounding in the distance; nor were they ever taught, like their parents during these air raid drills how to crouch under their school desks with their hands clasped behind their necks in case of a Soviet bombing attack, nuclear or conventional.

Dad's own political beliefs placed him firmly as a constitutional conservative. He was a firm believer that what made the American experiment successful was in the genius of the founding fathers and the U.S. Constitution. However, what made Dad's generation of Republicans, Democrats, and independents different was that all shared the common beliefs that America's freedoms are fragile and that they can disappear in as little as a single generation. His generation understood that America's success in self-governance by its citizens is an exceptional occurrence and an anomaly in the history of humankind. It was this common bond amongst all Americans that allowed the country to come together to tackle its challenges.

★ ★ ★

I started this labor of love on October 15, 2010, shortly after Dad recuperated from his stroke. I was at my parents' home every Saturday morning for two years with my tape recorder and notes in the hope of one day completing this book on his behalf. Before his stroke, it had been his dream to write it himself. Now it seemed that I was in a race against time as I wanted more than anything to hand him a completed book with his name on it. These Saturday mornings were the best thing that happened to Dad, Mom, and myself. Up until the night of his stroke, we had a strained relationship. I first started these visits out of a sense of duty, but they quickly became an enjoyable part of my week that I looked forward to. I found myself not only growing closer to my parents, but that evolution in my feelings for them expanded to include my brothers and sisters and their children. If for any reason I was not able to join them for our weekly meetings, it caused me a heavy heart and a feeling of guilt; Mom would tell me that Dad became very depressed if I was not able to make it as he looked so forward to our weekly sessions.

Dad passed peacefully on December 21, 2012, at eighty-four years old. He was laid to rest at Arlington National Cemetery with full honors including a twenty-one-gun salute, a Navy band, and a horse-drawn caisson. The day he was interred was a beautiful spring day, and scores of friends, family, and neighbors showed up to say goodbye. Elmer was a man much loved and adored by those outside our rather large immediate family. He never said no to a friend in need, always donating his time at others' homes to be of assistance. While Dad was never a religious man, I am comforted to know that he led his life as a highly moral and righteous man, just like his father before him. I am also comforted to know that he could see a draft manuscript of this book before he passed. He was thrilled beyond words with it, elated to finally have his book in a form that he could hold and read. It made him so happy that I asked Mom to have it buried with him.

I always had a fear that one day my parents would pass and I, being a horrible, emotionally distant son, would not feel anything, but I received a second chance in helping Dad with this book. A second chance to become best friends with my parents. A second chance to get to know my father as a very good and decent man who had led a very hard life and had sacrificed and worked hard to provide for his wife and children, a man I fell in love with. I thank God for the second chance I received. It feels good knowing that every time I think of him and how much I miss him, my eyes moisten.

APPENDIX A

Service Record

Naval Career Record:

1947, July 1—Enlisted in Jacksonville, FL—Rank Seaman Recruit (SR)

1947 July 5—Basic training Rank SR to Seaman Apprentice (SA)

1947, October 31—Hospital Corpsman training San Diego Naval Hospital. Rank from SA to Seaman (HN)

1948, November 6—USS *Repose* AH-16, Pacific Fleet, Rank from SN to HM3 (Hospital Corpsman 3rd Class)

1949, August 31—1st Marine Division, FMF, California & Korea. Rank from HM3 to HM2 (Hospital Corpsman 2nd Class) Weight 148 lbs

1951, June 8—US Naval Air Station, Memphis TN, Rank HM2

1951, August 24—Naval Air Tactical & Training Command (ATTC), Jacksonville, FL. Rank HM2

1952, February 25—US Naval Hospital, Jacksonville, FL – Patient.

1952, April 16—NATTC, Jacksonville, FL. Rank from HM2 to HM1 (Hospital Corpsman 1st Class)

1952, July 29—US Naval Hospital, Jacksonville, FL –Patient.

1952, October 14—NATTC, Jacksonville, FL. Rank HM1

1954, March 19—USS Banner AKL-25, Pacific Fleet. Rank HM1

1955, April 4—USS SLM 448, Pacific Fleet. Rank HM1

1955, April 13—USS Banner AKL-25, Pacific Fleet. Rank HM1

1955, November 18—USS Ingersoll DD652, Pacific Fleet. Rank HM1

1955, December 2—BB & CLT SCOL "C," Naval Med School, Bethesda, MD, Rank HM1

1957, March 8—Medical Research Institute, Bethesda, MD. Rank HM1

1957, July 3—Naval Medical Research Institute (NMRI), Bethesda, MD. Rank from HM1 to Chief Hospital Corpsman (HMCA)

1961, July 22—US Naval Station, Washington D.C.—Rank HMCA (Chief Hospital Corpsman)

1963, October 17—Antarctica Support Activity, McMurdo Station. Rank HMCA to Senior Chief Hospital Corpsman (HMCS)

1965, January 1—NMRI, National Naval Medical Center, Bethesda, MD. Rank HMCS

1969, June 30—U.S. Naval Support Activity, Da Nang, Vietnam. Rank Master Chief Hospital Corpsman (HMCM)

1970, July 27—NMRI, National Naval Medical Center, Bethesda, MD. Rank HMCM

1974, April 1—Retired

ELMER B. CUSTEAD HMCM USN RET.
Nine Years Sea Duty   5 Years Combat
Service: 1 July, 1947   1 April, 1974
Proudly Served America

APPENDIX B

Ribbon Legend

		1	Navy & Marine Corps Commendation Medal		
2	Presidential Unit Citation	3	Navy Unit Commendation Medal	4	Meritorious Unit Commendation
5	Good Conduct Medal	6	China Service	7	WWII Occupation
8	National Defense Service Medal	9	Korean Service Medal	10	Antartica Service Medal
11	Vietnam Service Medal	12	Republic of Korea Presidential Unit Citation	13	Republic of Vietnam Gallantry Cross Unit Citation
14	UN Korean Service Medal	15	United Nations Medal	16	Republic of Vietnam Campaign Medal

Note: Ribbons 2, 3, & 4 were awarded without corresponding medals.

1. Awarded for sustained acts of heroism and meritorious service in direct combat operations. The "V" is for valor in direct contact with the enemy.

2. Ribbon awarded to unit for extraordinary heroism in action against an armed enemy. Battle of the Chosin Reservoir, December 1950
3. Ribbon awarded to unit for distinguished outstanding heroism in action against the enemy. Battle of the Chosin Reservoir, December 1950
4. Ribbon awarded to unit for valorous or meritorious achievement or service in combat. Battle of the Chosin Reservoir, December 1950
5. Good conduct medal for three consecutive years of honorable and faithful service. The bronze star indicates it was awarded six times (once for the ribbon plus five additional awards).
6. Medal awarded to commemorate services in the Navy in China during World War II.
7. Medal awarded to commemorate participation in the European and Asian occupation forces during World War II.
8. Medal awarded for honorable service during a designated period of which a national emergency had been declared during a time of war.
9. Medal awarded for participation in the Korean War.
10. Medal awarded by the Department of Defense for service in Antarctica. The bronze device denotes wintering over.
11. Medal awarded for serving in Vietnam.
12. Medal awarded by the Republic of South Korea for outstanding performance in the defense of the Republic of Korea.
13. Medal awarded by the Republic of South Vietnam in recognition of deeds of valor or heroic conduct while in combat with the enemy. The palm designates that it was awarded to the armed forces of the U.S.
14. Medal awarded to those who participated in the defense of South Korea.

15. Medal awarded by the United Nations for participation in joint international military operations. The bronze star denotes a Presidential Unit Citation for the battle of the Chosin Reservoir.
16. Medal awarded by the Republic of South Vietnam for wartime service in support of operations in Vietnam.

Medals
(LEFT TO RIGHT)

1. Navy & Marine Corps Commendation Medal
2. Good Conduct Medal (6 times: June 30, 1950; June 30, 1953; June 30, 1956; June 30, 1959)
3. World War II China Service Medal
4. World War II Occupation Service Medal with Asia clasp for service aboard the Repose (January 25, 1952)
5. National Defense Service Medal
6. Korean Service Medal
7. Antarctica Service Medal with Bronze Wintered-Over Clasp
8. Vietnam Service Medal
9. Republic of Vietnam Gallantry Cross Unit Citation with Combat
10. United Nations Korean War Medal (August 4, 1953)
11. United Nations Medal with bronze star denoting a Presidential Unit Citation awarded to the First Marine Division for the Battle of the Chosin Reservoir (October 11, 1950)
12. Republic of Vietnam Campaign Medal

References

Chapter 1: My Story

1. U.S. Department of Veterans Affairs. *Data on Veterans of the Korean War.* June 2000. Retrieved from https://www.va.gov/vetdata/docs/SpecialReports/KW2000.pdf

Chapter 9: World War II

1. Unknown (1966, April 24). *Photo No. K-31496 USS Repose on 24 April 1966* [digital image]. Retrieved from: http://www.shipscribe.com/usnaux/AH/AH12-p.html
2. Chapter 11: Korea: The Inchon Landing
3. Taylor, Charles C. (Photographer) (February-November 1951). *Seoul City Limits* [digital image]. Retrieved from http://fayde.deviantart.com/art/Seoul-City-Limits-3802288

Chapter 12: Korea: The Chosin Frozen

1. National Museum of the Marine Corps. *Korean War: Send in the Marines: 1946-1953.* Retrieved from the National Museum

of the Marine Corps web site: http://www.usmcmuseum.org/Exhibits_SendMarines_p4.asp
2. Wikipedia. *Battle of Chosin Reservoir.* Retrieved from Wikipedia's web site: https://en.wikipedia.org/wiki/Battle_of_Chosin_Reservoir
3. *Aerial view of Chosin Reservoir* [digital image]. Retrieved from http://www.gunnygenes.koreanwar-educator.org/chosin_images.htm
4. Wikipedia. *Battle of Chosin Reservoir.* Retrieved from Wikipedia's web site: https://en.wikipedia.org/wiki/Battle_of_Chosin_ReservoirWikipedia. *Battle of Chosin Reservoir.* Retrieved from Wikipedia's web site: https://en.wikipedia.org/wiki/Battle_of_Chosin_Reservoir
5. Wikipedia. *Battle of Chosin Reservoir.* Retrieved from Wikipedia's web site: https://en.wikipedia.org/wiki/Battle_of_Chosin_Reservoir
6. Chang, Jung, & Halliday, Jon (2006). *Mao: The Unknown Story.* New York, New York: Anchor.
7. Wikipedia. *Battle of Chosin Reservoir.* Retrieved from Wikipedia's web site: https://en.wikipedia.org/wiki/Battle_of_Chosin_Reservoir
8. The U.S. Army Center for Military History (2007, January 10). *Map of the Battle of the Changjin (Chosin) Reservoir* [digital image]. Retrieved from https://commons.wikimedia.org/wiki/File:Chosin-Battle.png
9. Clavin, Tom, & Drury, Bob (2009). *The Last Stand of Fox Company: A True Story of U.S. Marines in Combat.* New York, New York: Grove Press.
10. Courtesy Photo (2013, March 29). The Battle of the Jangjin "Chosin" Reservoir was fought during one of the coldest winters in the history of the region [digital image]. Retrieved from https://www.army.mil/article/99795/Task_Force_Faith_veteran_remembers_heroic_leaderhttp

11. Wikipedia. *Battle of Chosin Reservoir.* Retrieved from Wikipedia's web site: https://en.wikipedia.org/wiki/Battle_of_Chosin_Reservoir
12. Wikipedia. Battle of Chosin Reservoir. Retrieved from Wikipedia's web site: https://en.wikipedia.org/wiki/Battle_of_Chosin_Reservoir
13. U.S. Navy (2005, October 10). *Photo # K-11771 Hungnam is blown up as USS Begor stands by, 24 Dec. 1950* [digital image]. Retrieved from https://commons.wikimedia.org/wiki/File:KoreanWar_Hungnam.jpg
14. Wikipedia. *Battle of Chosin Reservoir.* Retrieved from Wikipedia's web site: https://en.wikipedia.org/wiki/Battle_of_Chosin_Reservoir
15. Wikipedia. *Battle of Chosin Reservoir.* Retrieved from Wikipedia's web site: https://en.wikipedia.org/wiki/Battle_of_Chosin_Reservoir
16. Wikipedia. *Battle of Chosin Reservoir.* Retrieved from Wikipedia's web site: https://en.wikipedia.org/wiki/Battle_of_Chosin_Reservoir

Chapter 15: The USS Banner

1. Hockenhull, Bob (Photographer) FS-345, FP-345, AKL-25, USS BANNER (AGER-1) [digital image]. Retrieved from http://usspueblo.org/Background/Ship_History.html

Chapter 21: The Vietnam War

1. Headland, Andrew. (1968, June 5) *For the wounded, a place of hope.* Retrieved from https://www.stripes.com/news/for-the-wounded-a-place-of-hope-1.68070#.WPJhdKK1uUm

Chapter 22: Letters Home

1. http://archives.chicagotribune.com/1969/08/16/page/13/article/cia-ordered-100-killings-berets-attorney-charges)]

Chapter 24: Three Wars Later

1. Fenwick, John. "Communist Mercy." (1952) *Tranquility, Solace & Mercy*. [Illustration]. Retrieved from http://usstranquillity.blogspot.com/2012/03/combat-art-fenwick-drawings.html

Chapter 25: My Legacy

1. https://magoosh.com/cpa/cpa-first-time-pass-rates/